Building Leaders

Although the selection and development of emerging leaders is fundamental to organizational growth and success, many organizations are facing a troubling scenario—a striking gap between the leaders they need and the talent available to assume the mantle of leadership. This book, grounded in empirical investigations and philosophical insights into the study of leadership, is designed to help emerging leaders to bridge the gap between "new leader" and confident, respected difference-maker. From the development of leadership skills to the practice and application of successful strategies, scholars and leader-coaches Charles and Jason Stoner offer tools, ideas, and evidence-based advice to these up-and-coming leaders in an indispensable text that is direct, pragmatic, and action-oriented.

Charles R. Stoner is Robert A. McCord Endowed Professor for Executive Management Development at the Foster School of Business, Bradley University, Illinois. Dr. Stoner earned his bachelor's, master's, and doctoral degrees from Florida State University. An award-winning scholar and teacher, he has authored eight books and numerous academic articles. His most recent books are *A Life in Balance: Finding Meaning in a Chaotic World* and *The Adversity Challenge: How Successful Leaders Bounce Back from Setbacks*. A dynamic and engaging speaker and facilitator, Dr. Stoner works with a variety of businesses and organizations throughout the country, specializing in leadership, interpersonal dynamics, and change, as well as leader coaching for personal growth and reinvention.

Jason S. Stoner is Assistant Professor of Management at Ohio University. Dr. Stoner earned his bachelor's and master's degrees from Bradley University and his Ph.D. from Florida State University. His research interests primarily focus on individual differences influencing reactions to workplace stressors. Dr. Stoner's reseach has been published in *Human Relations*, *Human Resource Management Review*, *Leadership Quarterly*, *Journal of Occupational Health Psychology*, and *Journal of Vocational Behavior*.

Building Leaders

Paving the Path for Emerging Leaders

Charles R. Stoner and Jason S. Stoner

Routledge
Taylor & Francis Group

NEW YORK AND LONDON

First published 2013
by Routledge
711 Third Avenue, New York, NY 10017

Simultaneously published in the UK
by Routledge
2 Park Square, Milton Park, Abingdon, Oxon OX14 4RN

Routledge is an imprint of the Taylor & Francis Group, an informa business

Library of Congress Cataloging-in-Publication Data
Stoner, Charles R.
Building leaders : paving the path for emerging leaders / Charles R. Stoner & Jason S. Stoner. – 1st ed.
p. cm.
Includes bibliographical references and index.
1. Leadership. I. Stoner, Jason S. II. Title.
HD57.7.S756 2012
658.4'092–dc23
2012024627

ISBN: 978–0–415–89930–7 (hbk)
ISBN: 978–0–415–89931–4 (pbk)
ISBN: 978–0–203–18257–4 (ebk)

Typeset in Adobe Garamond
by Keystroke, Station Road, Codsall, Wolverhampton

SUSTAINABLE
FORESTRY
INITIATIVE

Certified Sourcing
www.sfiprogram.org
SFI-00555
The SFI label applies to the text stock.

Printed and bound in the United States of America by Walsworth Publishing Company, Marceline, MO.

Contents

Preface

This book is written for emerging leaders, young women and men in their twenties and thirties who are engaged in their first experiences of leading others in an organizational context. Our intent is to help these leaders bridge the gap between stepping into positions of challenge and responsibility and becoming confident and respected difference-makers. By taking a deep dive into the real world of the emerging leader, we strive to meet emerging leaders where they are and explore the issues that are most problematic for them.

This book has been a long time coming. It has been shaped by our studies of the disciplines of leadership and organizational behavior. It has been set in a foundation drawn from the exciting research and writing conducted by the brightest men and women in our field, as well as our own original work. As such, this book is grounded in solid evidence, drawn from the tapestry of empirical investigations and insights that highlight the study of leadership.

But most powerfully, the skills, models, and points of view that are presented here have evolved from working with and coaching hundreds of emerging leaders over the past thirty years. These interactions have come through our courses, through our broad-based consulting, and through the in-depth, multi-day workshops for emerging leaders, conveniently titled *Building Leaders*, that have now been running over ten years through the Executive Development Center at Bradley University. As we have listened to the questions and concerns, the excitement and demands, and the candid apprehensions and fears of these leaders, our thinking has been refined. These young leaders want ideas and they want actions. This book is for them.

Throughout this book, we turn to examples of leaders facing immediate challenges. We have been careful to capture reality while purposely camouflaging the specifics. As such, names have been changed and situations may be modified to ensure that the power of the example can be maintained and the identity of the participants can be protected. In a few instances, we have used composite profiles.

Many people have made important contributions to this book. For Chuck, I want to extend my thanks to my colleagues at Bradley University. A special call-out is in order for Dr. Jennifer Robin (who helped create and facilitate our original *Building Leaders* workshops and offered thoughtful input on this project) and Dr. Matt McGowan (my understanding and incredibly supportive department chair). Kristin Shanine, now a Ph.D. student at the University of Alabama, served as a much appreciated research assistant during the early stages of this project. A special note of thanks goes to Tom Bower of Mindset Consulting, who currently co-facilitates our *Building Leaders* workshops. Tom's impact is present throughout this book.

Thanks to the folks at Routledge and in particular our editor, John Szilagi. From our first meeting in my office to the final stamp, John has been a thoughtful and encouraging supporter.

I would be remiss if I did not express what an exciting honor it is to produce this book with a co-author whom I have known his entire life. Both of my sons, Jason and Alex, have chosen academic careers, and both are inspirations. And, as in past book projects, I must extend my gratitude to Dr. Julia Stoner, a renowned scholar in her own right. She has always been my staunchest advocate, my centering foundation, my very best friend, and my better half.

For Jason, I would like to thank my friends, family, and colleagues for their support and guidance. Specifically, I would like to thank my colleagues at Ohio University, especially Dr. Lenie Holbrook, Dr. John Schermerhorn, and Dr. Will Lamb. You have been very instrumental in my development as a professor and scholar. I would like to thank Dr. Pam Perrewe and Dr. Jerry Ferris for taking the time to train me and offer me advice over the last ten years. I would also like to thank my father and mother, brother Alex, and Gma for being pillars in my life. Lastly, I would like to thank Dr. Gabe Giordano, Annabelle Lamy, Dr. Matt Scott, Peejoe Johnson, Sammy Gee, Christy Pardieck, Vai Ky, Will deBeest et al. for "taking it for a ride" with me.

Challenge

The Playing Field Has Changed

Arguably, the development of emerging leaders may be the most critical challenge facing contemporary organizations. Although the selection and development of new leaders is fundamental to organizational growth and success, many organizations are facing a troubling scenario—a striking gap between the leaders they need and the talent available to assume the responsibilities of leadership. Further, this so-called "leadership talent crisis" is pervasive, spanning a global context (Wilson & Hoole, 2011).

Two primary factors have contributed to this gap. The first is demographically driven—the graying of our management ranks and the subsequent exit of seasoned leadership talent. As senior leaders leave in overwhelming numbers, we face a talent drain whose collective knowledge and experience cannot be replicated, at least in the short-run (Deal, Peterson, & Gailor-Loflin, 2001).

The second factor is economically driven. In recent years of economic uncertainty, many organizations chose to "batten down the hatches," engage in "trough planning," and trim expenses. Training and development budgets were frequent targets, and younger, emerging leaders were profoundly affected.

Today, on the heels of this demographic and economic double-whammy, organizations are battling to ramp-up the growth of a new cadre of leaders. There is little debate that the evolving, incremental development of younger talent must be accelerated. Consequently, emerging leaders, often in their twenties or early thirties, will have opportunities for challenging leadership roles that only a generation ago would have been years in coming. Therein lay both the challenge and the promise.

Consider, for example, a six-year study of over twenty thousand high-potential, emerging "organizational stars" from more than one hundred companies throughout the world that was recently conducted by the Corporate Leadership Council (Martin & Schmidt, 2010). Here, researchers found that nearly 40% of the internal job moves made by these promising young leaders ended in failure. The Council's study offered a striking explanatory finding. More than 70% of these high potential workers lacked "critical attributes essential to their success in future roles" (Martin & Schmidt, 2010, p. 56). In other words, these young leaders did not have the skills and perspectives needed for the challenges of contemporary leadership.

This story is not new. A 2005 report from Right Management found that about 30% of new managers and executives failed at their new jobs and ended up leaving their respective organizations within 18 months (Williams, 2010). Harvard Professor Linda Hill (2003), drawing from her insightful assessments of new managers, suggested that first line management is the level in the organization where we typically see the "most frequent reports of incompetence, burnout, and excessive attrition" (p. 2). Emerging leaders are often caught off guard when faced with the realization that well-honed skills that have assured past success now must be augmented by a new set of skills—skills that may have garnered scant attention and limited development (Ellis, 2004).

Interestingly, the development of new skills may be the easier part of the transition to leadership. Scholars argue that emerging leaders must develop "new attitudes," "new mindsets," and "new values" (Hill, 2003, pp. x–xi; Watkins, 2003). Importantly, new leaders must define a new sense of themselves and their role in the organization. Executive coach and author Marshall Goldsmith offers a catchy and pertinent assessment for our audience of emerging leaders in the book title, What Got You Here Won't Get You There (Goldsmith & Reiter, 2007). Accepting a new and more expansive role brings excitement, challenge, and a deeper sense of personal fulfillment. Concurrently, leadership is a new world, immersing some of our most talented people into an arena of uncertainty, frustration, interpersonal stress, and fear.

The Emerging Leader

This book is written for emerging leaders—those men and women who are experiencing their initial foray into the challenges of leading others in an organizational context. Emerging leaders may be asked to guide a project team, head a special assignment, coordinate a group of peers, or take responsibility for a group of direct reports. In some cases, this new leadership role is clearly defined. In many cases, it is a mixed role. That is, emerging leaders are often called to lead others while maintaining responsibilities as individual performers.

Assuming the mantle of leadership, one is not graced with an immediate and profound transformation of insight, emerging full-blown and full-grown—a leader in every way. Like all of life, leadership is comprised of a series of ebbs and flows.

As leaders, you will experience periods of success and unfortunately, you must endure inevitable stumbles. For example, you tactfully handle a tense and politically-charged battle over needed resources, and in the process, learn powerful lessons of respectful communication. You lose your temper with a team member over his failure to meet a deadline and recognize that firmness and anger rarely complement one another. You vow that holding standards of accountability must be coupled with appropriate impulse control. You learn, and you commit to grow.

We understand that leadership is a complex formative and developmental process (Nohria & Khurana, 2010). Importantly, for those who are perceptive, critical development is gleaned from both success and failure experiences, reinforcing the maxim that "there is no wasted experience" for the insightful leader.

Although emerging leaders may represent a range of ages, we have chosen to focus on younger leaders who are still in their twenties and thirties. While erecting this chronological boundary is admittedly arbitrary, we do so for two reasons.

First, younger leaders are likely to face issues, encounter complexities, and experience reactions (even push-back) that differ from the experience of their more senior colleagues. Second, there is a dramatic and pressing need for leadership development among this younger segment in our organizations. Faced with a mounting array of complex problems, leadership cannot be viewed as the exclusive purview of a small cadre, sitting atop the organizational hierarchy. The tone of impactful leadership must be present at all levels— underscoring the significance of our emerging leader audience (Bennis & Goldsmith, 1997).

While emerging leaders encounter a number of challenges that we will discuss shortly, the most profound of these challenges occur in the personal and interpersonal arenas. Accordingly, most of our attention will focus on these two key areas of change and growth.

Emerging leaders are not the champions of industry, at least not yet. Rather, you are women and men who are new to the experience of leading others, replete with the struggles and anxieties that are rarely discussed and addressed. However, certain challenges, needed skills and approaches, and even pitfalls are predictable, thereby allowing us to acknowledge and suggest ways of addressing these matters.

Most critically, emerging leaders want ideas, and they need actions—actions that can be put into place immediately. In short, this book is designed to help younger leaders bridge the gap between stepping into positions of leadership and emerging as confident and respected performers who create influence and impact.

Although experience is the master teacher, years of study and research indicate, rather conclusively, that well-designed interventions can lead to positive leadership change and accordingly, enhance one's leadership journey (Reichard & Avolio, 2005). Lessons can be gleaned and applied. Missteps can be thwarted. Skills can be practiced and incorporated into the leader's repertoire. And importantly, one can consciously choose patterns of behavior that define who they are and what they are becoming.

Our hope is obvious. We do not want you to simply meander through your new leadership role. We want you to grow and excel as a respected difference-maker.

What Is Leadership?

It's always a good idea to try to define the things you're going to be discussing. In the realm of leadership, there is no shortage of definitions, and every original study and new book offers its own unique wrinkle on the topic (Bass, 1991).

Some views are quite direct, stripped of pedantic undertones. For example, noted scholar and author Peter Senge (2006) has offered what is perhaps the sparsest look, noting that leaders inspire others. There is considerable merit to this simplicity, and we are a bit partial to this phrasing. The word "inspire" literally means "to breathe" or "to breathe life into." Indeed, our best leaders do "breathe new life" into people, teams, units, and organizations, enabling a level of movement and advancement that exceeds what was originally deemed reasonable or even possible.

Goleman, Boyatzis, and McKee (2002) add that "Great leaders . . . ignite our passions and inspire the best in us" (p. 3). We have all seen it in action. And, we have all lived through the depleting drain when it is absent.

With an admitted slant toward simplicity, we argue that the central characteristic of contemporary leadership is the process of "intentional influence" —influence that touches the feelings, emotions, thinking, and actions of others so that goals and visions are realized. This is hardly original (for example, see Gardner, 1995). From our perspective, equating leadership and influence is an expansive, not limiting, approach to our topic. Indeed, the challenge of influence is nuanced and complicated by the unique personalities, divergent interests and needs, and situational complexity we encounter.

There is an additional perspective that merits attention. Kouzes and Posner (2002) have emphasized that leadership is a process, not a position. To a large extent, that process and its evolving nature is the framework for this book. We accept that leadership is "an observable, understandable, learnable set of skills and practices available to anyone, anywhere in the organization" (Kouzes, 1998, p. 322).

The Impact of Leadership

Leadership matters. However, the question that has divided scholars for decades is how much leadership matters. Those with a more cynical tone contend, for example, that even the most talented leaders fail to stave off plunges in performance during periods of economic decline and market shifts. And, they counter that, during boom times, leadership acumen is largely the recipient of and not the driver behind performance spikes. In essence, the argument goes: broad factors beyond any leader's control (the nature of the industry, dynamics in the environment, and even organizational culture) are the real drivers of performance outcomes (Pfeffer, 1977; Thomas, 1988).

On the other hand, scholars and practitioners argue that leaders play a significant role in generating positive organizational outcomes. In fact, the bulk of research over the last twenty-five years suggests that leadership does matter and that leaders do, in fact, have important effects on performance (Bass, Avolio, Jung, & Berson, 2003; Judge, Piccolo, & Illies, 2004). No one affects the work experience of organizational members more (for good or bad) than the immediate leader.

Numerous studies have examined the qualities, characteristics, attributes, and approaches that differentiate successful from less successful leaders. As such, we have a wonderful tapestry of empirical investigations and philosophic insights that have been woven through fifty years of studying the field of leadership.

Understandably, we yearn for ways to improve and yield better leadership. Here, we must consider what is expected of our leaders. Good leaders map directions for transcending uncertain times. They provide inspiration and encouragement. They create environments where motivation can flourish.

They offer hope and resiliency during times of struggle. They provide fairness and justice when distributing the fruits of performance during times of boom. They move organizations to grow and improve and change, while recognizing that any change is, at its heart, a tenuous and fragile personal adventure. They can be firm and tough, demanding the highest of performance expectations and tight adherence to systematic processes. And they can provide authentic compassion and sensitivity and support.

Importantly, it is the situation-specific, idiosyncratic mix of these diverse perspectives that defines good leadership. The complexity of blending this mix in the proper proportions underscores why outstanding leadership is so rare. Does all this make a difference? Our experiences and our lives at work suggest providing a clear affirmative nod.

Although relatively few studies have focused, specifically and exclusively, on young, emerging leaders, we will draw heavily from those that have. Further, from a broader perspective, a number of general leadership studies and theoretical models offer important insights when applied to the needs of our emerging audience.

The Playing Field Has Changed

Ted Williams may have been the most gifted pure hitter to ever play the game of baseball. Through raw talent, an incredible work ethic, and plain old dogged determination, Williams defined excellence in baseball. He finished his career with an unbelievable .344 lifetime batting average. He hit .316 or better for 19 of his 20 seasons. He was the last player to hit over .400 for a season. With definitive punctuation, he even hit a home run in his last career turn at bat. Soon after his retirement, Williams was asked to manage—to lead young players to the same lofty levels he had achieved.

By nearly all accounts, Williams struggled as a leader. With a bias toward understatement, let's just say that the same intensity and single-minded focus that had led to personal success as a player did not quite connect with the less talented players who comprised his teams. He was impatient with their development. He had little understanding and even less respect for the idiosyncratic nature of pitchers—a breed of player he had hated as a hitter.

In many ways, the keys to successfully leading a baseball team—understanding unique personalities, developing players across a range of talents, making nuanced decisions based on the unique context of the game—were skills and qualities Williams had never really worried about and certainly had not honed. As an individual performer, Williams rightfully earned a spot in the Hall of Fame. As a leader, it was a new game.

Williams's story is common. It hits at the core of this book. It's the story of every outstanding individual performer who struggles carrying success to a broader team or unit. It's the story of a young man whom we'll call Mark. Armed with a Ph.D. in Electrical Engineering, Mark was a brilliant addition to the research arm of a large, global company. With fierce determination and an analytic problem-solving mind, Mark was lauded for his ability to bring creative and winning contributions to perplexing projects. Not surprisingly, Mark was only 29 when he was elevated to the position of team leader. Here, he was challenged to harness the talents of a five-person team to find solutions to a troubling product concern.

As we met, Mark was reeling, stunned by devastating feedback from his peers and a biting performance appraisal from his boss. In short, all reviews portrayed Mark as arrogant, intimidating, and dismissive. And the young superstar was now being eyed carefully as a flawed leader who was unable to deliver.

Interacting with Mark, one would quickly conclude that Mark, indeed, was arrogant, intimidating, and dismissive. He was also thoroughly competent and quick, seeing design issues and problems earlier and more clearly than his peers. However, he had little patience in waiting for others to catch up. He showed his irritation through nonverbal displays that clearly projected his disgust with less adept colleagues. Even more damning, Mark projected a "winning at all costs" attitude. If pushing the best or "right" answer meant a pointed exchange with colleagues, he welcomed it. Through intellectual force, he could bully folks into submission, forcing his views to prevail. Interestingly, his views were usually correct.

For Mark, the qualities of intensity and fierce determination to succeed had been the foundations for his individual success. Yet, when played out within a team leader context, he created frustration and resentment from those he needed to encourage to stretch in meeting challenging project demands.

Now here is the key. Mark had not changed. But he was now performing on a different stage, a stage upon which he had not previously walked. And, when the curtain went up, he floundered. When stepping into the realm of leadership, the playing field has now changed. It is more complex, more nuanced, and, most critically, it is decidedly not self-centric.

A Time of Transition

We all face points of transition throughout our lives and careers, and these transitions are a natural part of our evolving and developing nature. For example, you experienced a transition when leaving home to attend college, a transition bound in new challenges, opportunities, and responsibilities. You experienced the same transitional impact when you took your first job, made a commitment to a loved partner, or had your first child. Now, you face another transition as you become a leader.

We do not see your move to leadership as a dramatic transformation or reformation or metamorphosis. These terms suggest a radical or revolutionary change of behavior, literally changing from one thing into a different thing, a total alteration. This is not what we have experienced with young leaders we have worked with, coached, taught, and interviewed. Moving into leadership is really an evolution—a movement that, in many ways, is a natural progression for talented young people who wish to expand their realm of impact.

Ibarra, Snook, and Ramo (2010) describe transition as a "process of leaving one thing, without having fully left it, and at the same time of entering something else, without fully being a part of it" (p. 666). This is a wonderful description of what emerging leaders face, capturing the divergent tugs of attention and focus.

The classic work of William Bridges (1991) is helpful to us here. Bridges describes three stages of transition: (1) endings; (2) a neutral zone; and (3) new beginnings. Although your attention is logically geared to your "new beginnings" as a leader, there is power in the "endings," areas where you must "let go" and things you must "leave behind." These may be attitudes, behaviors, and practices that worked in the past but are now problematic.

Without a doubt, most of the qualities that have made you successful will continue to enhance your performance in a leader role. These will not be abandoned. But some changes must take place. Some shifts and some growth must happen. So we speak, rightfully, of evolving and transitioning.

An example may help. We worked with a talented emerging leader, selected to move from his "doer role" (salesperson) to a "leader role" (sales manager). He was selected to lead precisely because he had excelled in his doer role. Early in our conversations, he readily admitted how much he liked his work in sales. He loved it all—meeting people, understanding their needs, and helping create solutions that culminated in sales and long-term relationships. As a manager, he was being tasked to pull back on his direct sales role and in the words of his boss, "Build a sales team who are as good as you."

It won't surprise you that he had actively sought the leadership role, as it provided him advancement and expanded responsibility. However, it's also not surprising that he had difficulty leaving the sales role where he was so comfortable and adept. He wanted to stay close to his customers and maintain the relationships that had been forged. Soon, it became clear that he was spending too much time in his old role and not enough in his new leadership role. Not surprising and also not uncommon. This is not an indictment of one isolated sales leader. Instead, it is a reminder that transitions are rarely smooth, and there are often no clean points of delineation.

In the following sections, we will address four key transitions for the emerging leader. These are: (1) the transition from "individual performer to achieving performance through people"; (2) the transition from "an emphasis on technical skills to an emphasis on interpersonal and strategic skills"; (3) the transition from "focusing on micro-vision to focusing on the bigger picture"; and (4) the transition from "being a recipient of change to being an adaptive leader of change." Let's look, carefully, at each of these transitions.

The Transition from Individual Performer to Achieving Performance through People

Hill (2003), in one of the few in-depth studies of emerging leaders, analyzed the experiences of nineteen new managers during their first year of leadership. She noted that managers in her study experienced changes in identity as they moved from a "doer" who got things done through individual effort to an orchestrator and coordinator who got things done through others. She emphasized, emphatically, that this move typically became a "profound psychological adjustment" for new managers (Hill, 2003, p. 229). "First-time managers have to unlearn the deeply held attitudes and habits they had developed when they were responsible simply for their performance" (Hill, 2003, p. x).

Others have underscored this transition. Benjamin and O'Reilly (2011), in studying the early career experiences of MBA graduates, noted that, as we encounter things we have never encountered before, three transitions unfold: (1) role transitions; (2) business transitions; and (3) personal transitions.

Chatman and Kennedy (2010) look at this transition in even more emphatic terms. They argue that new leaders must embrace the "paradox of leadership"—that leader success is derived through others. In fact, these authors comment, "A leader's role in a team or organization is to set the context for others to be successful. Indeed, our 'acid test' of effective leadership is how well the team does when the leader is not present" (pp. 160–161).

Recently, Google took a serious look at the transition from engineer to manager at its organization. Google examined scores of company performance reviews, feedback surveys, and award nominations to produce a set of behaviors to emulate and a series of pitfalls to avoid. Number 1 on their list of pitfalls was having trouble making the transition from being a fantastic individual performer to being the leader of the team (Harrison, 2011).

Early career stages, even in team-dominated environments, reinforce individualism and self-determination. In fact, you have been recognized and rewarded for your individual competence, hard work, and performance. In many ways, you were permitted the luxury of focusing on yourself.

Leadership is different. Personal and individualistic thinking must be buttressed by collective thinking. Accordingly, individual domination must be supplanted with a focus on others and a search for fairness and collective justice. Leadership scholar Michael Useem (2010) sums this up nicely by noting that leaders must have a "commitment to common cause over private gain" (p. 507). In leadership, rugged individualism has its place, but only if it is carefully coupled with a strong sense of the collective and a sound belief in the significance of others.

The shift toward others does not minimize the strong tendencies and qualities of individualism. Rather, it creates an opportunity for development. Individual drive and intensity are not lost. Yet, the capacity to work through others to achieve outcomes takes center stage. Personal ego may need to be held in check. You may have to gear your pace to others and their capacity to assimilate and understand information.

Importantly, in the midst of a career, underscored by your personal success and importance, you must now accept that it is not just about "you" anymore. When the leader steps into a team meeting, he or she must be able to discern and truly believe that he or she is "the least important person in the room." This concern should not be minimized. It is a shift to which most emerging leaders are unaccustomed.

There is an additional theme that we will emphasize throughout this book. This theme has to do with growth, development, and reaching potential. So far in your career, you sought and put in place opportunities for personal growth. This came by volunteering for challenging assignments, asking for and receiving special training, finding informal mentors from whom you could solicit advice and guidance, and learning everything you could from the leaders you encountered.

Now, you must play a role—a major role—in the growth and development of your people. Now, you must be the one who spends time clearly explaining and clarifying expectations. You must be the one who aligns your people with projects and tasks that allow them to stretch without failing. You must be the "ear," available to help allay stress. You must be the coach who points the way and encourages development. You must take the time—time away from a busy agenda—to help others reach their potential. And, you must grasp, intellectually and psychologically, that all of this really is your new agenda.

We must inject a reality check. You may face this transition point and revert to what has always worked in the past. That is, you become the "doer," and you attempt to do it all yourself. The logic, at least on the surface, appears to be tight. "It's easier and faster to just do it myself." "I'm so much better at this than my people are." "I really do enjoy doing this myself."

The problem here is three-fold. First, your range of activities and responsibilities have expanded, thus rendering this option impractical. Second, your people will surely feel demeaned and unmotivated. They will counter, with good justification, that you are not willing to trust them. They will feel unappreciated and underutilized. Third, part of your leadership responsibility is to help your people grow and develop. The prospect for growth is virtually impossible if you hold the reins too closely or too tightly.

Many emerging leaders that we have encountered do not yet truly feel like leaders. At times, they even push back and argue that the leadership label is being applied a bit too liberally. Perhaps. Yet, once you are asked to align and move others, the demands and responsibilities of leadership are required.

The Transition from Technical Skills to Interpersonal and Strategic Skills

We begin with a fundamental premise, a premise that is supported by research and observation. The skills—generally technical and specialty skills—that you mastered to excel in earlier organizational positions are not the same skills you need to perform successfully in leadership. This can be a tough message for our audience. In short, the skills that got you here are still necessary, but they are not sufficient. Let's look at some of the research.

The idea that the skills needed for success shift as we advance in leadership roles is certainly not new. Katz (1955), in classic, groundbreaking work, argued that, as one rose higher in leadership, technical skills became relatively less important and conceptual skills became relatively more important. Interestingly, human skills—the ability to work with and through people— were seen as a key to success at all levels. In more recent years, the research team of Mumford, Zaccaro, Harding, Jacobs, and Fleishman (2000) has expanded our thinking regarding leader skills. They underscore the importance of complex problem-solving skills, solution construction skills, and social judgment skills.

In a study of more than 5400 new leaders, researchers identified leaders who were "struggling" in their roles and leaders who were "thriving" (Van Buren & Safferstone, 2009). Struggling leaders were found to exhibit five common behaviors: (1) "focusing too heavily on details" that led them to get bogged down in minutia; (2) "reacting negatively to criticism" that led to difficulty in addressing areas of relative weakness; (3) "intimidating others," especially prevalent among fast-rising stars who were enamored by their own success and brilliance; (4) "jumping to conclusions" which led to quick solutions and implementation instead of engaging others and gaining support; and (5) "micromanagement" that led to meddling in others' work.

By contrast, thriving leaders displayed (1) a strong focus on results and (2) superb change management skills. The study's authors used powerful phrases to describe the actions of the more successful new leaders, including (1) providing crystal-clear objectives; (2) building buy-in to a common cause; (3) showing people what's in it for them; (4) displaying empathy and understanding; and perhaps most important (5) building relationships that pulled the team together.

Researchers at the Center for Creative Leadership studied 191 successful executives from six major corporations, extracting key lessons or events that had a lasting impact on how they managed (McCall, Lombardo, & Morrison, 1988). Although leaders in this study do not specifically coincide with our "emerging" designation, the work is still quite useful for our purposes.

Five categories of leadership skills and ways of thinking emerged. These included: (1) agenda setting (such as determining direction, connecting goals and plans, innovative problem solving); (2) handling relationships (such as handling political situations, dealing with conflict, and developing people); (3) basic values (for example, guiding principles); (4) executive temperament (such as self-confidence, perseverance, and coping with ambiguity); and (5) personal insight (themes like self-awareness, recognizing blind spots, and recognizing weaknesses) (McCall, Lombardo, & Morrison, 1988, pp. 6–9).

We have already noted the work done by Linda Hill (2003). She found that the new managers mastered "four tasks of transformation" during their first year: (1) learning what it means to be a manager; (2) developing interpersonal judgment; (3) gaining self-knowledge; and (4) coping with stress and emotion.

One final and highly regarded study must be mentioned. Harvard Professor John Kotter (2001) highlighted three critical functions of leadership: (1) establishing direction; (2) aligning people; and (3) motivating and inspiring. Although creating a higher-level direction is generally not the purview of our emerging leaders, you will be tasked with creating a focus and agenda. However, Kotter's points about aligning people and motivating and inspiring will be central to your success as a leader.

What do these studies say to us as we explore the transitional impact for emerging leaders? In the broadest sense, two special skill sets emerge: (1) understanding and dealing with people and "interpersonal relationships"; and (2) setting and executing a "direction" for your team that aligns with broader organizational goals and vision. Accordingly, attention to these skills will frame much of our attention throughout this book.

The Transition from Micro-Vision to the Bigger Picture

Christopher Chabris and Daniel Simons (2010) developed a test of selective awareness that we have used in our workshops with young leaders. The test and its viral version have gained some notoriety in recent years in what has become known as the "invisible gorilla test." The video begins by instructing viewers to count how many times the players wearing white uniforms pass the basketball. Then, a set of players, some dressed in white and some dressed in black, weave through a segment passing the basketball to teammates. Our competitive audiences watch intently with aims of securing the correct answer. The video concludes by indicating that there were, in fact, fifteen passes from the white team.

But did they see the gorilla? In the video, a person dressed in a gorilla costume wanders into the middle of the players, pounds his chest, and then strolls off camera. In the original research, half of the participants missed the gorilla entirely (and our samples have done no better)! The authors note that we miss a great deal of obvious detail, especially when we've been led to focus on a particular problem, approach, or set of behaviors.

There is a powerful lesson for you, as a new leader. Thus far in your career, you have focused on "counting the passes," securing the right and proper solutions to the situations that you have encountered. Now, you must grasp the bigger and broader picture. Not only must you "get the answer," but you must "see the gorillas." The bigger picture always has nuance and complexity. You begin to realize that immediate, short-run successes must be pursued against a broader political context.

Let's provide another image. In Brazil, there is a fish, commonly known as the four-eyed fish. In reality, the fish has only two eyes, but the curvature of the eye lenses allows the fish to see under the water and above the water at the same time.

The image provides metaphorical impact for our exploration of leadership. The leader must see the organization that is. Yet, at the same time, the leader must see the horizon of opportunities and threats and envision what can be. More importantly, the lenses must be brought into clear focus so neither domain is clouded or provided differential influence over the other. That ability to see and project clarity about "what is" and "what can be" is unique to the character of leadership.

This metaphor can be applied at a deeper, micro level. Most people see others as the sum of their actions—what they say and what they do. But leaders must have the insight to gaze beneath the surface and consider, within each person, a creative possibility—what they can be. Leaders see potential, while others are restricted to history. Accordingly, leaders are always searching for ways that they can help people "play at the top of their game." And, we are always looking for ways in which the game can be expanded, extended, and enhanced.

The Transition from Being a Recipient to Being an Adaptive Leader of Change

In today's rapid-fire organizational world, change is the rule, not the exception. Your leadership world is one of turbulence and change, and the rate of change is accelerating at a rapid pace. As an individual performer, you were certainly aware of change, and you felt the impact when change touched you or your team or your unit.

For a leader, everything is ramped-up. You are immersed in the swirl of change, battling to creatively craft a future for your team, while attempting to offer clarity and assurances that will, hopefully, mitigate the barrage of stress that your people face. You must now lead your people through a world of change, and we will discuss this undertaking in more depth in a later chapter.

Here, we focus on the transitional demand to be an adaptive leader of change. In fact, Bennis and Thomas (2002) suggest that this adaptive capacity is one of the key attributes that leaders must possess in our dynamic and ever-shifting environment. At the most basic level, this means that you must learn to be flexible and adaptable without being inconsistent. You must be able to change course without losing sight of the eventual goal.

Chatman and Kennedy (2010) emphasize that leaders must have astute diagnostic capabilities—being able to recognize the various nuances of different situations and being able to understand the unique leadership needs that the situation demands. Further, they note that leaders must develop a broad and flexible behavioral repertoire to respond to the nature of the situation. One is not being disingenuous, nor is one assuming a chameleon-like nature. Further, core values and character are not mitigated. Flexibility does not change who we are or what we believe in. Instead, it is a respectful adjustment in behavior.

Let's look carefully at the first two points. Emerging leaders must learn how to carefully and accurately "read the situation" with all its rich complexity. This complexity often arises from the interpersonal and political undertones that exist in all situations. Being able to correctly assess and understand the situation or context you face is always a challenge. And, understandably, it is an incremental activity.

It's important for emerging leaders to engage in reality testing; that is to see the situation as it really is. Max DePree (1989) aptly notes, "The first responsibility of a leader is to define reality" (p. 11). Daniel Goleman (2006) refers to this as "objectivity," recognizing and understanding what is really going on. In short, Goleman argues that we must see events as they truly are and not just the way we would like them to be, a process that takes time and study.

Second, leaders must be able to adapt, be flexible, and modify their carefully developed plans based on shifting demands. This is a particularly challenging transition for young leaders. Think of what is occurring. You have studied the situation, worked with your bosses, involved your people, and defined a set of challenges for the next year. You have communicated the needed direction, set the agenda, and aligned your people. In the midst of your team's march toward success, a crisis hits, and the path must be changed. Can you adjust? Can you adapt? Can you help your people adjust? Can you still produce successful team outcomes? Transitional challenges, indeed.

With a leaning toward over-simplicity, we have often told our leader audiences that, at its essential core, leadership demands two things. First is the ability to understand the situation and the unique demands it presents. Second is the capacity to flex—that is, the ability to adapt so that demands can be addressed in the best way possible.

A Perspective on the Leader's Journey

As we have seen, a number of thoughtful studies have explored the opportunities and struggles that new leaders face. While some of these studies may have not targeted emerging leaders, the outcomes and perspectives of these works are important nonetheless.

Harvard Professor John Gabarra's work is one such example, as he has studied the factors that cause managers to succeed or fail in new positions. Although the research that is reported in his book, *The Dynamics of Taking Charge* (1987), focused on higher-level, general, and functional-level managers, broader applications are present.

Gabarra described five stages of transition that managers face when taking on new leadership roles, and we find that these stages are important for you to consider. These stages are: (1) "taking hold"—a period of orientation and learning; (2) "immersion"—a period of reflection, where learning moves to a deeper level; (3) "reshaping"—a period of action and change, where the leader begins to adjust and implement based on what has been gleaned in the first two stages; (4) "consolidation"—a period where changes are meshed or consolidated; and (5) "refinement"—a period of tweaks and fine-tuning (pp. 6–7).

Critically, Gabarra's work reminds us that there will be a "settling-in" period, where we gain understanding and perspective of our new leadership situation. And, he reinforces the importance of the sequence—study, reflection, and understanding should precede action.

There is a twist here, and it is revealed in the work of Michael Watkins (2003). His book, *The First 90 Days*, is a popular read for many new leaders, and it is a favorite among corporate trainers. Watkins discusses what we all know and have experienced. Everyone is watching the "newbie" to see how you handle yourself and how you handle your people across an array of situations. Further, Watkins asserts that the first three months are fundamental to the tone you set and the image of leadership that you establish. Although he offers a number of sound ideas, his emphases on building relationships, connecting with people, and creating coalitions of support are particularly noteworthy.

At times, emerging leaders, drawing from their action-preferred backgrounds, may underplay the importance of establishing and developing these interpersonal networks. It is critical to get to know your people—to know their skills, their talents, their passions, and their loyalties. What excites them? What frustrates them? What do they need and expect from you as a leader?

It is just as important to get to know your peers, your boss, and the key players that will touch your realm of influence. Get to know them for the people they are, as well as the points of organizational perspective they represent. Find out what they are dealing with; what they are up against; their "hot-button" issues. It is all part of your growth and development.

A Preview of Coming Attractions

This book is grounded in solid evidence, drawn from the rich tapestry of empirical investigations and philosophic insights that highlight the study of leadership. However, this book is written with an applied, pragmatic, action-oriented focus that speaks clearly and directly to you, our emerging leader audience.

This book addresses skills and ways of approaching situations that can be put into practice immediately. We emphasize ideas, actions, techniques, and approaches that will help you be a difference-maker, a person of impact, and a successful leader. Be prepared, you can expect a deep dive. We will not shy away from the complex and tricky themes of the emerging leader equation; themes that rarely garner attention; themes such as character, confidence, conflict, and resilience.

Our choice of topics for this book is, of course, selective. However, the selection is driven by our desire to focus on topics that seem most critical and most problematic for emerging leaders. With that backdrop, here is a very brief look of what is coming—our preview of coming attractions.

In Chapter 2, we will look at "Character: The Inside Game of Leadership." You will recognize that there is always a battle between character and expediency, and we will discuss how you can build covenants of respect, integrity, authenticity, and value-driven trust.

Chapter 3 will address "Confidence: The Capacity to Lead with Assurance." You will see that, for emerging leaders, competence is rarely the issue. Underdeveloped confidence often is the issue. In this chapter, we will help you gain the perspectives necessary to experience healthy self-confidence.

In Chapter 4, we discuss "Clarity: The Foundation of Crystal-Clear Expectations." Here you will see that clear expectations, expressed and shared, are the building blocks for success.

Chapter 5 addresses the sticky topic of "Conflict: The Power of Successful Conflict Encounters." As a major concern and stumbling block for many emerging leaders, we will help you learn how to deal with interpersonal conflicts and handle troublesome and difficult "problem" people.

In Chapter 6, we emphasize "Connection: The Language of Understanding." Here, we will emphasize reciprocal understanding through deep listening, open-ended questioning, engaged dialogue, and responsive coaching.

Chapter 7 looks at "Commitment: The Strength of Performance through People." Here, we will explore how to build motivation, commitment, and engagement, enabling your people to experience challenge, energy, fulfillment, ownership, and high performance levels.

In Chapter 8, we look at "Change: The Call to Opportunity and Possibility." This chapter will help you move your people to grasp the opportunities and potential that reside in turbulent times, and you will understand how you can be a respected leader of change in your organization.

In Chapter 9, we face the crucible of "Crisis: Developing through the Cauldron of Adversity." You will recognize the developmental impact that adversity holds for those who learn from it, and you will understand how the tests of resilience can be addressed.

Finally, we have labeled Chapter 10, "Codas and Continuations." Here, we offer some summary thoughts for your ongoing development and growth.

Character

The Inside Game of Leadership

It may appear tangential to begin our journey by focusing on character, especially for an audience of emerging leaders, anxious for bottom-line strategies. Yet, this is where we must begin. When addressing emerging leaders, there is a tendency to be sure that all the right skills and perspectives have been provided, assuring that each of you have the proper provisions in your leadership "toolbox." This chapter is less about the toolbox and more about the person who is carrying it.

We live in an age of contradiction, confusion, mixed messages, and uncertain character. The media are littered with examples of leaders who stumble because of questionable character. Powerful business titans, highly-placed politicians, athletic icons, and even members of our clergy have had reputations tarnished and careers ruined. The vestiges of these missteps have led cynics to conclude that those in power rarely look beyond their narrow self-interests. Leaders, at all levels, pay the price.

Against this backdrop, we encounter a puzzling reality. In a number of cases, those with exposed flaws of character have ascended to lofty positions of influence. Many retain their swagger even in the face of apparent character deficiencies. This disconnect is troubling and confusing. We are left wondering. Does character deserve deep consideration in the somewhat complicated and hectic world of the emerging leader? Perhaps character is some vague, internal quality that descends to a lesser status when set against the challenges of attaining peak performance. Perhaps statements of character are needed to assuage public opinion, while actions of expediency get results. And we are left questioning. Does character really matter? Does character really count?

These are fair questions. We argue in this chapter that character counts, and it counts in ways more prevalent than one may expect. Interestingly, some of our most respected leadership authorities, people like Warren Bennis, James Kouzes, and Barry Posner, all see character as the "cornerstone" of true, difference-making leadership (Bennis, 2003; Kouzes & Posner, 2002).

Drawing from assessments of 25,000 leaders, Zenger and Folkman concluded that character is the "center pole" of leadership and argued that developing and displaying "high personal character" is a key to becoming a great leader (Zenger & Folkman, 2009). Management guru Dave Ulrich echoes this sentiment: "Everything about great leadership radiates from character" (Zenger & Folkman, 2009, p. vi). Beeson, in exploring the "unwritten rules" for leader advancement, highlights factors that are "nonnegotiable," such as displaying integrity, ethics, and character (Beeson, 2009).

Importantly, the qualities of character may have heightened significance in our ramped-up, contemporary organizational world. For example, Posner recently presented a broad study examining the values of American managers over a nearly thirty-year period. Among other key findings, he reported that in turbulent times, amid conflicting views and demands, strong values provide a source of direction—underscoring the impact of clear, unmitigated character (Posner, 2010).

There is another important dimension to consider. Character seems to matter deeply for our employees. When employees decide to voluntarily leave an organization, many factors are typically at play. However, the #1 reason for choosing to look for another job is a feeling among employees that their bosses lack integrity and cannot be trusted—again, a dimension of character (Deloitte, 2010).

Although personal character is the underpinning of all leadership, the quality of character assumes special significance for emerging leaders. In part, this is because people have fewer touch points for assessing your true character. People know that you have faced fewer trials, adversities, and crises that test and reveal one's true character.

Accordingly, you are somewhat "under the microscope." People are watching, and they are drawing assessments from their perceptions of what they see. Followers, peers, bosses, customers, and clients are learning about who and what you are. They hear your words; they evaluate your actions; and they decide whether the two connect. They are trying to get a fix or a read on you. It's not a case of distrust. Rather, it's a case of needing more evidence to provide clarity, continuity, and assurance. Make no mistake. These key constituencies are trying to determine the nature of your character.

Among the questions your contacts are pondering is one regarding your "focus of concern." Your team, your boss, and others are attempting to decide which dominates: (1) your "concern for self"; or (2) your "concern for others." Employees express this most clearly. One picture emerges from comments like

this: "He's more concerned about getting ahead than he is about helping us."
A far different picture is drawn from the following: "He stood up for me in
front of the boss; he's got my back."

As we will discuss throughout this book, there is nothing wrong with
healthy self-interest and personal, growth-oriented career drive. We would
expect nothing less from strong emerging leaders. Yet this natural concern for
self can never come at the expense of your broader leader responsibility of
concern for others.

Defining Character

Nailing down, with any degree of precision, a quality that is as ethereal and
encompassing as is character can be a daunting undertaking. However, let's
attempt to add some clarity to what we're dealing with here.

Character is comprised of both an "inner dimension" and an "expressed
dimension." From an inner perspective, character is comprised of that unique
and highly personal set of core values, standards, and rules of behavior that
define (1) who we are; (2) what we believe in; (3) what we stand for; and (4)
how we propose to behave. More simply, character is what we are like at our
core—that deep and personal level that shapes us and how we act. Carefully
reflecting on this inner dimension of character is fundamental. Kouzes and
Posner (2002) remind us that "to effectively model the behavior they expect
of others, leaders must first be clear about their guiding principles" (p. 14).

There is a stronger and more tangible level at play here too. In the leadership
classic *On Becoming a Leader*, Bennis (2003) offers a critical perspective on
character:

> By the time we reach puberty, the world has reached us and shaped
> us to a greater extent than we realize. Our family, friends, school,
> and society in general have told us—by word and example—how
> to be. But people begin to become leaders at that moment when
> they decide for themselves how to be . . . Know thyself, then,
> means separating who you are and who you want to be from what
> the world thinks you are and wants you to be.
>
> (pp. 47–48)

This becomes a challenge of character for every emerging leader. What kind
of person and what kind of leader do you want to be? Indeed, deciding "how
to be" may be the essence of the inner dimension of character.

Let's dig more deeply. When you were offered a role of leadership, your reasons for accepting were, no doubt, multi-faceted. First, if we are perfectly candid, part of it was probably ego—that ego reinforcement that comes when others recognize that your past performance and your promise of potential make you "worthy" of a leadership assignment. Second, you probably recognized that this initial leadership assignment was an essential step on the ladder of career progression.

In all likelihood, there was a third and more central reason. You experienced excitement about being in a position where you could have a stronger impact and contribute more broadly to making a difference. That may have involved doing things just a bit differently, just a bit better, tweaking here and there. In short, you had a sense of the kind of leader you wanted to be and the kind of impact you hoped to offer. That deep personal sense of "the kind of leader you want to be" is your touch point of inner character.

There is a second dimension of character. Character is revealed through its expression. True character must be a living concept—an action—an observable practice. We realize that those around us infer our character from our expression—from what we do, and what we do not do. Regardless of the laudable nature of one's inner convictions, failing to display consistent evidence of those convictions renders one little more than a well-intentioned hypocrite. Stephen Covey (1989) offers a cogent and applicable perspective:

> The real key to your influence with me is your example, your actual conduct. Your example flows naturally out of your character, or the kind of person you truly are—not what others say you are or what you may think you are. It is evident in how I actually experience you.
>
> (p. 238)

Further, character is revealed when things get hard; when stress is high; and when emotions are raw. The finely honed veneer of pretense is stripped away during adversity, revealing what's under the surface—our foundation—our character.

We've hung on to two quotes that may be helpful or, at least, thought-provoking. The first, once again, comes from Warren Bennis (2003): "Everything the leader does reflects what he or she is" (p. 132). The second comes from a far different source, theological scholar Robert Mulholland (1993): "Being and doing are integrally related, to be sure, but we have to have the order straight. Our doing flows out of our being" (p. 30). Indeed!

The Dilemma of Expediency

There is always a tension between character and expediency. This tension is prompted by organizational realities—the reality of deadlines, competitive pressures, political agendas, battles for limited resources, and a world of people who would rather "play hardball" than "play nice." These realities are part and parcel of the leadership life. These realities may not challenge our inner character, but they certainly do challenge our courage to engage and exhibit our expressed character.

The expedient route, at times, can be easier, shorter, and less time-consuming. In many cases, an argument can be made that no one will really notice. And, in other cases, the argument can be expanded to suggest that no one really cares, as long as performance expectations are consistently maintained. Of course, such judgments represent a step onto the proverbial slippery slope of expediency over character.

It is easy to get trapped in a pattern of expediency. A well-known psychological study may be helpful here. Over forty years ago, psychologist Stanley Milgram created a laboratory setting where research subjects were told to administer shocks to a research volunteer that they had just met (Milgram, 1963; 1974). Subjects were led to believe that these shocks were intended to enhance learning and recall. Although the volunteers receiving the "shocks" were accomplices or confederates (members of the research team) and all shocks were bogus, manipulation checks indicated that the subjects were unaware of the guise. In short, most subjects believed they were administering increasingly severe shocks to an unwilling and confined fellow person.

Amazingly, nearly two-thirds of the subjects continued shocking the confederates through all stages of the experiment, despite cries of pain and pleas to stop from the "shock inflicted" confederates. And why? Well, the lead experimenter, dressed in his white lab coat, told them to do so. This presumed authority figure even assured the subjects that he would take responsibility for any harm that came to those receiving the shocks. Watching the filmed experiments is a tension-filled and exasperating experience.

It is probably not surprising that Milgram's original motivation in undertaking the study was to understand how seemingly "normal" people could commit atrocities (such as those of the Holocaust) on their fellow person. Milgram explained the results by arguing that the research subjects had entered a state of absolution which he termed as an "agentic state." In this state or condition, subjects saw themselves as acting as the agent of the clear authority figure (in this case the lead experimenter) and, accordingly, were able to disassociate themselves from their actions. During debriefs, it became apparent that the experience had not had a negative effect on the subjects' self-images. In fact, they still saw themselves as people who would never harm another.

Some leaders experience a similar agentic state, often justifying their actions as simply what the organization requires and their bosses demand. Personal responsibility is absolved when one assumes such an agentic role.

When WorldCom's Cynthia Cooper and her team of internal auditors unraveled the largest corporate fraud in U.S. history, the amazing factor was not the depth of deception perpetrated by those at the top of the organization. Rather, it was the array of people throughout the organization who had evidence that something was amiss but refrained from acting. As Cooper (2008) notes in her book, *Extraordinary Circumstances*, these were not bad people. But they were people who submitted to the pressures of expediency. How can an emerging leader be expected to withstand the pressures of expediency when such pressures take the face and voice of the firm's most senior executives? This, in stark terms, is a challenge of character.

There is a common conception (or misconception) that argues that, when we are faced with real and immediate challenges of expediency, we will then engage in deep tests of our character. Well, perhaps. In most cases, we do not begin to explore and test our character when pinned down by some crisis of expediency. The test must come well in advance of the crisis.

Behaving with character in the face of pressures to do otherwise requires not only a clear understanding of what is important but the courage to act accordingly. On June 2, 2010, Detroit Tigers pitcher Armando Galarrago was on track to tossing the rarest of baseball feats—a perfect game.

With two outs in the final inning, only Cleveland Indian shortstop Jason Donald stood between Galarrago and perfection. However, on what should have been the final out, Donald was called safe at first base by veteran umpire Jim Joyce. Television replay clearly revealed that Donald was out. Joyce had blown the call, costing Galarrago his perfect game. Of course, umpires are human and mistakes happen. The uniqueness, the character, comes in what followed.

As the game ended, Joyce did not retreat to the showers, and he made no attempt to slink out of the park. Instead, he asked for and received permission to meet with Galarrago. Face-to-face, Joyce admitted that he was wrong and offered his personal apology to the young pitcher. Galarrago, despite being emotionally devastated, was gracious. Galarrago noted, "There's no doubt he feels bad and terrible. I have a lot of respect for the man. It takes a lot to say you're sorry and to say in interviews that he made a mistake" (Walker, 2010). The next day, in a further expression of character, Detroit manager Jim Leyland allowed Galarrago to deliver the line-up card prior to the start of the game to none other than Jim Joyce. There, in front of all the fans, Joyce gave Galarrago a hug, and the two men shook hands.

What strikes us most about this episode is that neither man allowed his personal pride, intensity, or ego to supersede his consideration for his fellow man. There is an interesting footnote here. At the end of the 2011 baseball season, the major league baseball players voted Jim Joyce as "the best umpire in the game."

In summary, we must realize that our foundational character cannot be bifurcated. That is, deep, underlying character cannot shift with the winds of expediency, used when it's easy to do so and discarded when pressures mount. Let there be no doubt. When this path of expediency is traveled, compromised values and standards of behavior follow. Personal integrity is diminished. Eventually, you become a shell of the leader you sought to be—a leader devoid of authenticity and credibility.

How Character Shapes Behavior

Nan Keohane, former president of Wellesley College and Duke University, addresses the linkage between the power of leadership and the qualities of personal character. "Holding power does have distinctive impacts on a person's character, for good or ill (and sometimes both). But character also determines how one will react to the experiences of holding power" (Keohane, 2010, p. 195). As noted in the previous chapter, stepping into the leadership role brings a set of unique challenges, demands, and pressures. Character provides the grounding for sifting through and addressing these concerns.

Character counts by shaping behavior in at least three ways. Namely, character establishes commitments, sacrifices, and boundaries. More specifically, character establishes the commitments that we "must" keep; the sacrifices that we "are willing" to make; and the boundaries within which we "must" operate.

The Commitments That We Must Keep

As a new leader, people need to know where you stand, and they need to know what is important. Probably the best way to create clarity regarding the centrality of commitments is by articulating, clearly and unambiguously, the core values that will not be shaken or altered. In essence, you are conveying to others two things: (1) how we should be operating and (2) what practices we will live by.

The Sacrifices That We Are Willing to Make

Part of the legend of Southwest Airlines came from founder Herb Kelleher's famous commentary that the customer is not always right. Kelleher explained that at times customers can become so outrageously demanding that they infringe on the respect of his employees. Kelleher said that such disrespect toward his people would not be tolerated—even if business was lost! This statement of sacrifice became a foundation among Southwest's people, indicating that the boss was truly looking out for them (Freiberg & Freiberg, 1996).

Harvard Business School Professor and best-selling author Clayton Christensen provides another vivid example. The starting center on the Oxford University basketball team, Christensen's team had an undefeated season that culminated in the final four of the British collegiate basketball tournament. Approaching the championship game, the schedule revealed that the game would be played on Sunday. However, Christensen had made a personal commitment that he would never play on Sunday. Despite prodding and pressure from his coach and teammates, Christensen, a deeply religious man, refused to play. Would it have hurt to make an exception just one time, especially for something so seemingly important? Christensen's assessment, "If you give in to 'just this once,' based on a marginal cost analysis, . . . you'll regret where you end up. You've got to define for yourself what you stand for and draw the line in a safe place" (Christensen, 2010, p. 51).

The Boundaries Within Which We Operate

The examples presented above indicate that character provides for each of us a set of boundaries, establishing the context and range of our behavior. Everyone needs clear boundaries, as we emphasized in the preceding chapter. This means that you must first understand your personal boundaries. Second, you must convey these boundaries to your people so they understand.

One of the more interesting exchanges we had in interviewing emerging leaders for this project involved a young woman who had taken on the leadership of an established team. After getting her bearings and assessing her team, she concluded that one of the senior team members was hurting the team. As she described example after example, we concluded that the member in question was well liked but an underperformer. She described him as a "great guy," but a team member whose work was consistently of low quality and who regularly missed timelines on meeting team commitments.

Importantly, she realized that the behavioral issues this member displayed had not suddenly materialized. In fact, as she learned, he'd been like this for years. His behavioral pattern was not new. Now here is the rub. His behavior had not been formally addressed in the past. As a result, his destructive behavior had been tacitly accepted and reinforced. What can and what should a young, emerging leader do against such a history of neglect?

We asked her to consider the impact, the downside, and the risks of addressing this senior team member—a task she undertook with careful reflection. However, her conclusion was unwavering, "I can't build the team we need if his behavior does not change. Besides, it's [the behavior in question] wrong and does not fit with who we are." The team member was "riding his charm" and in the process, was forcing team members to pick up the slack.

She knew the boundaries. It would be nice to report that all went smoothly, but it did not. Yet, she was unwavering. Like so many problem situations, progress was slow and incremental—two steps forward and one step back, with plenty of backsliding. However, the clarity of her character and unwillingness to accept behavior that was "outside the boundaries" was a stance that had a strong positive impact with the rest of the team and helped solidify her credibility as a leader.

What Are the Qualities of Character?

As a leader, you are a role model of character. As such, the qualities of character that others encounter as they interact with you will shape how they regard you as a leader.

Recently, James Sarros and Brian Cooper completed a study of Australian business leaders that explored the relationship between character and leadership. Noting that "personal values lie at the core of character," the authors identified "integrity," "cooperativeness," "fairness," and "self-discipline" as the key attributes of character (Sarros & Cooper, 2006, pp. 2, 15).

In a similar vein, Linda Hill (2003), drawing from her interviews with new managers, identified a set of prime qualities of managerial character that included "self-confidence" (the subject of our next chapter), the "willingness to accept responsibility," "patience," "empathy," and the ability to "live with imperfect solutions" (p. 167).

Burchell and Robin, in their study of the best places to work, underscored the importance of five factors: (1) "credibility" ("I believe in my leaders"); (2) "respect" ("I am a valued member of this organization"); (3) "fairness" ("Everyone plays by the same rules"); (4) "pride" ("I contribute to something really meaningful"); and (5) "camaraderie" ("The people here are great"). They further noted that credibility, respect, and fairness together comprise trust. The authors emphasized that building trust, pride, and camaraderie in the workplace is the "central task of today's organizational leaders" (Burchell & Robin, 2011, p. 7).

The following qualities of character are proposed as a set of guides. Our list may not fully define either your character or your situation, and our list, most assuredly, is not exhaustive. Barlow, Jordan, and Hendrix (2003), studying the differences in character across management levels, found that "there are different levels of character attributes needed at each level of leadership" (p. 577). As such, we have chosen elements of character that seem to be particularly important or problematic for emerging leaders.

Setting and Maintaining High Standards of Performance

All leaders are judged by performance. Accordingly, it would be both unwise and disingenuous to begin our quest for the qualities of character in any other direction. Holding yourself and others to the highest standards of performance is critical for success. But high standards also create challenge and help establish a culture of pride and commitment.

Respect and Significance

In a pioneering and now classic series of field studies, researchers from Harvard University studied the effect that lighting had on workers performing manual tasks. You have probably heard of this work. As the levels of illumination were increased, performance increased, as expected. Finally, it was suggested that in order to assure sound investigative methodology, the lighting should be decreased so that the corresponding plunge in performance could be observed. So the level of illumination was reduced . . . and performance went *up*. Another reduction in lighting led to another *rise* in performance. Finally, employees were working in little more than moonlight before performance began to decline (Roethlisberger, 1989).

The explanation given to this phenomenon has become known as the "Hawthorne effect," named after the facility where the studies took place. Apparently, the workers were not responding to illumination but to the immediate attention they were being shown. The workers felt like they were part of an important study and, thus, they felt important and significant.

Fast forward three-quarters of a century to the world of software giant SAS—recipient of the #1 ranking for 2011 in *Fortune's* annual survey of the "Best Places to Work." Recognizing the company's legendary perks such as affordable childcare, on-site healthcare, high-end gym, or even their beauty salon, one starts to get the picture. Yet, perhaps more impactful were the sentiments offered by one of the company's managers, "People stay at SAS in large part because they are happy, but to dig a little deeper, I would argue that people don't leave SAS because they feel regarded—seen, attended to and cared for" (*Fortune*, 2011). These are expressions of respect and significance.

More than an expression of character, it is your responsibility, as a leader, to treat people with respect and significance. Meeting this challenge is both complicated and rather simple. It begins with a raw understanding of people. We all need to feel that we are significant—that is, we count; we make a difference; we're important; we're needed; we're valued. We must feel that we are more than a link in the organizational array of activities. We must believe that we make a difference, and that we have an impact. Make no mistake, this sense of significance is a powerful motivator and provides meaning to our efforts.

We've all seen leaders capture the energy and passion of their people by offering an honest and sincere "thanks," recognizing and affirming meaningful contributions and significance. And we've seen leaders crush spirits by their dismissive posture toward the hard work and dedicated effort of their people.

Damning interpersonal effects arise when any party feels that they have been treated disrespectfully. Some forms of disrespect are overt and blatant. These forms include bullying, intimidating, and belittling behaviors— behaviors that are all too common in today's pressure-packed climate. Other forms of disrespect are more subtle, with a passive-aggressive tone. Here we see behaviors that are perceived by others as cold, insensitive, abrasive, dismissive, self-centered, aloof, and bitingly sarcastic. Quite a list. Such perceived threats generally elicit a "fight or flight" syndrome.

We've all seen this. In the face of disrespect or diminished significance some of us assert ourselves—strongly—in essence demanding that the other party pay attention and accord us our just due. Or, we retreat and shut down, psychologically (and at times even physically) slinking away to lick our wounds. Damage has been done and relationships have been tainted. Rare is the person whose ego can withstand the smacks of disrespect and cuts of insignificance. Piled on, time after time, people are remolded. They become confused. They become hurt. They become resentful and angry. And ultimately, they become disengaged.

In an era of high demands and challenging performance expectations, some leaders confuse the duality of possessing high standards and engaging with the highest levels of respect and significance. Sometimes, we fool ourselves. Respect and significance are often espoused, lauded for the fine imperatives that they certainly are. Yet, it's often just words, void of depth and meaning and lacking any vestiges of tangible impact. Statements of core values may decorate the walls, but action is missing. Emerging leaders must build a foundation of respect and significance that differentiates your people and ultimately your organization from the rest.

Integrity

Integrity refers to consistency. In leadership, integrity usually plays out in two ways: (1) "value consistency," or the consistency that exists between our core values and personal principles and the actions we take; and (2) the "commitment consistency," or the consistency that exists between what we say we will do and what we actually deliver.

Commitment consistency is what others see. It is played out and revealed through our day-in-and-day-out actions. As such, it can be easy to overlook or dismiss the impact of these seemingly small statements of integrity. For example, do you follow through on your promises? If you say a report will be completed by the end of the week, does it happen? If you tell your people that you'll research and get back to them on a request, do you do it in a timely manner? If you promise one of your people confidentiality as they share a concern, will you keep that commitment without wavering? These are the true tests of integrity.

Fairness

The research basis of this dimension of character is quite sound, drawing from years of solid scholarly work dealing with theories of equity and justice

(Adams, 1965; Walster, Bercheid, & Walster, 1976; Weick, 1967). We'll have more to say about the motivational impact of these factors in a later chapter that deals with building commitment.

Fairness takes many faces. Generally, we believe that perceptions of fairness or justice involve two components (Cropanzano & Folger, 1987). The first component, known as "distributive justice," involves one's perception of whether outcomes or rewards have been allocated or distributed fairly. The second component, known as "procedural justice," involves one's perception of the fairness of the process or set of procedures that are used when making the allocation decisions.

In this regard, you may feel that it is unfair that your unit did not receive additional resources (the distribution), given the high level of performance your unit has attained. However, when your boss explains the budget constraints that he is facing and the need to correct a two-year underfunding problem in a sister unit, the rationale and decision (the procedure) make sense and seem reasonable and fair. In short, if we feel that the procedures are fair, we tend to assume that the system and its leaders are behaving fairly, thereby ameliorating dissatisfaction or other negative outcomes (Cropanzano & Folger, 1996).

This example underscores the value of clear and open communication. Without procedural explanations, people are left guessing and often assume that favoritism has overshadowed fairness and equity. We favor "pre-emptive procedural communication." For example, if you have selected one employee over another to attend a sought-after, out-of-town training retreat, it may be prudent to explain to the non-selected employee how and why your decision was made. Not only may this contribute to perceptions of fairness, it is also a statement about respect.

There is a special category of fairness that is quite relevant for emerging leaders. It deals with making sure that you play "no favorites." This can be tricky for the emerging leader. It is natural that you will feel closer and more comfortable with some of your employees than you do with others (Graen & Uhl-Bien, 1995). It is also natural to want to be close to your people, building open, friendly, and considerate connections.

However, some degree of "social distance" must be maintained. You are the boss. You can be "friendly" without being close "friends." Limited socialization with your people may be a good idea, but socializing with select members and excluding others can be risky. We mentioned earlier the work of Nan Keohane, drawn from years of study and leadership experience. She encourages leaders not to develop close personal ties with those they are leading, arguing that "accusations of favoritism may arise and the leader can lose her objectivity" (Keohane, 2010, p. 202).

Remember that the fairness issue has an edgy duality. First, you must be fair; second, and considerably more complex, those around you must perceive and believe that you are fair.

Patience

Because emerging leaders are generally intelligent, high achievers with plenty of drive, speed rather than patience has probably been reinforced. Accordingly, patience may be under-cultivated. Remember, as individual performers—the doers of the organization—the ability to work at a quick pace was beneficial. In many cases, you were lauded for your capacity to be a "quick study." That capacity should not be diminished, and it will continue to be essential as you lead.

However, as you work with others, you may find that their ability to process information, ascertain connections, and reach decisions comes a bit more slowly. In fact, in coaching emerging leaders who have just received 360-degree feedback, we find that "patience with others" is generally toward the top of the list of developmental needs.

Patience has an interesting link to a leader's character or at least the perception of character. Recipients of the leader's impatience may view the leader as dismissive, rude, inconsiderate, or even arrogant. Further, people tend to believe that the leader cares only about action and results. In short, when the leader behaves with impatience toward others, the perception drawn is almost always negative.

Strikingly, emerging leaders may be unaware of both their impatience and its impact. A typical response follows what we heard in a recent workshop from a 30-year-old high-potential new leader. "I know I'm already three steps down the road. But I don't say a word. What are they talking about?" We suggested that a number of tell-tale non-verbal signals undermined his attempts at self-containment. These included rocking in his chair, his rapidly shaking leg, his visual disengagement from the group, and a general facial expression that included the proverbial roll of the eyes and a provocative smug smirk. We did not even mention checking messages on his I-phone.

Humility

In his popular book *Good to Great*, Jim Collins (2001) speaks of level-5 leaders, that small cadre of outstanding leaders who excel beyond others. In his research, he found that these top leaders exhibit two defining qualities. One is a fierce and unwavering resolve to make sure that their respective organizations succeed at the highest levels. The other is humility. Collins's descriptions of these leaders included terms like "gracious," "mild-mannered," "unassuming," and "modest." It may seem a bit paradoxical when these adjectives are included with "fierce" and "unrelenting." The blend of high and unwavering expectations, coupled with personal humility, is a formula for emerging leaders as well.

Level-5 leaders demonstrated their humility by openly recognizing and giving credit for successes to those whose had work hard generated the success. Presumably, these leaders were so sufficiently self-assured and confident that their egos did not need to be assuaged by added attention and praise, which was instead extended to others.

Candor

Strong emerging leaders have both a point of view and a willingness to express it. In one of our initial forays to the executive table at a mid-sized organization, we were struck by the tone of discussion around a strategic issue. In turn, each of the top leaders took great care to say essentially nothing, crafting innocuous language without tipping their preferences. However, once the president weighed in, all other leaders fell in line, espousing strong statements of agreement and support. Two questions arose. First, doesn't anyone have a point of view here? And second, if they do, why are they so reluctant to express it? Undoubtedly, there were some well-understood political dynamics that stifled any authentic discussion.

As we got to know the characters better, we found that some of the leaders did, indeed, possess strong and well-conceived opinions. But they had learned, over time, to refrain from taking chances. Other leaders, perhaps because their ideas had been dismissed previously, formed no opinions until they could gauge which way the political winds were blowing. We're not sure which leader is more troubling and dangerous. To the president's credit, he readily asked for input and at least professed a desire to hear and consider differing points of view. It's hard to know what's really going on here. But this we do know, the resulting collective actions are likely to be destructive, and the organization is likely to progress no further and no faster and with no greater innovation than the president permits—the proverbial disaster in the making.

Leaders are expected to assess situations, study the options, consider value and cultural issues, listen to informed input, and emerge with a point of view. Let's be crystal clear here. This is an *expectation* of leadership. And leaders are *expected* to have the courage of conviction to express their point of view in a timely, direct, and respectful manner. These are not naïve claims. Risk is involved. Study is required. An honest and respectful tone of delivery is essential. And the reality of "no" must be understood and accepted.

Recognize that your growth as a leader, both in your eyes and in the eyes of those around you, is tested and defined by the point of view you bring to the table and the manner in which you share that point of view. McCall, Lombardo, and Morrison (1988) offer insight: "It's OK to say, 'I don't know,' but it's not OK to back off a point you've carefully prepared. Then people begin to wonder what you're doing there if you have no point of view" (pp. 38–39).

Compassion

Compassion involves two activities—one that is emotional and one that is behavioral. Emotionally, compassion is a feeling—an awareness and under-standing of the emotional state of another. Although such feelings of compassion are commendable, they possess limited impact unless they are behaviorally reflected through some action. Accordingly, true compassion extends beyond a feeling to convey efforts to help others. In most cases this help involves an effort to ameliorate or reduce another's pain. In this regard, one's claims of compassion are always measured against the acts of compassion that are provided.

Sometimes, we see compassion played out in sweeping and even heroic ways. For exmple, when NBA Hall of Famer, Jack Twyman, saw his team-mate, Maurice Stokes, strike hs head as he crashed to the floor during a game, Twyman certainly had no idea of what would follow. Yet three days later, Stokes, a victim of undetected brain trauma, suffered a seizure; lapsed into a coma; and emerged permanently paralyzed—unable to move or talk. Although only 23 years old at the time, Twyman stepped forward to become Stokes's legal guardian, raising thousands of dollars to help pay the medical bills and remaining a dedicated friend until Stokes's death twelve years later.

Far more common, however, compassion is displayed in less dramatic ways. Like most leadership practices, it is experienced through the details of day-to-day life. At times, compassion is expressed by taking time to have lunch with a colleague who is struggling through a divorce. At times, it is demonstrated by your willingness to volunteer your time, talent, and energy to community causes that have special meaning for you. At times, it is simply setting aside your busy schedule to listen as a peer shares his or her concerns about his or her child's development delays.

Finding the Authentic Leader

Any discussion of character must venture into the territory of authenticity. We've all seen leaders who espouse all the right things, asserting with seeming conviction that "our people are our most important assets." They speak easily about engagement, relationship building, developmental coaching, and all the greatest and latest behavioral ideas. Yet, there is something missing. We often wonder, if we scratched beneath the surface just a bit, what would we really see once the finely polished veneer was removed? It's really a question of authenticity. CEO and author Bill George (2003) boldly shares: "I believe that leadership begins and ends with authenticity" (p. 11).

But what makes a leader authentic? And, importantly, what makes others perceive a leader as being authentic? In simplest terms, authentic leaders have strong and deep personal convictions and are willing to behave so that there is consistency between their values, beliefs, and actions (Walumba, Avolio, Gardner, Wernsing, & Peterson, 2008). Yet, in order to be helpful and practical, we need to dig a little deeper. A relatively new arena of leadership research has centered on the topic of authentic leadership. While the research in this field is still evolving, we lean toward the developmental view of authentic leadership that argues that authenticity is not fixed or static, but develops and is shaped by major life events and conscious leader decisions (Avolio, 2010).

Research tells us that authenticity is drawn from four leader attributes: (1) core self-awareness; (2) an internalized moral perspective; (3) balanced processing; and (4) relational transparency (Avolio & Gardner, 2005). Let's look at these attributes more carefully to discern what they mean to emerging leaders and the quest for character.

"Core self-awareness" is the ability to be in touch with our core values. These are the values that define who we are and what is truly important to us.

Core self-awareness also includes the capacity to understand how your values, emotions, and needs affect the way you see things.

Remember that our core affects how we perceive and interpret events. For example, one of our strongest core values is respect. When we encounter someone being rude or dismissive toward another, our core value of respect is touched, and, accordingly, we see a person who violates our sense of appropriate respectful behavior.

People who lack core self-awareness struggle with authenticity because they lack a clear sense of what they truly believe in and hold dear. It is easy to bend to the expediency of the moment when a clear centering of self-awareness is lacking.

An "internalized moral perspective" is a carefully refined internal barometer that allows us to exercise self-regulation and self-control. Here, we use our core values and internal moral standards to guide our behavior rather than allowing outside demands and pressures to have unnecessary sway. And, as discussed earlier, these demands and pressures always have some degree of leverage, affecting people and the bottom line.

Authenticity builds as we choose the proper course—the value-laden course over the expedient course. At the 2010 Verizon Heritage PGA golf tournament, Brian Davis and Jim Furyk were tied for the championship at the end of the regulation seventy-two holes of play. Shooting from the rough on the first playoff hole, Davis thought he might have touched a loose reed during his backswing—a rule violation. Davis immediately summoned the PGA tour tournament director and voiced his concern. Only after consulting slow motion TV replays were officials able to confirm Davis's fear, resulting in a two-shot penalty assessment that cost Davis the title and nearly $400,000 in prize money. In all likelihood, no one would have known had Davis remained silent. But the internal barometer defies such circumstance-based morality. Davis knew!

"Balanced processing" is the ability to objectively and rationally evaluate what others are saying. The key here is for the leader to remain open to various viewpoints and think through the merits of each position, even if there is disagreement.

Finally, authenticity builds when leaders are able to connect with others through "relational transparency." In simplest terms, this means being able to present your core self (your true self) to others. This is often a difficult challenge for both seasoned and younger leaders. In part, the challenge arises from the stereotypic image of the leader as a stoic and confined person who presents a strong front and never shares his or her true concerns. Indeed, there are times when leaders must project fortitude and there is often some level of information that should not be shared. However, our call here is for "appropriate self-disclosure."

Relational transparency through appropriate self-disclosure means a willingness to share your thoughts and express your emotions honestly. Unfortunately, some leaders assume a pattern of emotional retreat when issues become heated.

The opposite of authenticity is hypocrisy. Hypocrisy arises when we profess to have certain beliefs, values, and standards that we really do not have. As such, hypocrisy involves deception—or, more correctly, a conscious act of deception. Understandably, perceptions of hypocrisy destroy legitimate authenticity. Yet, the effects can be even more wide-ranging and pervasive. For example, evidence indicates that, when perceptions of hypocrisy increase, so do employees' intentions to leave their jobs (Philippe & Koehler, 2005).

Building Trust

Trust is a key quality for all leaders. In this regard, building and maintaining trust will be one of the special challenges you will face as an emerging leaders. Quite simply, trust is a belief or sense of confidence that another can be counted on to do what they say they will do. Trust is a relationship between people and always involves some level of uncertainty and risk. Trusting another, we are placed at risk, perhaps even the risk of losing control (McCauley, Moxley, & Van Velsor, 1998).

We encourage you to keep three points in mind as we begin our brief discussion of trust. First, trust is conditional. Practically no one trusts another unconditionally unless there is a history replete with overwhelming evidence. Second, trust is built incrementally, in stages, through our encounters and exchanges with others. And third, your trust is tested continually. People watch what you say and do, and they are gauging your trustworthiness all the time. And let's not be naïve, everyone is not pulling for you to pass the test!

A number of studies have helped us understand the correlates of trust, and these include many of the qualities of character that we have already discussed (Galford & Drapeau, 2003; Gilbert & Tang, 1998; Hoy & Tschannen-Moran, 1999; Perry & Mankin, 2004). Our intent here is to show you how trust is built in practical and real terms.

Tendency to Trust

The first consideration affecting whether your people will trust you has little to do with you. It has to do with them and their tendency or propensity to trust others. That tendency has been shaped and molded over the years. In part, the tendency may be affected by personality. However, to a larger extent, it is a function of experiences. When people risk trusting another, only to be deceived and violated, their tendency to trust again has been modified. A higher standard of evidence is needed.

We worked with a wonderful emerging leader, a young woman of impeccable character, as far as we could tell. She lamented that while she was working hard to build trust among her people, she could not help but feel that they were still holding her "at arm's length," apparently fearful to extend more than the simplest levels of trust. The young leader pleaded that she could not understand what she was doing wrong.

We suggested that, perhaps, the situation had less to do with her and more to do with the boss who had preceded her—a destructive and manipulative manager who regularly "pulled the carpet out from under his people." You see, her people had become jaded by their experiences and quite logically, were being quite careful about vesting trust in the next leader.

Next, your people look at you and make three critical assessments—the three "C's" of trust. They assess: (1) your "competence"; (2) your "character"; and (3) your "consistency." "Competence" is others' perceptions of whether you have the skills and capacity to do the things you say you'll do. Be careful here. Emerging leaders often fall prey to a tendency to over-promise and, in the process, may exceed their capacity to deliver. People see this. Accordingly, while they trust your intent, they begin to question whether you possess the capacity to deliver.

We have spoken at length about "character." The key here is others' perceptions of your intent. Do they find you benevolent—attempting do what is right for others and the team? Or do they see you as driven by vested self-interest? This dimension of character becomes a critical factor in the trust equation.

Third, others evaluate your "consistency"—your record, over time, of following through on your commitments. These judgments come in small ways, and even the slightest of commitments should not be minimized. Logically, people reason that, if you cannot be trusted to keep day-in-and-day-out commitments, why should they risk more important issues?

There is another, practical dimension that must be addressed. How do you rebuild trust once it has been breached or broken? The work of Reina and

Reina (2006), in their groundbreaking book *Trust and Betrayal in the Workplace*, offers great insight. The authors present categories of breaches, ranging from major and intentional acts of betrayal to ones that are relatively minor and unintentional.

It is the latter category that captures our interest. Most young leaders we encounter are solid organizational citizens who do not casually and willingly undermine trust. Most of their trust violations are unintentional. However, the impact for the party who feels betrayed can be devastating. The key here is what you do to address broken trust when it arises. And, try as hard as we might, these unintentional breaches will occur.

Often, these breaches are acts of omission rather than acts of commission. For example, we forgot to include a person on an important internal email memo; we did not check with a colleague before an important issue was discussed, leading him to feel "blindsided" in front of his peers; we did not follow-up on an employee request by the end of the day, as we had promised; we got busy and forgot that we had agreed to meet for coffee. Importantly, if these are not addressed, they fester; they build; and future encounters are seen, ever so slightly, through a tainted lens.

Here is your prescription for rebuilding frayed trust. First, honestly and reflectively assess the situation to determine the part that you played in creating the perceived breach of trust.

Second, once emotions have settled, meet one-on-one with the other party. Trust must be rebuilt through eyeball-to-eyeball conversations rather than less personal avenues, if at all possible.

Third, describe the situation and apologize for the part you played. Be clear and specific here—"I did not keep you in the loop, and I apologize for that."

Fourth, clarify your intentions for future behavior. For example, "I did not check with you ahead of the meeting. I should have done so. It's my intention to keep people informed. I intend to do so in the future."

Fifth, you can expect some emotion from the other party. We encourage you to listen, refrain from following the emotional path, and again, clarify your intentions.

Sixth, give it some time. This is tough. People who apologize often assume that the issue is now behind them, and all parties are back to square one. That's inconsistent with how people think and behave. Just as trust is built incrementally, it is rebuilt incrementally, and reinforced by a pattern of consistent behaviors over time.

Concluding Thoughts

Leadership is hard. When real, authentic leaders move into uncertain waters, what guides them? Certainly, the quest for performance is central. However, as we have argued in this chapter, true difference-makers are guided by an intense sense of character, demanding that performance be achieved by doing the right things.

Hopefully, your values are so well honed that you will not succumb to the temptations of expediency. This does not mean that you will not be tempted by the devils of expediency. Indeed, you will. It does mean that your values and qualities of character are so deep and real that you will readily recognize the demons for what they are and move courageously to battle against them.

Confidence

The Capacity to Lead with Assurance

Self-confidence has long been accepted as an important factor for leader effectiveness (Conger & Kanungo, 1987; Khurana, 2002). Self-confidence affects individual performance, satisfaction, and overall leader effectiveness (Gist & Mitchell, 1992; Stajkovic & Luthans, 1998). Additionally, self-confidence is correlated with higher levels of motivation, as those who approach tasks with confidence tend to work harder and put forth high levels of energy (Benabou & Tirole, 2002; Hollenbeck & Hall, 2004). Individuals with solid self-confidence are likely to pursue ambitious goals and persist when confronted with adversity (Benabou & Tirole, 2002).

On the other hand, low self-confidence can lead to timidity, inappropriately low assertiveness, a reluctance to act, stressful self-doubt, and overly wrought self-questioning. Although there is some evidence that women may have lower levels of confidence than men in early adulthood, confidence levels between genders tends to converge as we age. Generally, self-confidence rises over our working careers (at least up to about the age of 60), as people experience more and more success (Orth, Trzesniewski, & Robins, 2010). In fact, nothing boosts self-confidence more than the experience of success—or what is popularly known as "successive successes."

Not surprisingly, emerging leaders may struggle with self-confidence. At times, self-confidence issues may be part of a leader's make-up, one of those idiosyncratic dimensions of personality. However, at least to some extent, it is due to the fact that emerging leaders have had fewer opportunities to gain work-related experience than their more senior colleagues. We are not here to explore the psychological underpinnings of low self-confidence. Rather, we want to be sure that self-confidence does not become a debilitating factor to your success. Further, we want to help you understand the significance of this concept, recognize the various facets that are at play, and engage in practices to build healthy self-confidence.

Finally, as we will explore in this chapter, self-confidence can be a double-edged sword. Too little and we are left with self-doubt and indecisiveness. Too much, and we may display a cavalier over-assessment of our capacities and an attitude of arrogant disregard for others and their views. So, for the sake of accuracy, emerging leaders should not simply be concerned about having self-confidence. Rather, the deeper concern is achieving the proper balance of healthy self-confidence.

Foundations

An alternative high school is just that—an alternative or last chance for students who have either left or been dismissed from their regular or traditional high school. Some have been in trouble with the law; some have been consistent disciplinary problems; some have left their traditional schools because of pregnancy. In short, these are students whose life choices have landed them in an alternative school. Often, these students are bright and have solid potential. However, they are living with a series of heavy consequences and consuming stress.

Apart from the obvious educational goals, experts tell us that something deeper and much more fundamental is generally at play in alternative schools (Brown & Beckett, 2007). These students have experienced rejection, failure, and disapproval on a regular basis—at least part of it due to their own actions. Sadly but importantly, they have been "thumped on the head" and told they were failures so often and so consistently that they have come to believe it. Too frequently, the internal message that loops through their minds is, "I'll probably mess this up too."

Among other concerns, these students struggle with self-confidence or what researchers call self-efficacy. The pioneering work of psychologist Albert Bandura (1982) in the field of self-efficacy is widely known. Bandura (1986) notes,

> Unless people believe that they can produce desired effects and forestall undesired ones by their actions, they have little incentive to act. Whatever other factors may operate as motivators, they are rooted in the core belief that one has the power to produce the desired results.

(p. 228)

In short, without a solid foundation of self-confidence, that core belief in themselves and their abilities, the students would remain unmotivated and their long-run job prospects would likely remain dim.

This is not just a story about a select group of students. Rather, it is the backdrop for presenting a lesson for each of us. Some of you may be dealing with the unsettling pangs of low self-confidence. More broadly, some of the people you are now being asked to lead may be boxed-in by their own efficacy concerns. In this regard, confidence issues surface as a point of awareness for the informed and thoughtful leader.

The Context of Confidence

Let's dig a little deeper. Self-confidence may be defined as a personal judgment based on our perceptions of our capabilities to execute or perform a specific task challenge in a specific context (Hollenbeck & Hall, 2004). There are a number of important themes in this definition. However, the most useful for emerging leaders may come from the ending phrase, which looks at self-confidence as a "task specific" rather than a "general" trait.

Most of us are not confident all the time and across all situations and challenges. There is nothing unusual here. Consider an analogy. It's amusing to watch the seasoned actor, talented musician, or respected sports figure who appears on a late night TV talk show, admitting to being nervous and unsure about the conversation that is about to take place. There is little doubt that these stars are quite confident of their "capabilities to perform" in their chosen fields. However, the territory of unscripted questions and answers leads them to question whether they can be effective performers on a TV stage, facing a live audience, while chatting with a professional entertainer. We would not conclude that these persons lack self-confidence. Quite the contrary. However, their self-confidence in the specific talk show context may be low.

This is what we see among emerging leaders. You have mastered many technical skills and have achieved performance success in most (if not all) of your assignments. Yet, as we noted in our opening chapter, leadership presents new challenges, and leadership demands new skills and perspectives. You may be quite self-confident in your technical arena and, at the same time, you may feel less self-confident in your new leadership role.

Again, it is important to recognize that these perceptions are reasonable, common, and anticipated. They should not be interpreted that "you're not up to the task of leading." Further, our perceptions and beliefs change with experience. Consider the following story.

Jeff is an emerging leader in his early thirties who has been promoted from leading a small technical team to overseeing an entire unit. His scope of responsibility has changed dramatically, as have the expected results. His new metrics now include profit and loss goals for the unit. Two weeks into the job, he felt overwhelmed and questioned his ability and desire to stay in the position. He even shared that he had mentally decided to "give it until the end of the month," but certainly expected that he'd be requesting a return to a more technically specific role in the business where he had experienced a record of consistent achievements.

Jeff's story is one of frustration and eroding self-confidence. Working with Jeff, we offered an observation and a request. First, we reminded him of all the successes that he had amassed over his years with the business. It's easy to dismiss or minimize that record as the current pressures mount. And second, we asked him to give himself a little more time. The end of the month (which was just another two weeks) was not really sufficient. We asked him to set a four-month goal. This came with our promise that if he felt in four months that he still wanted out, we would work with him to make a smooth transition to something else.

He accepted this request; although it's a good bet that he expected that he'd being exercising the "safety-valve" option. You know what happened. Things looked different as he got his arms around the job, and slowly his self-confidence began to grow. (We might add, parenthetically, that while four months is probably too brief a time period, we felt he would reject, outright, a time horizon much beyond that.) In all fairness, Jeff's path was not without its share of rough spots, but he had gained enough experience and perspective to believe he could survive and thrive.

We'd be remiss not to mention a common misstep that emerging leaders can make at this juncture. At times, faced with flagging confidence in the leadership realm, there is a tendency to retreat back to do more of the technical work from the past. Of course, this is a return to a context where you have succeeded and have confidence in your ability to perform. Accordingly, this tendency is understandable. It is also dangerous, especially when the technical focus takes away from the developmental time that should be targeted on your new leadership role.

Enter a bit of theory. There is considerable research that looks at the need to achieve and the need to avoid failure (Atkinson & Feather, 1966; McClelland, 1967; 1976). Individuals with a high need to achieve are motivated by challenge. Moreover, they tend to gauge their chances and enjoy challenges that are moderately difficult but have acceptable probabilities of success. On the other hand, people with a high need to avoid failure shy away from challenging assignments because of the fear or risk of failing.

Faced with daunting new assignments, aware that scrutinizing eyes are gauging every move, some emerging leaders become timid and cautious. The need to avoid failing seems to step ahead of the need to achieve. Here, it may be useful to reframe your concept of confidence. Envision a slightly different look at confidence as not being paralyzed by the fear of failure. In short, you must have faith in your abilities, and you must permit yourself to stretch and push your boundaries of comfort. Recent research acknowledges that successful, high potential leaders have an "enterprising spirit" and readily take on "stretch assignments" (Ready, Conger, & Hill, 2010).

There is a business sage adage that applies. Two senior managers were discussing whether a young, up and coming colleague should be promoted. "I'm just not completely sure he's ready," commented one manager. The other countered, "If you wait until you're absolutely sure he's ready, you've waited far too long."

Building Self-Confidence

As we have noted, for most new leaders, the issue is not a generalized sense of low self-confidence. Rather, the concern is low confidence in the context of the new leader role. There are ways to build self-confidence but there is no good alternative to time. A young leader nailed it when she told us, "My boss is so self-assured, but he's been in leadership positions for 25 years." I wish there was a pill that would give each of you twenty-five years of experience over night. Because our pharmaceutical companies have not quite reached this level of achievement, let's look at some other options.

We will look at six methods or approaches for building self-confidence. While certainly not an all-inclusive or exhaustive list, these methods draw from the best and most widely accepted research on the topic.

Mastery Experiences: The Power of Successive Success

Restating an earlier point, nothing builds self-confidence more strongly than experiences of success. As we all know, confidence grows from a series of successes or what has been termed "successive success." In simplest terms, successful experiences breed confidence, and unsuccessful experiences diminish confidence. As such, these mastery experiences are the most important way to build healthy self-confidence (Bandura, 1982; Gist, 1987).

Building high levels of self-confidence in the leadership realm may take a little time. We are seeking realistic and accurate self-confidence, not some hyped-up version that does not square with reality. We even encourage emerging leaders to not be too tough on themselves. Mistakes happen. You will not have all the answers. The key here is to be "failure-tolerant" with yourself. Do your homework; study the issues; make the call; and learn the lessons that are revealed when mistakes arise. And yes, don't make the same mistakes again.

There is a wrinkle here. Enter a phenomenon known as the "negativity bias." In simplest terms, this bias or perception recognizes that most of us pay far more attention to and are more influenced by negative information than by positive information (Vaish, Woodward, & Grossman, 2008). The negativity bias even affects the way we draw judgments and make decisions, as we tend to weigh negative factors in a situation more heavily than positive factors (Kahneman & Tversky, 1984). The impact on one's self-confidence can be dramatic.

For example, we see the negativity impact when using 360-degree feedback assessments. A leader may glance over a page of feedback, containing evaluations on perhaps twenty or more desired leader behaviors. Nineteen of those twenty may be positively affirmed as strengths. However, if there is even one negative or developmental item on the page, your eyes and attention go there. At times, folks can weigh that single item so heavily that the overwhelming positive picture can be diminished.

The same thing can happen when emerging leaders are evaluating and judging their personal track record. A series of successful decisions and encounters can be trumped by a single sub-par performance. For example, a leader may have done a great job planning and analyzing a proposed course of action. Yet, the presentation before the executive team came across as tenuous and uninspired. You know the judgment—an overall low appraisal.

Given this, what are we to do? First, recall that self-confidence is a "perception." Immediate impressions and the resulting self-talk (frequently negative self-talk) should be placed in proper perspective. Perceptions of one's capacity to perform should be weighed against the evidence and the record, not a single, glaring negative event that may be over-valued anyway.

It is important for emerging leaders to do a fair and objective assessment of their achievements. Your path of progress is laden with a number of important challenges and accomplishments. Recognize and experience pride in your successes.

Modeling or Vicarious Success

Vicarious success or modeling assumes that we gain personal self-confidence by observing the successes of comparison others—people similar to us in talent, background, and experience. Logically, we reason that, if the "relevant comparison other" can approach a situation and succeed, we should be able to do the same. Therefore, our perceptions of capacity are influenced by the others' accomplishments. The key, of course, is that the other party must be viewed as a true, relevant comparison.

Verbal Persuasion

Verbal persuasion is generally viewed as the third best way to enhance one's self-confidence. Verbal persuasion is a somewhat formal term that's given to the praise and encouragement that we receive from others.

There are two key factors here, credibility and realism. First, the verbal persuasion must come from a credible source, namely someone who knows and understands the task or work that has been accomplished. Often, this is the immediate boss. However, it could come from a peer with whom you have worked closely who truly recognizes and admires the results you have produced. The more credible the source, the more credence their statements of praise hold, and, accordingly, the more likely that self-confidence will be enhanced.

Second, the praise and encouragement must be perceived as realistic—that is, commensurate with the actions and outcomes that have been achieved. A key here is whether we think the praise that is being offered is sincere and deserved. Over-the-top ingratiation does little, and it may even be detrimental.

In this arena, little things can mean a lot. At a recent workshop, Brenda, one of our emerging leaders from a small firm, was surprised when her CEO stopped in to say hi at the beginning of the day. We asked if he wanted to say a few words to our group before we started the day's activities. He spoke for perhaps two or three minutes, at the most. During that time, he told the group what Brenda did for the company, extolling how critical her role was and how proud he was of the way she executed her role. His comments were direct, specific, on-target, and complimentary. Later, as we worked in a coaching session, I commented to Brenda about how nice it was to have the boss stop by and say such nice things. Brenda responded, "You have no idea what that meant coming from the CEO. My self-confidence just leaped off the page, and I've been on a high ever since."

There is a major lesson here for you as you interact with your team and your reports. Recognition and praise are important for many reasons, not the least of which is enhancing the confidence of those with whom you work. However, to have its greatest impact, praise should be provided in clear and specific terms—emphasizing the achievements that are being recognized. It should be deserved. The recognition should be consistent with the accomplishment. The recognition should be closely tied to the achievement. Big time lags between the achievement and the recognition reduce the impact and overall effectiveness. And finally, there is no need to overdo it. An honest, sincere, and timely "thanks for doing such a great job on that project" means a lot, even if you do not have the means or capacity to incent the job in any other way. Further, these actions, when done authentically, will build rapport, respect, trust, and increase the chances that positive, desired behavior will continue.

Acceptance of Ambiguity

Consultant and executive coach Marshall Goldsmith advises emerging leaders to "make peace with ambiguity in decision making" (Goldsmith, 2010, p. 8). This is great advice. Much of leadership involves working in the "gray area," where the exact "right" action is muddled, mixed, and open to interpretation. We rarely have all the information or all the time we would like. In fact, we have argued that decisiveness—making decisions with incomplete information—is a key quality for leader effectiveness.

Equally important is what we call "avoiding the loop." We work with many emerging leaders who make a decision and then replay the decision over and over again in their minds. Although it is productive to learn from each situation and each decision, such constant "looping" tends to breed self-doubt and negativity.

Of course, this is an easy thing to say, and a much tougher thing to do. Our guidance is to catch the loop of negativity before it becomes consuming. Realize that every leader faces the same kinds of uncertainty and decision-making ambiguity that you do.

Finding Guidance from Senior Leaders

DePree and Wright (2006) have written an insightful piece that is especially relevant for emerging leaders. They recognize the powerful role that mentoring can play, while acknowledging that formal mentoring programs often fall short of their intended goals. Accordingly, DePree and Wright advise young leaders to find their own guidance through informal exchanges with respected and trusted senior managers. These should be leaders who are in no way vying competitively with you. These are the talented "good citizens" that populate all organizations.

Here is how this approach can work. Let's say, as an emerging leader, that you have trouble running good, tight, and productive meetings. You have noticed a senior manager who seems particularly adept at this task. Approaching the manager, you might share, "I need to get better at leading team meetings. I've been impressed with how deftly and effectively you run meetings. I wonder if you would be willing to meet me for coffee and let me pick your brain for a few minutes?" Keep the conversation brief. Pay for the coffee. If the exchange goes well, ask if you could meet again down the road. There is no need to ever talk about a mentoring or coaching arrangement. Even in an era when everyone's schedule is packed, most senior leaders are flattered to share with younger talent.

There are several advantages here. First, you will gain some practical insights and lessons of experience. Second, you are tipping senior leaders to your authentic desire to grow and your willingness to reach out to others for help. Third, as you talk through issues, you will recognize that your concerns and struggles are not unique. Fourth, talking through issues with those who have mastered them helps make the issues less ponderous and helps to disarm your anxiety. In short, the entire process can be a confidence builder.

There are some obvious caveats too. First, make sure the leaders you work with are trusted colleagues who seem to be interested in your growth and development. Second, keep the discussions relatively brief and issue-focused. Third, don't go to the well too often. Finally, let your senior "guide" know of your progress and your appreciation. Even a short email can do the trick. For example, you may share, "We just had a team meeting, and I used many of the ideas we discussed over coffee. I liked the way the meeting went. Thanks." Senior leaders gain reinforcement from both their own ego satisfaction and the realization that they are helping younger talent in the organization.

Overcoming Obstacles

Obstacles, adversities, and roadblocks are part of the fabric and challenge of leadership. No one—regardless of status, experience, or intelligence—is immune. In this regard, Wood and Bandura (1989) offer important insight: "To gain a resilient sense of efficacy, people must have experience in overcoming obstacles through perseverant effort" (p. 364). In other words, if success comes too easily, quick and easy successes become expected as the norm. Consequently, one quickly becomes frustrated when struggles or even failures arise.

Recent research on the theme of psychological capital is relevant here. Although some argue that psychological capital may be an old idea packaged in a new way, it boasts some interesting studies that add punch to the themes of dealing with obstacles.

In short, psychological capital is viewed as a positive psychological state characterized by "(1) having confidence (self-efficacy) to take on and put in the necessary effort to succeed at challenging tasks; (2) making a positive attribution (optimism) about succeeding now and in the future; (3) persevering toward goals, and when necessary, redirecting paths to goals (hope) in order to succeed; and (4) when beset by problems and adversity, sustaining and bouncing back and even beyond (resilience) to attain success" (Luthans, Youssef, & Avolio, 2007, p. 3). Importantly, advocates of psychological capital argue that the four attributes of efficacy, optimism, hope, and resilience interact synergistically (Luthans & Youssef, 2004).

If all of this sounds a little too pedantic, hold on. These four attributes are, to some extent, just part of our personality. We see this readily. Some people just seem, as a matter of who they are, to be more confident, optimistic, hopeful, and resilient than others.

However, we also believe that these attributes can be developed and enhanced through training, coaching, and careful and thoughtful attention. OK, no sane person relishes the prospect of confronting and battling through adversity. Yet, when struggling with and working through obstacles, we learn three critical lessons: (1) we are not defined by obstacles or setbacks in our path, but by our broader journey—an overall pattern of success; (2) obstacles and adversities are natural occurrences that can be reframed into opportunities and challenges; and (3) each obstacle that is surmounted provides greater self-assurance that the next obstacle can and will also be mastered (Stoner & Gilligan, 2002).

These points warrant some additional discussion. Reframing obstacles into opportunities and challenges represents a mindset that can inject energy and drive into a set of circumstances. There is solid research that indicates that approaching obstacles and adversities as challenges has a positive and transformational quality (Maddi & Kobasa, 1984; Stolz, 1997). Further, this reframing capacity appears to be learned, and it can become habitual (Stoner & Gilligan, 2002).

We have also suggested that, when we surmount current obstacles, subsequent obstacles are faced with greater confidence. In part, this occurs because we have an "adversity memory." That is, we remember the feelings and sense of discomfort we have previously encountered. But we also remember surmounting the emotions and circumstances. Accordingly, we surmise that we can and will do it again.

The Dark Side of Confidence: Too Much of a Good Thing

We know that the relationship between self-confidence and performance is not linear. Instead, it follows a curvilinear or inverted-U pattern. As such, higher levels of self-confidence enhance performance to a point, at which time increased self-confidence can actually lead to a decline in performance. This may seem quizzical and intuitively unlikely.

Overconfidence

Is it possible to have too much self-confidence, to be overly self-confident? Well, yes. Research indicates that high levels of self-confidence can lead to overconfidence that, among other things, can contribute to groupthink, persisting with strategies and approaches that are failing, laziness in devoting the proper levels of time and study to tasks, and overall poor performance (Grant & Schwartz, 2011; Vancouver, Thompson, Tischner, & Putka, 2002). In fact, Bandura and Locke note that, "In preparing for challenging endeavors, some self-doubt about one's performance efficacy provides incentives to acquiring the knowledge and skills needed to master the challenges" (Bandura & Locke, 2003, p. 96). We are reminded and cautioned that our biggest problems can arise from what we don't know but think we do.

Consider an example and analogy from the study of eye physiology and vision. All of us, in our normal field of vision, have an area of diminished or absent vision; the proverbial blind spot. The technical term for this blind spot is "scotoma." Even these so called "normal scotomas" can be exacerbated by various conditions and diseases of the eye.

Importantly, we all confront the scotoma imagery in our leadership roles. There are always blind spots—things we do not see; matters we do not understand; and issues that we do not attune to with the proper degree of attention and concern.

All leaders must face the reality of their personal scotomas. This is why we seek input and solicit feedback. Stated succinctly, overly confident leaders may not do enough to reduce their blindspots, and, in the process, they can become victims of their scotomas.

Another factor is at play. There is a fine line between confidence and arrogance—a delineation that is particularly important for emerging leaders. The image of the young, brash, and cocky leader is reinforced through TV and cinematic characterizations. In some circumstances, those working with the leader are waiting (and hoping) for a misstep and stumble—allowing the leader to get his or her comeuppance. Clearly, the leader's strident tone diminishes open communication and reduces others' desires to work with the leader.

The overly confident leader may be accused of hubris—an exaggerated sense of self-confidence and self-pride that results in excessive pride, arrogance, and haughtiness. Such leaders are so self-centered that they may take actions that belittle or humiliate others. This element of hubris is a form of destructive self-centeredness.

Narcissism

Our discussion of the dark side of confidence would hardly be complete if we did not address the tricky issue of narcissism. Commonly, we think of narcissism, from its origins in Greek mythology, as an excessive fascination with oneself that evolves into excessive vanity, self-centeredness (self-love), and extreme ego-centrism.

However, the issue is more complex and nuanced when applied to the realm of leadership. Like other aspects of confidence, the relationship between narcissism and leader effectiveness is curvilinear. Research has helped us recognize that "a solid dose of narcissism is a prerequisite for anyone who hopes to rise to the top of an organization" (Kets de Vries & Engellau, 2010, p. 193). However, too much of a narcissistic tendency can be toxic, debilitating, and generally destructive for relationships, trust, collegiality, and overall organizational effectiveness.

Daniel Goleman offers an excellent distinction between "healthy" and "unhealthy" narcissism. In short, Goleman offers seven characteristics of unhealthy narcissism. These include: (1) a craving to be admired and adored by others; (2) a need for constant praise and affirmation; (3) an internal drive to achieve that is largely motivated by the personal glory it brings the leader; (4) a tendency to pursue goals aggressively with little regard for how others are affected; (5) a reluctant and closed approach to criticism; (6) a tendency to view criticism (even constructive criticism) as a personal attack; and (7) a desire to exclude messages other than those that confirm the leaders' success and greatness (Goleman, 2006).

Unhealthy narcissists are unwilling to share power or seek the counsel of others, preferring to surround themselves with yes-men and be in control of all decisions (Kets de Vries & Engellau, 2010, p. 195). Their response to the typical ebb and flow of business outcomes is predictable. When successes occur, they bask in the limelight. When failures arise, they blame others and find scapegoats.

Healthy narcissism, on the other hand, meshes closely with our conception of appropriate self-confidence. Leaders who exhibit healthy narcissism are ambitious, with high levels of self-regard and self-confidence. Yet, they also: (1) exhibit self-confidence that is consistent with their talents and skills; (2) are self-reflective; and (3) are open and receptive to criticism (Goleman, 2006). Importantly, these leaders (as opposed to unhealthy narcissists) are likely to excel when faced with challenges and adversities. Not surprisingly, healthy narcissism is linked to overall success.

It is hard to determine the apex or the tipping point for the right mix of narcissism. However, Goleman offers a key. He notes, "Whether a narcissist is healthy or unhealthy can be gauged by their capacity for empathy. The more impaired the person's ability may be to consider others, the less healthy is their narcissism" (Goleman, 2006, p. 119).

The Imposter Syndrome

The original studies of this syndrome were conducted among highly successful women. Psychotherapists Pauline Clance and Suzanne Imes recognized that, despite clear and outstanding records of success, these women maintained strong beliefs that they were not intelligent and had "fooled" those around them (Clance & Imes, 1978). In essence, they saw themselves as imposters, and the resulting phenomenon has been called the imposter syndrome.

Today, we believe that the imposter syndrome is not gender-specific. The syndrome describes individuals who are quite accomplished but seem unable to accept their achievements and successes. Instead, they discount the evidence and see themselves as "phonies" or "frauds" whose competence and abilities have been far overrated and overestimated by others. In addition, they possess a gnawing sense that they will be "found out" at any moment and that their "true competence" will be revealed in all its embarrassing splendor.

Our attempt here is not to delve into the psychological underpinnings of this phenomenon or even to suggest premeditative responses. Instead, we want to attune and sensitize you to what you may be experiencing. We have observed tinges of what seem to be imposter phenomenon among a segment of the emerging leaders with whom we have worked. In most cases, the evidence supporting this conclusion has come during successive, in-depth coaching sessions.

Initially, these young leaders speak of low self-confidence. However, when we recall their achievements and accomplishments, the leaders minimize, discount, and, at times, even dismiss what seems to be obvious successes. The words "fooled" and "lucky" are bandied about, eventually leading these leaders to share that they "fear" they will soon be "revealed for who they really are."

Again, there may be deeper and nuanced psychological issues that are percolating, exceeding our skills and training. We simply encourage leaders to engage in some objective self-reflection and self-awareness. Unravel your record based on evidence and outcomes. Ask, "What would others see, and what evaluations would they draw?"

The Inside-Out Job: The Importance of Projecting Confidence to Your Team

DeCremer and van Knippenberg (2004) suggest that the "leaders' display of self-confidence in pursuit of collective goals communicates the likelihood or expectation of collective success" (p. 142). In other words, when a leader expresses and shows confidence, others are affected and, presumably, their sense of confidence in getting the job done is raised (DeCremer & van Knippenberg, 2004). You can begin to see the close connection between self-confidence, optimism, and even resilience.

Your team and your followers must have confidence in you. That means that you must not only feel a sense of self-confidence, you must also be able to project that confidence to others. In this manner, others gain assurance that following your lead makes sense. If leaders display self-doubt, followers are less likely to trust the leader, and they are less likely to be committed to the goals that the leader wants them to pursue (Kirkpatrick & Locke, 1996).

From time to time, all leaders will face situations where they must "project" confidence that they do not necessarily "feel." This act of projecting confidence can be particularly challenging for younger, emerging leaders. The intent here is not to be disingenuous or manipulative. Rather, the leader must carry an attitude of optimism and resilience. Far from a shallow Pollyanna, the leader acknowledges events for what they are, while sending clear signals of resolve and expectations of success. Not surprisingly, "rookie managers are often so internally focused that they are unaware of . . . the image they project" (Walker, 2002, p. 99).

Consider the following example. Faced with a decline in sales and a bare-bones budget, Ben knew his team was nervous and fearful of what the next two quarters would bring. Yet, he also knew that the signals he sent at the next team meeting would set a key tone for his group. He carefully shared and clarified the facts, allaying rumors, but never dismissing the reality that was revealed in the numbers and projections. Then, he talked about what steps would be necessary and how those steps could be achieved. He asked for input. Importantly, he projected a "move-ahead mentality." Rather than let his team wallow in a depressing situation, he focused on the next steps and the near-term future. He expressed confidence in his people, and projected an attitude that collectively the team would weather this storm.

Realistically, Ben was far from 100% assured that the outlined direction would work. But he knew it was the best that could be done at the time. Further, it would be naïve to believe that all (or even any) of the team members pushed their fears aside in a blitz of motivational zeal. But he did three important things.

First, he sent a signal that he was confident in his team—a statement of assurance that was needed. Second, he projected confidence in the company and its leadership. Ben, like all leaders, is an agent for the organization and demonstrating confidence in the organization and its strategies is an important responsibility. Third, Ben projected confidence in the future. Note that he recognized and did not skirt the facts. The next year would be rough and some sacrifices would be needed. But he encouraged his team to consider that they would survive and revive their strength again.

The need for confidence and projecting confidence is always important. However, the need is even more dramatic during periods of change. The leaders' confidence can provide calming assurance during these times of uncertainty. Self-confidence generally helps leaders feel and project a capacity to tolerate and handle the stresses that accompany change. We'll talk more about leading change in a later chapter.

Reflecting on the Lessons

Part of your development as an emerging leader is that you are learning about and gaining insight into yourself, or at least we hope you are. We want to encourage you to make this process more explicit. Reflecting on your experiences and learning from the lessons of experience are critical to building self-confidence.

Sometimes we miss the big picture. Kris was a 27-year-old engineer with only four months in her first leadership role when she received her first 360-degree feedback. Although her 360-degree feedback data were overwhelmingly positive, she dismissed the results. She argued, for example, that the people had not worked with her long enough, and that they were just being nice. While we agreed that their exposure was rather brief, we noted three facts: (1) she had received data from a broad range of people at various levels (direct reports, peers, and boss); (2) all respondents indicated that they felt like they knew her pretty well; and (3) the data were consistent.

Kris was particularly taken off-guard by her boss's positive responses. She revealed that, in one of her first challenges, she had handled a key client in a fairly clumsy and inexperienced manner, requiring the boss to "bail her out." Why weren't the boss's impressions colored by this event? After being encouraged to talk with her boss about the matter, she returned with a different take on the story. Yes, she had made a mistake. However, the boss was swayed by how she responded to the mistake, learned from it, and worked to rebuild rapport with the client. He was impressed with her resilience and how she adapted her style and approach. Reflecting back, she realized that the deep lesson was not in the mistake, but in how she pulled herself up and dealt with the mistake. Her frame of mind was on the mistake. The boss's frame was on the ability to adapt.

Without some reflection on what we are experiencing and how we are growing and developing, we miss these lessons and the confidence that they can bring. Further, because our growth is incremental, we often take for granted or attribute scant regard for some pretty formidable advances that we have made.

There is another factor at work here. Bright, young, emerging leaders are often their own toughest critics. At times, this may be because you hold yourself to quite high standards. However, at other times, your experience base may not be broad enough to allow an honest evaluation of what you truly do know and have accomplished at this stage of your career. In short, you have no adequate frame of reference.

So, how do we make reflection be a real and meaningful activity? First, we are fans of journaling. Admittedly, journaling can be a tough discipline to enact in your fast-paced world. That being said, chronicling your lessons of experience in a journal format can be a powerful developmental tool. The journal is especially important when reviewing your progress.

Second, we are also fans of support groups—folks with whom you can talk through your experiences. Support groups should not be confused with either mentoring or coaching. Support groups may be made up of people from your organization, but frequently they are not. The key is that the group: (1) is committed to provide reciprocal help to one another; (2) will hold all matters in strictest confidence; and (3) have enough similarity to one another and work-related insights that they can offer meaningful support and advice.

Concluding Thoughts: The Limits of Your Capacity

There is a practical, bottom-line question that we must consider as we conclude this chapter on confidence. What do you do when you reach the limits of your skills, your strengths, and your capacities? For example, you will face some tricky interpersonal issues beyond what you have experienced—issues where all options are less than optimal. You'll hit some roadblocks where carefully honed and analytically sound recommendations are blocked by upper management. You'll face the intransigent peer who simply refuses to work collaboratively for the good of the business. You'll face a disheartened senior employee whose motivational engine seems incapable of recharge. And we repeat, what do you do?

Realistically, you will likely face some degree of self-doubt. In fact, once we scratch through the bravado, even leaders who seem to be paragons of confidence will admit that they experience periods of uncomfortable questioning and troubling second-guessing. So, the first lesson lies in the realization that nobody has all the answers. Indeed, those who believe they have mastered the leadership domain are simply arrogant and delusional—not confident.

Once we accept the reality of this first lesson, we can then seek to progress. The second lesson comes when you have the courage to reach out and ask for help. Here, you are neither throwing in the towel nor are you capitulating on your role as a leader. Think of it this way. You are seeking additional input, viewpoints, and ideas to help you make the best informed decisions possible. Your challenge is to seek input, actively consider and evaluate that input, and make the best call you can. That's all anyone can ask, and it's all anyone can do. No one succeeds alone!

The third lesson comes when we can reflect on what we are learning and how we are growing. Although it's a bit trite to assert that we are all works in progress, it is still true. When coaching emerging leaders through those pesky, inevitable downturns, we always ask, "What have you learned through all this, and what will you do differently next time?" This is the key, and it is an unspoken dynamic for all confidence. What are you learning? Where will you turn for help? What must you do differently? Soon, you will see a burgeoning maturity and if we might be so bold, a realistic and healthy self-confidence.

Clarity

The Foundation of Crystal-Clear Expectations

As we have stated earlier, emerging leaders rarely engage in elaborate, long-term visioning. However, the clarity of your expectations and how these expectations are expressed and shared is fundamental to your success as a leader. Crystal-clear expectations are paramount in today's fast-paced environment where needs and priorities change frequently. Bruce Tulgan (2007) offers succinct insight. "Your number one responsibility is to make sure that every person you manage understands exactly what he (or she) is expected to do" (p. 90).

Leadership pioneer Bernard Bass's definition of leadership provides important insight and guidance. Bass (1990) suggests that "leadership is an interaction between two or more members of a group that often involves structuring or restructuring the situation and the perceptions and expectations of the members" (p. 19). It is the second part of that definition that we find intriguing, as it highlights the leader's role in providing structure and expectations. Indeed, clear expectations are building blocks for success. However, through either deficiency or negligence, unclear expectations erect stumbling blocks of misdirection, frustration, and ineffectiveness.

One of the first questions we ask when working with new leaders is, "Has your boss been crystal clear about what is expected of you? Do you know what outcomes are expected? Do you have a clear sense of the metrics being used to measure your performance? Do you have a good sense of expected timelines? Do you have enough clarity that you can set solid priorities?" Too frequently, the answers to these questions are nebulous at best. One leader even commented, with only a slightly facetious tone, "When I get called on the carpet for not doing something, I assume that it's my responsibility."

There is considerable research attesting to the positive impact of clear expectations (Chen & Bliese, 2002; Lang, Thomas, Bliese, & Adler, 2007; Whitaker, Dahling, & Levy, 2007). Much of that work surrounds the concept of role clarity. In simplest terms, role clarity (as opposed to role ambiguity) deals with the extent to which people know what is expected of them (Katz & Kahn, 1978).

Evidence indicates that role clarity, especially regarding job responsibilities, job duties, and performance expectations, leads to higher levels of job performance (Taylor, Fisher, & Ilgan, 1984; Whitaker, Dahling, & Levy, 2007). In a fascinating study involving Army cadets, researchers found that cadets who were experiencing high job demands reported less physical and psychological strain when they had high role clarity (Lang, Thomas, Bliese, & Adler, 2007). In short, role clarity appears to moderate the relationship between job demands and strain (Bliese & Castro, 2000). Clarity has even broader impact. Classic research has indicated that clear role expectations resulted not only in less tension, but also in higher job satisfaction (Kahn, Wolfe, Quinn, Snoek, & Rosenthal, 1964).

Consider the other side of this equation, when clarity is absent and ambiguity prevails. In a recent meta-analysis of forty-two studies, role ambiguity was found to be negatively related to organizational citizenship behaviors—those important discretionary actions that people take for the good of the organization (Eatough, Chang, & Miloslavic, 2011). Not surprisingly, clarity is also an important factor as organizational newcomers adjust and are socialized into their new environment (Bauer, Bodner, Erdogan, Truxillo, & Tucker, 2007).

Clear expectations provide reasonable boundaries so your people know what is within their purview of activity and what is not. Again, we turn to Bruce Tulgan (2007), who offers, "If an employee's job is to be creative, the biggest favor you can do for that employee is to be clear about what is not within the employee's discretion" (p. 99). Establishing clear boundaries does not diminish motivation, initiative, or innovative thinking. To the contrary, expectations offer the context that permits the enhancement of motivation, initiative, and creativity.

Emerging Leaders and the Clarity Bias

Although emerging leaders generally grasp the significance of establishing clear expectations, they often fall short here. There are two reasons why this happens. First, young leaders have a tugging concern, even a fear, that they not be perceived as micro-managers. Consequently, they may not provide enough specifics and enough clarity.

For years, we have asked the young leaders in our workshops and classes to describe the worst leader they have ever had and exactly what has led to that labeling. At the top of the list is the overly domineering micro-manager who limits and underutilizes people by holding them too closely in check. There is well-reasoned logic for this concern. True micro-management can be associated with lower levels of morale, higher levels of turnover, and critically, it can be a potential career staller (Chambers, 2004). Further, the tendency to micro-manage can signal a lack of trust in your people. Consequently, many young leaders hold back being too explicit with expectations for fear that others will think they are over-thinking and over-managing the situation.

There is also a second reason. Young leaders assume, at times incorrectly, that people prefer and work best with less direction rather than more. This belief is probably an outgrowth of how you prefer to be treated. And yet, this is generally a misread, and, as we will see shortly, it's inconsistent with research (Latham & Locke, 2007). Most people need clear expectations and a clear set of boundaries in order to have the discretion to work progressively and productively. The words of Computer Associates CEO Charles Wang (1989) ring true, "We must tell people what we expect. And if they don't meet the expectation, we have to tell them, and tell them why, so they can improve" (p. 331).

The Case for Clarity: Goal-Setting Theory

One of the more useful approaches to understanding the importance of clarity was originally advanced by Ed Locke (1968). Locke's research produced "goal-setting theory," an approach that has been both well-studied and highly-regarded (Latham & Locke, 2007; Locke & Latham, 1990; 2002). Goal-setting theory debunks the myth that we are better off providing people with loose, nebulous, "do your best" goals. Instead, the theory emphasizes that "clear, specific, and challenging but attainable goals" lead to higher levels of performance and employee fulfillment.

The issue of challenging but attainable goals, of course, can raise some concerns because of its particularly idiosyncratic nature. Creating just the right amount of challenge allows people to experience their highest sense of utilization. But if the challenge is too lofty or is perceived as being out of reach, people can give up, refuse to extend effort, and motivation can wane. Consistent with what we have learned from studying achievement needs, it's best that goals are moderately difficult but potentially achievable (McClelland, 1971). In other words, people must feel stretched and challenged, and they must believe that their achievement results from their own efforts rather than luck, fate, or chance. Leader sensitivity, through open communication, is important here.

There is an additional and critical point to consider. Goals have their biggest motivational impact when they are "accepted" by your people. This point warrants some additional discussion. How does a leader increase acceptance of a goal? One of the things that you can do is allow followers to participate in the goal-setting process (Erez, Earley, & Hulin, 1985).

This can be a tricky proposition, and we recognize two caveats. First, as the leader, you must have a clear idea of where you want to go—the goals that seem reasonable and appropriate for what you want to accomplish. As such, it is your responsibility to focus the participation. You do not want the participation process to be such that the goals are shifted too far from your original intent or, worse yet, that they be allowed to run counter to organizational goals. Second, you have to facilitate the goal-setting process to assure that it is challenging and offers appropriate stretch. If left to their own devices, many people may set goals that are below their potential, thereby assuring that the goals can be attained.

The research is clear that, if people are allowed to participate in goal-setting rather than being told what to do, a psychological shift occurs (Erez, Earley, & Hulin, 1985). When individuals are asked to participate (rather than being told what to do), and they feel this request is genuine, they feel included and special. Even if you do not go along with their suggested goals, as long as people believe that their opinions have been listened to and considered, they are more likely to accept the goal.

You should not assume that goals must be established solely by you and thrust on a waiting audience of followers. You are far better off working with team members and direct reports to clarify goals and expectations rather than imposing them. Again, if people have a hand in setting goals, they will be more committed to seeing that goal attainment occurs. Of course, the process of setting mutual expectations is often a negotiating activity.

Although clear goals and clear expectations must prevail, levels of goals must be considered with a careful eye on the audience. While annual or even long-term goals are important metrics for you, you will probably need to shorten the time frame and think more about incremental or feeder goals for your people. These are those close-in and more visible goals that must be sequentially attained so that our longer-term goals can be realized. Although you understand that a 2% increase in volume is needed this year, your people need to know that the Jones Company project must be completed by the end of the month, and they must know why this is so important.

Finally, there is merit to the well-known S-M-A-R-T goals. This approach asserts that goals should meet five conditions. Goals should be: (S) specific; (M) measurable; (A) attainable; (R) relevant; and (T) timely or time-specific. Keep in mind that these conditions must be assessed from the perspective of your people. For example, what seems attainable to you may not to them. What appears quite relevant to you may be obscure to them. Accordingly, careful communication that explains and clarifies each of the five conditions is a must. And, perhaps most important, put all of this in writing.

Reality Check: The Case of the Psychological Contract

The concept of psychological contract surfaced in the leadership literature over twenty years ago, but it has seen a resurgence in recent years (Jafri, 2011; Rousseau, 1989; Zhao, Wayne, Glibkowski, & Bravo, 2007). It is probably more than coincidental that this rebirth has coincided with the bleak economic period that has clouded our business climate. A psychological contract exists when an employee perceives or believes that his or her contributions to the organization create a reciprocal obligation to which the organization should conform (Rousseau, 2001; Rousseau & Tijoriwala, 1998). The key here is that employees feel that there have been "promised obligations." Although the terms of these obligations (the contract) are not discussed and not formally agreed upon, employees still emerge with a set of working expectations regarding what the organization should do and how it should act. Further, these expectations deepen as they are reinforced over time.

If all this sounds quite esoteric and theoretical, you'll soon see that it is not. First, consider the emerging leader who has been promoted to head a department of her business, a department plagued with a series of performance issues. The department head soon assesses (correctly) that the existing talent base does not match the department's needs. Although the current employees are loyal and dedicated, they broadly lack the technical skills necessary to turn the department around. Now, overlay on all of this a company tradition of being strongly family oriented and caring for its people—a tradition that has been reinforced by never having a reduction in force and rarely exercising a termination.

In essence, a psychological contract has been forged in the employees' minds—if you are loyal to this company, the company will take care of you. Further, that expectation has been reinforced through years of consistent behavior. This awareness does not eliminate the department head's perceived need for change, but it certainly injects a complication into the mix for the prudent leader.

Are the employees' expectations reasonable? Do they make sense given the department's current situation? Does all this make sense given the economic climate of cutting-edge performance that all organizations seek? To an extent, it does not matter. The employees have an expectation, an unwritten psychological contract, within which they behave, and that contract has been solidified through a history of action (or inaction).

There is considerable research looking at what happens when managers and organization breach and violate this psychological contract. Among the outcomes are lower job satisfaction, lower company commitment, increased levels of mistrust, greater turnover intentions, and lower performance (Lester, Turnley, Bloodgood, & Bolino, 2002; Restubog, Hornsey, Bordia, & Esposo, 2008; Robinson, 1996; Shore & Barksdale, 1998; Zhao, Wayne, Glibkowski, & Bravo, 2007). Given these dramatic possibilities, the impact of these unwritten contracts should not be minimized.

There are at least two key points that this discussion should raise for our emerging leaders. First, you should never underestimate the impact of the psychological contract on the attitudes and behaviors of your people. The contract represents what they have seen and what they expect. Deviating too far from these expectations will be countered by resistance. You will hear the oft-uttered commentary, "That's not what we signed up for"; "He's trying to change everything"; and of course, "She just doesn't understand how things work around here."

Given this, here is the second point. You may have to begin the process of mapping out new expectations for your people, especially if you find the existing perceptions to be inaccurate or incompatible with organizational needs. The best way to do this is to begin by clarifying with your people "what will not change." For example, let them know that core values of respect, dignity, and appreciation of our employee partners will not be sacrificed. However, let them know, in performance-related terms, what must become part of their new expectation set.

Finally, you are not in this alone. Shifting expectations that require a reframing of the psychological contract are usually broad, and they are typically unit or even company-wide initiatives. Accordingly, your stance should be reinforced throughout the leadership ranks.

Signaling Expectations

Chatman and Kennedy (2010) have indicated, "Because leaders can influence employees' fate, employees attend vigilantly to leader's behavior, even to the mundane aspects such as what leaders spend time on, put on their calendar, ask and fail to ask, follow up on, and celebrate" (p. 171). As such, they remind us that leaders are sending signals about "what counts" all the time. Accordingly, it is important to realize that employees are reading expectations through both our words and our actions.

In fact, our behaviors may trump our language as an indicator of what's really important and what's really expected. It seems that leader behaviors provide employees with a much clearer picture of priorities than do formal vision statements or policies (Chatman & Kennedy, 2010).

When our people see inconsistency between formal expectations and leader actions, they are confronted by competing cognitions or competing awarenesses, what has been termed cognitive dissonance (Aronson, 1992; Berkowitz & Devine, 1989; Festinger, 1957). Dissonance is conceived as an "aversive motivational state," meaning that we are compelled to reduce the dissonance when we experience it. One way of doing this is to discredit or minimize one of the competing cognitions, thus eliminating the source of inconsistency.

We've all experienced the vestiges of this inconsistency and dissonance. It starts early. The high school teacher who hammers home the importance of preparing for the pop quiz that never comes is signaling (consciously or not) that all that preparation is a waste of time.

We see it in our organizations too. Time-consuming reports that are rarely used force the hand of time-sensitive employees. The boss's words say the reports are important, but the behavior (or lack of behavior) suggests they are not. Consequently, why are we surprised when the reports remain undone?

There is a further issue at play here. The leader's inconsistency may be perceived as hypocrisy (as opposed to authenticity)—a theme that has seen considerable research attention in recent years (Walumba, Avolio, Gardner, Wernsing, & Peterson, 2008). When values are at stake, perceptions of hypocrisy can undermine the leader's credibility.

It's a safe bet that these issues of signaling and consistency are highly relevant for emerging leaders. People are always trying to figure out what the leader really wants, and, even more critically, what the leader will reinforce and reward.

The Role of Feedback as a Form of Clarity

Part of gaining and assuring clarity depends on how you use feedback. Feedback to your people should be frequent and specific. This provides reinforcement, keeps them informed, and keeps progress toward goals clearly on the front burner.

There can be a tendency to get people involved, set a clear course, and then let people go too long without feedback. Without regular updates, check-ins, and progress assessments, people lose a sense of what's going on. They may even begin to drift.

Relying on 360-degree assessments, we have noted a tendency among emerging leaders to be criticized for their lack of "follow-through." Investigating this result, we often find that young leaders set a path of clarity and help their people get on board. And then, feedback wanes or even disappears for a time. In most cases, the leader is working hard and pursuing a meaningful agenda, but people do not see the behind-the-scenes activity. All they know is that they have not heard anything for a while. So they begin to construct meaning. They may surmise that the leader is not dependable, does not really care, and in some cases, trust can be frayed. In short, when feedback lags, people will construct their own stories about what's going on. Some are realistic; some are extensions of reality; and some are unsubstantiated rumors. But this is all part of their sense-making.

We encourage emerging leaders to meet regularly, preferably weekly, with their direct reports. This is in addition to the numerous, ad-hoc, problem-solving or issue-oriented meetings that arise. Weekly meetings are planned and scheduled get-togethers.

These meetings should focus on accomplishing three things. First is the personal, one-on-one contact. It's hard to estimate the impact of this time, but it can be huge. It is a form of connection that should not be underplayed. The opportunity to meet with your people one-on-one sends an important message to your folks. It says that you want to be accessible. It says that, even though you are busy, time with your people is a high priority. It says that you want to hear from them and that you value their feedback. You are making a statement here about you, what you value, and how you will lead.

Second, these meetings give you an opportunity to offer reinforcement, thanks, recognition, and encouragement for the positive actions your people have taken. Leaders may be reluctant to offer such "praise" for fear that this feedback will be dismissed as just a series of "atta-boys." However, these statements need not be over-the-top, and they should be tied to specific behaviors. Don't miss the small things. "I know you stayed late yesterday to get that report done. Thanks." "Your analysis on that project was really solid. Nice job." Will people reach a satiation point with such feedback? It's unlikely if the recognition is earned and the feedback is sincere. Most leaders err by expressing too little appreciation, not too much.

Third, these meetings provide opportunities for discussing needed "course corrections." Course corrections should be a joint process between you and your people. Progress can be discussed openly, and needed adjustments can be determined. The goal here is not to assess blame when adjustments are needed, but to ensure that targets are met and goals are accomplished. The tone is one of problem-solving and progress. The focus is on moving ahead to provide the greatest opportunity for success.

Course corrections are not synonymous with micro-managing. Instead, they are forms of refining and clarifying expectations. It is important for emerging leaders to make sure that people do not wander too far off course. Additionally, you may find ways to help your people when they encounter problems that deter their progress in meeting expectations. Through conversation, you may find that they have hit a roadblock where you can help. Or they may need additional resources or extra help that you can help arrange. When this is done openly and sincerely, your people will see you as working to facilitate their progress in meeting expectations—not imposing yourself to tighten control.

Attaining Personal Clarity: Building Your Expectations and Roles

Amid all the discussion regarding clarity of expectations, it is important that you are clear on the behaviors and roles that are expected of you. They come at you from differing levels and angles. Hill (2003) has referred to this as a "constellation of expectations," where you as a leader and all those around you have conceptions (and perhaps even differing conceptions) of what your role(s) should be. Hill's insights are illuminating, and we are certainly influenced by her research. Let's look at each of the key players that typically contribute to the mix.

The Boss

Of course, it is critical to understand what your boss expects of you. You must know what outcomes and results the boss wants—in short, your realm of responsibility and accountability. When we meet with new leaders, working to get their arms around the job, we always ask, "What are your metrics?" The metrics are the benchmarks against which your boss is measuring and evaluating you. These metrics should be clear. This is your "performance role," and it is the foundation against which your leadership success is judged.

In some cases, the boss's expectations here are perfectly clear. However, as often as not, the boss's metrics may lack the detail and direction you desire. Here, we encourage our emerging leaders to define their own metrics, even if the boss has not done so explicitly. These can be shared with the boss, providing evidence that bottom-line outcomes or performance are important drivers for your leadership.

Of course, hitting the performance metrics is only part of the game for the boss. In addition, the boss expects you to create a tone or culture where people are engaged and committed to their work, and the interpersonal spirit is positive and flourishing. If you feel that the descriptors of "tone" and "spirit" seem a bit fuzzy and imprecise, you are correct. However, we cannot escape the "interpersonal role" that the boss desires.

The Subordinates

Your subordinates or direct reports will have their own ideas of what you should do as a leader and how you should do it. Some of the subordinates' expectations are based on their past experiences (good and bad); some expectations are based on what would make their work and their working lives more meaningful and more productive; and, frankly, some of their expectations are based on wishful thinking—what they hope they can extract from the "new kid on the block."

Hill (2003) has reported that subordinates, fundamentally, believed new managers should provide support for the subordinates. This support included solving problems, creating a positive work environment, and contributing to the subordinates' overall development and success. In short, although it is quite broad, we like this notion of a "supportive" role when discussing subordinate expectations.

Every leader wants to support his or her people. So, this role is understandable and legitimate. It also seems to be a logical and reasonable expectation for subordinates to hold. However, providing support, while finding appropriate boundaries, is a challenge that all emerging leaders will confront. Remember that even the best and most loyal subordinates are likely to test the boundaries. There are no clear and absolute answers here, but certain themes typically arise. Accordingly, we will highlight three boundary issues that we often encounter when working with emerging leaders.

Problem-Solving versus Employee Development   The first issue is the boundary between solving problems and encouraging subordinates' development. Without a doubt, there are some problems that subordinates bring to your attention where you must take ownership. Often, these involve conflicts between units of the organization or concerns that require the attention of those higher in the organizational hierarchy. They may involve particularly sticky interpersonal issues where the nature and range of the conflict demands your attention.

With these caveats in mind, we suggest that your goal, generally, is not to solve problems for your people, but to help them solve their own problems. We often recant the time-worn phrase, "Most people are more than happy to have you solve their problems for them if you are willing to do so!" It's an easy trap because our intentions are pure—we want to help others, and we want to make things easier for our people.

Subordinates come to you with a "monkey on their back," wanting you to "take the monkey off and put it on your back." Pretty soon, you've got a lot of monkeys weighing you down. But even more critically, your people are not developing and growing and learning how to solve their own problems. We encourage taking time with subordinates, listening carefully, asking questions, offering suggestions, and offering reasonable help. This becomes developmental coaching in its best form. However, we want your subordinates to emerge from this meeting with their own plan for dealing with the problem.

We encourage emerging leaders to meet, one-on-one, with every subordinate. Do it early and do it regularly. Ask, "What can I do to help you do your job better?" Again, listen and question. There will be things you can do; things you need to do; and things you want to do. However, you will also uncover requests that are neither realistic nor in the best interests of the business and the long-term growth of your people. This is where boundaries begin to be created.

Friend versus Boss   Second is the boundary between being a friend and being the boss. Emerging leaders ask, "How close should the leader be with the team of subordinates?" The answer is always influenced by the nature of the people, the situation, and the culture of the organization. As such, there is no standard and certainly no "correct" stance. Further, exceptions abound—all purporting excellent outcomes. The question here deals with an arena of management that is commonly known as "social distance." Stated fully, "What is the proper social distance between leader and follower?" Let's unpack this sticky question.

Leaders need to know their people. They need to be open. They need to be approachable. They need to consider the needs of their people from both organizational and extra-organizational perspectives. We do not hire a set of skills. We hire a whole, complex person. To make this decision even more problematic, some of the people you are now leading have been colleagues and friends from the past. In many cases, you and your families socialized together.

Understanding all of the above, we would still argue that some degree of social distance is needed. An example may be helpful. Working with a leader in his early thirties, I asked about his relationships with his subordinates. He reported that most were his friends. He enjoyed socializing with them. That socializing included playing on a softball team; going out for drinks afterwards; and getting together after work at a local watering hole for a round or two of drinks to unwind. He asserted that he saw only positives and no negatives from these encounters. I asked only one question. "Do these relationship inhibit, in any way, your ability to make tough, objective decisions, even including disciplinary decisions?" He thought only a second and replied honestly. "Yes." In fact, if we are honest, the answer is almost always, yes. So what guidance can we offer? Well, be careful and judicious.

There has been a wonderful line of research over the years known as "leader-member exchange theory" or its more colloquial label, LMX (Graen & Uhl-Bien, 1995). It suggests, among other things, that most leaders have a tendency to build special bonds with a few of their people, a selection that has been termed "the in-group." Often, people become part of the in-group because of the interests and values they have in common with the leader. They build a special bond because of their love of golf, yoga, college basketball, NASCAR, or opera.

However, LMX suggests the following happens. The in-group develops a special and closer relationship with the boss than do other team members. They spend more time together, communicate more often, and feel a more trusting relationship. They have the boss's ear. There is nothing necessarily wrong with this relationship.

However, certain considerations come into play. How do the other subordinates, those not part of the in-group, feel? Do they feel they are being treated unfairly? Do they feel that special concessions and certain privileges are extended to the in-group? Do they feel that in-group members get an extra edge when assignments are made? How about when resources are allocated? Once again, all of the above highlights the need for sensitivity and careful boundaries.

Tolerance versus Corrective Action   A third boundary issue is that between tolerance and corrective action. Because we do hire whole people whose lives extend beyond work, every employee will encounter periods when they are "off their game." Even the highest-level performer will go through periods when their attention and energies are diverted by the vagaries of life. These may include such far-ranging themes as personal and family health issues, marital struggles, trouble with children, changing family dynamics (such as responsibility for an aging parent), or financial difficulties. In many cases, these events lead to slides in performance. These slides may be deviations that represent stark contrasts to a pattern of acceptable, high-quality performance.

So the question becomes, how tolerant should we be? How much slack do we cut folks given that we know what they are facing? When is it time to pull in the reins? How do you draw a line and say "enough," without the risk of being perceived as insensitive, callous, or non-responsive to the life-issues of our people. After all, aren't we supposed to exercise flexibility?

This is tough, and we will not attempt to paint it any other way. We are confronting one of the ever-trying dilemmas of leadership. Here are the horns of the dilemma. We must respond with compassion, understanding, and tolerance, and we must assure that performance is attained. Two examples may be helpful.

Within a few months of assuming his position of leadership, Bill's administrative assistant informed him that she and her husband had separated and would be getting a divorce. Bill demonstrated concern and understanding, recognizing that some level of distraction was inevitable and some time away from the job was likely. Bill demonstrated his support by offering to take a couple items off the assistant's plate for a couple of months. Note, the work had to be done. However, Bill, realistically, took a pro-active stance to assure a continued flow of performance.

A second example is even more dramatic, and it is one of our favorite stories. Dan led a production team that included four hourly-paid machine operators. Although the operators were all in their late thirties and early forties, Dan had built respect and rapport with them in his first eight months on the job. Tragically, one of the operators lost his teenage daughter in a horrific traffic accident as she was driving to high school. Dan contacted the family, offered his sympathies and support, but did not thrust himself into their personal situation. A bereavement period was stipulated in the employment contract. However, the interesting twist to the story is how Dan responded to the other operators.

He went to the area where they worked, called them together, and openly shared his personal sorrow. In addition, Dan told the operators that he knew all of them were close friends. He understood that they were probably experiencing their own grief. Dan noted that while the contract stipulated parameters for time off in these circumstances, he would understand if they needed more time off and would approve whatever made sense to them. He only asked that they communicate with him so he could figure out how best to handle production goals during this crisis. Two hours later, the operators reported that they had created a rotational system that would keep production running while each took turns being with their grieving colleague. You can imagine the impact this had on respect and trust.

But there is a deeper issue—one we encounter in nearly every workshop we conduct. When is enough really enough? When does tolerance and sensitivity become taking advantage? When does tolerance become code for failing to step up and pull your weight? We cannot provide that answer. To do so would suggest a formulaic approach that is inconsistent with our understanding of people and work and their complicated interconnections. However, we can offer some factors to consider when making your decisions.

First, how are others receiving and accepting the concessions and tolerances that you are extending? This is critical because, in most cases, they are the ones who are being asked to step up and cover the slack. If you sense that the rest of the team is feeling victimized, or if they feel that fairness and equity have been breached, it may be time to rethink your approach.

Second, what sort of progress is the target person making? We all deal with crisis differently and our capacities for resilience vary. However, it is reasonable and fair to assess whether progress is being made. Perhaps different strategies are needed. Leaves of absence may even be needed.

The Peers

Emerging leaders may be so focused on meeting the expectations of the boss and subordinates that they fail to consider the needs and expectations of peers. Peers approach one another expecting an accurate sharing of information, a willingness to work together for the best interests of the unit or organization, and a willingness to weigh in with support on certain critical issues. As such, most peers expect a "collegial role" of one another.

Collegiality permits peers to interact across lines of formal authority and, as such, engage one another beyond the constraints of a strict hierarchy. One acquires a level of political savvy in this arena, learning what can and should be shared and what cannot be discussed. Further, political skills and techniques, such as coalition building, are refined among peers. This can be tricky in environments where peers are competing for limited resources.

What You Expect of Teams

Emerging leaders often work with and through teams. Accordingly, issues of clarity become important for the team. Obviously, the leader should be clear about what is expected of the team in terms of outcomes, deliverables, and necessary timelines.

Consider the following example. As a leader, you need to select a new source of supply for one of the items in your production process. You assemble a team and give them the charge of screening and evaluating five potential suppliers. Here, the leader might assert, "I'd like the team to evaluate each supplier. You can select the criteria for evaluation, but quality, consistency, and dependability must be heavily weighed. I want to see pros and cons of each with supporting data, along with a ranking of suppliers, and your proposed best choice. We need to move with some haste here. I need a final written and oral report in four weeks. I think you have all the access to data that you need, but don't hesitate to ask me for information or input if I can help." Of course, there will be questions and further refinement and clarification in this initial interaction.

Note that you are not boxing-in the team, and you are not minimizing their input and influence. Instead, you are providing parameters and clarity on the key items you must have: (1) a recommendation that can be supported through analysis; (2) a ranking that provides a pecking order for consideration; and (3) a timeline. The team can now proceed confidently because they know what is expected.

There are additional team dimensions to consider. Hill and Lineback (2011) provide valuable help here. Regarding teams, they suggest that the leader must ensure that: (1) the team members are clear about their individual roles so that team members know who does what; (2) the team is clear about the practices and processes that it will use as it does its work; (3) the team is clear about how it will interact, collaborate, and work together so that norms of collaboration are established and practiced; and (4) the team is clear about how it will ensure and report its progress.

The leader should not dictate, but you should influence and help assure team clarity. You may offer some influence if you sense that the team is faltering in any of these areas. More likely, though, you will influence teams through the example you set when you lead teams. To the extent you are clear and focused on performance outcomes, you help the team reach its potential.

Accountability

We live in an age of accountability (Meyer & Kirby, 2010). For a new leader, accountability assumes a new and daunting edge—what Hill (2003) refers to as "the full pressure of having to make the bottom line" (p. 72). Obviously, your ability to establish and maintain personal and team accountability will be critical to your success. We view accountability as comprised of two components: (1) establishing clear and meaningful performance metrics; and (2) assuring that people are held to the standards of these metrics. Each of these components is distinct and challenging.

First, organizational life is framed around standards of measurement. As such, you must establish, communicate, and monitor these metrics. Certain metrics are outlined by your leaders. These may be sufficient, but often they are not. We encourage emerging leaders to create their own "scorecard," comprised of the key metrics that will be tracked as you evaluate performance and adjust your actions. There is merit in the adage that "what gets measured gets done."

The question here is straightforward, but may require considerable reflection—"How will you know if you are succeeding?" Further, your scorecard must be checked regularly and necessary adjustments must be made. As we coach emerging leaders, we always want a check-in, "How are you doing in terms of your scorecard?"

As we have framed in this chapter, your people need their own scorecards— their metrics. We have built the case that such indicators have positive effects on both motivation and performance.

However, there is a second component to the accountability formula, and it is even more nuanced and problematic. People must be held to their metrics. They must understand where they are succeeding and where they are not.

They must understand that deviations must be corrected. And, most importantly, they must accept that the responsibility for adjustment rests with them. Many leaders, especially new leaders, do a better job establishing metrics than with holding their people to these metrics. When this occurs, accountability is lost.

Generational Considerations

Over the past several years, much has been made about the blend of generations that we are experiencing in our workplaces. The mix of Baby Boomers (generally accepted to be those born between 1946 and 1964), Gen Xers (born between 1965 and 1980), and Gen Y (born between 1981 and 1995 and often referred to as millennials) raises some interesting questions and challenges. Since our emerging leaders fall into these younger cohorts, it's important to take a look at how generational issues are likely to come into play.

Some of the more credible studies in this arena come from Jean Twenge (2006). Twenge assessed generational impact by holding age constant. In other words, she asked, what were 20-year-old Baby Boomers like and how does that correlate with 20-year-old millennials? The data do offer points of divergence. However, many of the claims bandied about do not pass the muster of research.

Drawing from Twenge and others, three themes emerge that seem especially relevant for our emerging leaders (Deal, Peterson, & Gailor-Loflin, 2001; Twenge, 2006; Twenge & Campbell, 2009). As we embark, we must cautiously remind ourselves that we are speaking about general composites, not conditions that will be experienced in each and every situation.

The first theme has to do with the "centrality of work." In general, Baby Boomers tend to have a strong work-role salience. That is, their identities are tied closely to their work. Gen Y, on the other hand, are less likely to feel that work is the central dimension of their lives. For them, work plays a more instrumental role—work is the way to make a living.

Recently, a senior executive confided his concern about many of the young managers with whom he worked. "They just don't have that fire in the belly that I do." We reminded him that, while that fire had brought business success, it probably also played a role in his premature heart attack and his divorce. "Perhaps they see the fire and don't want to follow that path."

It seems that younger leaders embrace "work-life balance" as more than an overworked, feel-good phrase. This should not be interpreted, as it has been by some, that emerging leaders are not hard workers. However, emerging leaders do not want work to consume them at the cost of other life dimensions, such as family, friends, and taking care of oneself.

The second theme concerns the "immediacy of gratification." The Baby Boomer generation, as well as many workers in their forties, have practiced and honored a progressive model of reinforcement. The pattern suggests that one works hard, sacrifices, "pays one's dues," and then reaps the harvest of their labors. Emerging leaders and younger employees desire more immediate gratification. One emerging leader confided to us that she been a project leader for two years, had mastered the tasks, and was getting bored. Clearly, she was not feeling challenged and, consequently, she was getting restless.

This can lead to assumptions about loyalty. Younger leaders have grown up during eras of organizational and social cutbacks, economic troughs that have forced downsizings, and broad uncertainty about the potential and timing of recovery. Many see the hard work and dedication of their parents result in unexpected furloughs and wrenching career disruption. Many have first-hand experience with the pain and trauma of these events. Not surprisingly, many have grown unsure of the intentions of upper management. In the worse case, organizational loyalty seems to be a worn-out concept of a distant era. In the best case, it is a tough sell.

The challenge here for emerging leaders is to gain perspective. The tendency to push too hard, too fast can be viewed by others as a sign of arrogance, and evidence suggests that this tendency can also lead to leader derailment. It is important to keep in mind that, while company loyalty may be on shaky ground, loyalty to one's immediate boss becomes even more significant. This can be a powerful awareness and a point of impact for emerging leaders.

There is a deeper concern here. Evidence suggests that you may be less likely than your more senior counterparts to demonstrate respect for people simply because of the position or formal authority they hold (Hays, 1999; Holtz, 1995). This attitude often signals "disrespect" toward elders in general and bosses in particular (Deal, Peterson, & Gailor-Loflin, 2001, p. 9). Similarly, adherence to following the chain of command can also be an issue. Gen Y can be prone to disrespect the chain of command (Lipkin & Perrymore, 2009). Care should be taken here. Obviously, such moves have pervasive impact, and people have long memories.

The third theme deals with forms of connection. Growing up in an age of instant contact through rapidly evolving technology, it is no surprise that emerging leaders may eschew face-to-face contact that more senior people use and prefer. The disparity here can be striking. "Let's get together and discuss it" is often seen as "a major waste of time." In fact, the high value given to technological connection often dissuades emerging leaders from face-to-face contact.

There are good sides to this argument. Many meetings occur for the wrong reasons, and excessive time and expense is, no doubt, lost. However, tone and intent are often lost through technology. For example, building interpersonal trust is fundamentally an eyeball-to-eyeball activity.

The key here is to know what form of connection is needed in each situation. It's important to ascertain when sending a text or email is too risky and is the absolute wrong thing to do. Emerging leaders may have to "pace down" and have a one-on-one personal meeting, not because it's the best way to garner needed information and direction, but because the other person's emotional state demands it. We'll have more to say on this topic in Chapter 6.

Finally, there are some personal characteristics of both Boomers and Gen Y that will be helpful. First, as Boomers age, their need for relevance and significance must be maintained. Second, many Boomers are facing a set of uncertainties they had not anticipated. Given broad advances in wellness, Boomers have the capacity to work longer. Many Boomers are questioning whether they'll experience boredom and lack of fulfillment in retirement. Increasingly, Boomers are recognizing that their financial situations have made retirement problematic. Emerging leaders must understand these issues and sensitivities.

Gen Y employees, on the other hand, bring their own unique challenges. As a cohort, Gen Y tends to have high levels of self-esteem and narcissism (Twenge & Campbell, 2009). They often have inflated self-concepts and, accordingly, have difficulty accepting criticism. It's not surprising that some have unrealistically high expectations of what the organization can and should do for them. Clarity of expectations is essential here.

Concluding Thoughts: What You Expect of Yourself

We end this chapter with what may be the most important theme regarding expectations. Namely, what do you expect of yourself? Your answers here are shaped by the expectations of your boss, your subordinates, and your peers. But they are also affected by your values and your character, as revealed in an earlier chapter. Further, your expectations are affected by your special passion and drive, what we have often referred to as your unique "voice."

This unique voice grows from a desire to be a difference-maker who moves the team, the unit, and the organization forward. Perhaps the saddest commentary for any emerging leader is to be labeled as a "caretaker" who holds the troops together and maintains what has already been achieved. Most leaders want more, and they expect more of themselves.

Emerging leaders experience a shift in identity, a theme that we have mentioned previously. In their work on leadership "passages," Dotlich, Noel, and Walker (2004) contend that this shift may be most difficult for those with strong professional identities. For example, those coming from accounting, engineering, and information technology possess strong and deeply ingrained professional affiliations. Accordingly, when they assume a position of leadership, they may feel that their professional identity is being subjugated or lost.

Emerging leaders understand that their technical skills are not lost. However, the new leadership identity may lead to concerns that your technical skills will not remain sharp or cutting edge. In all honesty, there is merit to this concern.

In all likelihood, your initial expectations will center on technical issues and performance standards. However, your focus will increasingly move toward the personal and interpersonal realm. Knowing what needs to happen is one thing. Making it happen through people is a far more complicated endeavor.

Leaders want to invoke change that will lead to improvements. You want to move your group from point A (where we are now) to point B (where we need to be). There are issues to be considered here. The pesky question of "how much and how fast?" almost always arises.

Three factors affect this decision. The first deals with the nature of the situation you encounter. We often ask, "What is the cost of not being at point B?" This question calls for an assessment of how bad the current situation really is. If the situation is dire and the red ink is flowing, prompter rather than slower action seems appropriate.

The second question is, "How far is it from point A to point B? Are your changes minor tweaks? Or are they major shifts?" As the distance between these points increases, the need for progressive, incremental steps is enhanced. This is built on a classic tenet of behavioral theory known as the "law of successive approximations."

The third question deals with the nature of the people and their level of receptivity to the changes that are needed. "Do you anticipate general acceptance or broad resistance?" Remember that people can support, and they can destroy the best of plans. Never underestimate the level of pushback that accompanies change—any change.

Conflict

The Power of Successful Conflict Encounters

We have chosen to address the topic of conflict relatively early in our discussion of *Building Leaders*. There is good reason for this decision. Drawing from our workshop data extending over twenty years (and including over two thousand participants), the theme of "dealing with conflict" consistently ranks at the top of developmental needs for emerging leaders.

For emerging leaders, the concern with conflict is usually neither strategic nor long-term. It is immediate. It is encountered in our daily exchanges which are peppered with all the elements of a ripe conflict. Are we able to confront others with respect? In the midst of conflict, can we show sensitivity to others' points of view? Do we shy away from potential conflict? Do we minimize and subjugate our needs to avoid what may be an unpleasant exchange? Can we work effectively with others who disagree with us? Do we think in terms of trade-offs and win-win outcomes, or do we engage in abrasive and antagonistic win-at-all-cost positions? And, perhaps most critically, can we extract the functional parts from conflict without being destroyed by the dysfunctional parts? To a large extent, the image that others have of a leader's character, style, and credibility are drawn from how he or she addresses conflict.

The Power and Value of Conflict

Conflict cannot and should not be avoided. There will always be disagreements between well-intentioned people who are vying for limited resources. There will always be honest differences of opinion. Moving forward in ways that create the greatest value for the organization is the key in such situations. We've all encountered leaders who hunker down, take adamant stances, and "win" the immediate case. In the process, ill-will can be stoked, and relationships can be damaged. We try to remind these leaders that "there is always a tomorrow" that must be considered. Sometimes, leaders, and especially younger leaders, fall victim to the adage that they "have won the battle and lost the war."

There are a number of advantages that come from functional conflict. For example, when conflict is addressed openly, it can provide the spark to break ingrained and stale patterns of thinking and acting. Additionally, the presence of conflict can be the impetus for creative inquiry that generates real innovation and growth (Jehn & Mannix, 2001). Much of this potential seems to depend on how conflict is accepted and handled. For example, in a recent study of 378 executives from 105 organizations in China, researchers found that the approach that management teams took in handling conflict powerfully impacted the leadership of organizational innovation (Chen, Liu, & Tjosvold, 2005). Here and in other studies, a cooperative conflict style was associated with positive organizational outcomes and overall effectiveness (Chen, Liu, & Tjosvold, 2005; Song, Dyer, & Thieme, 2006).

Further, when conflict is addressed and respectfully considered, it can provide a needed system of checks-and-balances. Let's consider an example. We have worked with a creative young entrepreneurial leader in her mid-thirties. Beaming with new ideas and ground-breaking innovative projects, she carefully runs each new venture by her team of five other colleagues. The team is more cautious and conservative, and they are prone to respectfully "poke holes" in the leader's enthusiastic options. One might see this as a disaster about to explode. But it works! And it works largely because of the leader's attitude and approach. She understands the limiting reality of groupthink and, accordingly, encourages dissent and constructive conflict. She wants others to share their candid reservations. She welcomes the debate and exchange. She realizes that, if she can't convince her team of the value of her projects, she is unlikely to be able to convince anyone higher in the organization.

There is an added advantage that arises out of conflict—an advantage that is often not fully appreciated. When leaders openly and respectfully confront and address conflict, authenticity and credibility grow. Relationships may become deeper and more meaningful. Teams can become stronger. And perhaps most powerfully, trust can be enhanced (Chen & Ayoka, 2011).

The preceding discussion points in an interesting direction. Hopefully, it helps shape an attitude or view of conflict that is relevant for leadership in a complex organizational world, comprised of increased diversity, escalating global connections, shifting assumptions about where and when work must occur, and pressing demands for greater efficiency.

However, despite all these potential advantages, the prevailing approach of many emerging leaders (as well as leaders in general) toward conflict is the same—avoidance. Sometimes, avoidance is born out of the conviction that, with time, things will get better or work themselves out. Of course, timing can be critical, and this argument is not without merit. Yet, avoidance often results from one's unwillingness to address what may be a difficult encounter. As Stone, Patton, and Heen (2010) point out, this reluctance may come from one's perceived inability to have a difficult conversation that is typically laden with emotion.

Creative and respectful conflict encounters can be functional. However, the inflection point that moves conflict from functional to dysfunctional is hard to define. Generally, it is recognized after the fact, once things have begun to spin off in an undesirable direction. As such, the emerging leader faces a daunting task—keeping the innovative aspects of conflict moving, while keeping the head-banging, destructive aspects in check. These destructive pieces are almost always about people and interaction, demanding that interpersonal conflict be understood and managed. Accordingly, the arena of interpersonal conflict will be our focus in this chapter.

The Structure of Conflict

We begin with a direct example of how conflict can arise. A few years ago, we conducted a workshop for the mid-level and upper-level managers of a mid-sized organization. The organizational leaders had rented a beautiful training facility in the North Carolina woods, just a few miles from their headquarters. The facility had all the latest technology. Even more striking were the amazing ceiling-to-floor windows, giving one a panoramic view and the feel of being in the middle of nature.

During a mid-morning exchange, one of the managers got up and left the discussion. To make matters worse, we could see exactly what he was doing (remember the windows). He was standing outside, smoking a cigarette and talking on his cell phone. Soon, he finished his smoke and returned to the training room. Heads turned as he moved through the group. Not more than 15 minutes later, he went through the same routine. It was just one of three trips, all replete with smokes and phone conversations, which took place over an hour's time.

Let's unpack this scenario. What do we know is going on? What facts do we really have? Well, we know that he left the room three times. We know that each time he smoked a cigarette and talked on the phone. We know that he returned each time. We know that his comings and goings were momentarily distracting to the rest of the group and to us. But, really, we know nothing else.

These are all the facts that we have, what experts label as first-order realities (Nardone & Watzlawick, 2005). Most critically, they are also "personal facts" and may not represent the full spectrum of facts surrounding this situation.

Already, the complex cognitive processes of perception and interpretation are set in motion, as we begin to carve some sense of meaning from the facts that we have. You've probably already gathered in this book that respect is pretty important to us. That value factors in and affects our interpretation of what is going on in this workshop situation—a determination that the manager in question was rude and disrespectful. Of course, this too is simply a "personal interpretation," and it may not be an accurate attribution of what's really occurring.

While these processes are unfolding, "personal emotions" were activated. In our case, we responded as we do to most evidences of what we perceive as blatant disrespect. We became angry.

It's interesting how quickly our facts, our interpretations, and our emotions coalesce and prompt our actions. Here, we must admit with embarrassment that we were rather dismissive toward the manager the rest of the day. Nothing over-the-top, but we really made no effort to encourage his involvement, as is our normal practice. "Personal actions" were simply extensions of personal facts, interpretations, and emotions.

This is the set-up or structure of our interpersonal conflict encounters. In rapid succession, our facts lead to our interpretations (second-order realities), which prompt our emotions and our actions (Nardone & Watzlawick, 2005).

That evening, as we reviewed the day, we were disappointed at our lack of emotional control. After all, we were the leaders in this situation. We decided to address the situation the following morning before the workshop began. But what followed was the shock. The manager sought us out first, offered an apology for his previous-day actions, and then shared his explanation. "I'm sorry I had to leave. I probably shouldn't have attended the workshop, but I know they wanted the whole management team here. I thought it would be disrespectful not to attend." (His choice of words here was really interesting.) Then he continued, explaining the rest of the story—his story. Apparently, he was dealing with a family emergency that was not only dramatic but was unfolding with increasing intensity as the day progressed.

There is a critical lesson here. Our facts are never all the facts. There is always another side to the story. And it's incumbent on us to check out the facts when the evidence we have does not connect with the behaviors we are encountering. Leaders have to read situations, interpret facts, and do so quickly. Yet, we must make sure that we are reading the situation with the most solid factual base possible. Jumping to quick conclusions without checking all angles to get a solid factual base can be a trap for emerging leaders. So, we offer a simple beginning. Check the facts. There is always another side to every story.

Conflict and the Skills of Emotional Intelligence

The story offers further depth, as it highlights three qualities of emotional intelligence that are quite relevant for conflict situations. These qualities are: (1) "emotional self-awareness"; (2) "reality testing"; and (3) "impulse control." As you are probably aware, emotional intelligence has gained momentum in recent years. Research has suggested emotional and relational qualities are critical to successful leadership, and that the absence of emotional intelligence skills may inhibit or thwart one's growth and progress as a leader (Goleman, 1998).

Let's look at these emotional qualities in more depth. Emotional self-awareness deals with the ability to recognize one's emotional state and the ability to see the connection between these feelings and how they affect our thinking and actions toward others. In fact, it is generally accepted that awareness of our emotions is the foundation for regulating those emotions (Mayer & Salovey, 1997). (In the case above, recognizing the presence of anger and understanding how that anger can funnel and stymie logic-based patterns of thinking is part of emotional self-awareness.) Leaders with high levels of emotional self-awareness tend to be "attuned to their inner signals" (Goleman, Boyatzis, & McKee, 2002, p. 253). In essence, emotional self-awareness helps us be aware of what is happening, and how it is likely to play out. This awareness may also help us to recognize the limiting effects the anger emotion can have and motivate us to pace ourselves for more emotional control.

Reality testing deals with our ability to see situations as they really are. We've all worked with people who read far too much into situations. And we've worked with folks who seem unable to glean the impact of what is right before their eyes. Both can be damning for a leader, as both undermine your ability to respond with accuracy and fairness.

Finally, there is the tricky skill of self-control or impulse control. Researcher Rueven Bar-On explains this as "the ability to resist or delay an impulse, drive, or temptation to act . . . or to react appropriately without uncontrolled anger"

(Bar-On, 2002, p. 18). It's not surprising that the lack of impulse control can derail leaders and thwart further advancement. The response in anger or the errant comments are part of the collective memory of the group. Research sponsored by The Center for Creative Leadership emphasized that "Managers who don't feel a responsibility to others, can't handle stress, are unaware of their own emotions, lack the ability to understand others, or erupt into anger easily are viewed as likely to derail due to problems dealing with people" (Leslie, 2003, p. 4).

It is also not surprising that struggling with impulse control can be a concern for talented, intelligent, and achievement-oriented emerging leaders. Keep in mind that people read your credibility and your character with how you respond under pressure, when anxieties and tensions are escalated. These people reason that anyone can put on their game face when things are going smoothly. However, when conflicts arise and emotions escalate, others may believe that our "true colors" come out.

Conflict Styles

Much of the research on interpersonal conflict has examined differing conflict styles and how these styles can be applied across situations. The most common approach looks at five conflict styles—forcing, avoiding, accommodating, compromising, and collaborating (or problem-solving) (Sternberg & Soriano, 1984; Thomas, 1992). Each style varies along dimensions of "motive" ("concern for self" versus "concern for others"), "approach" ("competitive" or "cooperative"), and "outcome" (who ends up "winning") (Rizkalla, Wertheim, & Hodgson, 2008). There are some very useful and practical points to this situation-based approach.

For example, when time is very short or when emergency measures are needed, the more assertive and coercive "forcing" style may have to be used. There really is no other recourse. Action must trump discussion. Here, you assure that your needs and interests are met in what becomes a win-lose scenario with the other party. Of course, applying this style too liberally, as some leaders do, can destroy engagement and motivation and eliminate the power of functional pushback.

An "accommodating" style involves the strategy of "yielding," where you back off and let the other party have what they want. There is no doubt that some leaders use this style simply as an act of capitulation—a way to refrain from dealing with unpleasant issues. Of course, we cannot condone that approach. However, strategic accommodating is often needed, and it can be a mark of a politically-savvy leader. For instance, this approach may make sense when you realize that the issues at hand are far more important to the other party than they are to you. Further, a leader may decide to yield on an issue in order to gain a degree of "social credit" with the other party—a credit that can be called-in on more important matters down the road.

In a similar vein, an "avoiding" or "postponing" strategy may make solid strategic sense. For example, if you find yourself relatively underprepared for a conflict deliberation, postponing may be prudent. Sometimes, we avoid discussing some items because other, more critical, items demand our focus and energy. Even more critical, when the emotions of either (or both) parties are running so high that the risk of interaction is dangerous, avoiding makes sense. Recognize that this is not a long-term or ongoing strategy. We are deferring interaction, not eliminating some eventual interaction when the timing is better.

Given these considerations, our discussions will center more on styles that work toward "compromise" and "collaboration." Both of these styles look for ways in which the important needs of each party can be met. Although we will not use these exact terms in the discussion that follows, you will still see elements of these styles coming into play.

The Foundations of Interpersonal Conflict

Here is an approach that we use in workshops to probe more deeply into the nature of interpersonal conflict. Think of a recent conflict in which you were involved. Be careful that you were one of the active participants and not just an observer. It will not matter whether this is a work or non-work episode.

Next, ask yourself, "Why did this conflict occur?" This is your sense of cause—your interpretation of why it happened. Next, try to sense and name the emotions you felt when you were in the midst of the conflict. Finally, what was the first action you took when addressing the other party. We emphasize the first step because that first step has a disproportionate effect on all that follows. Here you have the key factors in interpersonal conflict—precipitating events, interpretations, emotions, and actions—similar to those we described earlier in the North Carolina training example.

There are many possible causal factors. At times, conflict arises because people approach conflict with differing interests and needs. At times, it arises as we struggle over limited resources. At times, conflict comes from parties representing differing points of view, each of which may be quite legitimate.

However, we begin to experience conflict or feel the presence of conflict when our expectations (which are always reasonable to us) are blocked or dashed by the other party's behavior or lack of behavior. That's a powerful sentence, worth another look. Our expectations are blocked or dashed by the other party's behavior or lack of behavior.

Now here is the tricky part. In some cases, the expectations have never been carefully and fully clarified and communicated. In other cases, expectations are vague and are open to varied interpretations. The joke about the parent who asks his son how he is doing in college comes to mind. The young man replies, "Good." The father astutely queries, "Is that my A-level good or your C-level good?"

In a similar vein, "I need that report as soon as possible" means vastly different things to different people. "I need that report by Monday afternoon" removes much of the interpretive ambiguity. Accordingly, as a starting point, clarity and assurance of expectations should be emphasized.

Emotions are always interesting and complicated to unpack. Most of you probably described your episode with negative emotions—frustration, disappointment, confusion, anger. But a small percentage of you experienced conflict as a challenge, and you were even energized by the conflict episode. It's an intriguing and stretching experience to work with people who find energy in conflict. Sometimes, it seems that they go out of their way to create some level of conflict in otherwise mundane situations. At best, they enjoy debate, asking penetrating questions, and pushing the boundaries. Although they may spark creative discussion, they can easily exacerbate emotions that are already elevated.

Now here is the key factor. What did you do? How did you respond? You may also want to evaluate the relative effectiveness of that response. A first-line supervisor once inquired, "What should I do when one of my folks gets in my face?" Perceiving a baited question, I asked what he usually did. "I do the only thing a strong supervisor can do. I get right back in his face, and I get the last word." Sensing his agitation, I asked him if that approach seemed to work effectively. "Hell no. He says something; I come back; he yells; and I yell louder. Everyone hears it, and soon I'm doing damage control." Then he asked a really penetrating question, "Why do I fall into that trap every time?"

The answer, like most behavior events, is nuanced. But the long and short of it is this: most people, in the presence of conflict, assume a fairly habitual response. That is, we use the same behaviors that we've used before without much regard for its effectiveness (or ineffectiveness) in previous situations. Indeed, research evidence suggests that most people have conflict styles or dispositions that are relatively stable over time and across situations (Blake & Mouton, 1964; Sternberg & Soriano, 1984)

There is good reason for this consistency. Conflict comes with intensity. Emotions are heightened and arousal levels are spiked. If we were able to drain all the emotion from a conflict encounter and approach the encounter analytically and strategically, we are all smart enough to make good action choices most of the time. But that is not the way it works. So we all fall into similar, often ineffective behavioral patterns.

There is hope and help here. We can modify behaviors, and we can utilize practices to give us the best chances of navigating successfully through conflict episodes. Importantly, these behavioral practices can be learned. Becoming aware and mastering these behavioral options early in your leadership career will be an advantage that enhances your growth for years to come. It will be a key to helping you become the credible difference-maker you want to be.

The Principled Outcome Base

Thomas Jefferson once decreed, "Differing points of view do not necessarily mean different principles." There is considerable insight here. In the face of interpersonal conflict, what is the principled outcome that all parties agree needs to be achieved? In other words, at the bottom line, what are we trying to accomplish here?

Consider a series of recent studies looking at the dynamics of court-mandated mediation during divorce proceeding (Perry, Marcum, & Stoner, 2011; Stoner, Perry, & Marcum, 2011). In some states, if divorcing couples are unable to agree on child custody and visitation issues, they are required, by law, to submit to outside mediation before the court system becomes formally involved. The intention, of course, is to save the time, money, and trauma that typically accompany formal court proceedings.

Court-approved mediators face a complicated conflict situation. Here we have two people who presumably loved one another at some point, but do not any longer. Their emotional intensity runs high, and angry exchanges often dominate their communication. In many cases, interpersonal conflict is about as intense as one can imagine. Posturing and self-vested demands are par for the course. How do you get these two parties, each combatively struggling with the other, to come together and reach a joint decision?

There is only one approach that works. The mediator must get the parties to agree on a guiding, underlying principled outcome. As you probably guessed, that outcome is "to do what is in the best interests of the children." Once such an agreement is struck, progress, hackneyed as it may be, can begin. Without this agreement, the mediation, in almost all cases, fails.

There is an important parallel for emerging leaders. When faced with a strained and unwavering conflict of positions, look for principled outcomes—those underlying foundations that all parties can agree must be attained. Think in terms of points of agreement. If conflicting parties can find some initial points of agreement, they will likely be predisposed to search for and expect more agreement. As you see, this is only a slight variant of the classic negotiating strategy that encourages parties to focus on interests rather than positions (Fisher, Ury, & Patton, 1991). Accordingly, if the parties can agree on some degree of fundamental joint-interest, the odds of successful exchange improve.

Leading Respectful Conflict Encounters

Before we present our model for respectful conflict encounters, there are some important, upfront considerations to note. While we have indicated that many people have a strong aversion to engaging in conflict encounters, every episode of conflict certainly does not warrant a conversation or encounter. Some situations really will get better with time. And some situations simply do not rise to the level where they need to be addressed. Minor bumps and differences are par for the course, and effective leaders may reasonably conclude to "let it go." In short, emerging leaders have to decide whether the situation rises to the level where a conflict encounter is needed. We recommend two considerations.

First, think through the impact of the conflict. Is this conflict intense? Are people highly disturbed? Is it affecting our ability to work together or our ability to meet customers' (internal and external) needs? Is the conflict disturbing me, the other party, or those who observe and work with us? In some ways, we are asking you to weigh the "cost" of the existing conflict.

Second, consider the probability that things will improve without an encounter. Honesty is needed. One cue is whether you have had conflict with this person in the past. Another cue is whether the current conflict represents a recurring set of circumstances, such that a similar conflict is likely to spring forth in the future. Much of this has to do with how frequently the parties are required to interact.

Here is our suggestion. Conflicts that are high in intensity, where continued interaction is required, where the likelihood of recurrence is high, and where the cost of conflict is high should be addressed through a respectful conflict encounter.

An additional caveat must be entered. Don't expect too much. While the ultimate purpose of a conflict encounter is to achieve resolution, intermediary steps may be necessary. For example, it seems unreasonable that long-standing conflicts can be truly resolved through a single encounter. Tough interpersonal conflicts do not emerge over night, and, consequently, they will not be resolved over night. Smaller and more incremental steps may be necessary. Perhaps just meeting and talking is a good first step. Clarifying needs and expectations may be the best that can be achieved in a single encounter. In such cases, the goal is to achieve a positive, progressive interaction that will lead to a follow-up meeting.

A Model for Respectful Conflict Encounters

The underlying desire of the conflict encounter is for you to express your thoughts, beliefs, and expectations in a direct and respectful way, so that your needs can be met without violating the needs of the other party. Importantly, the encounter must be carefully communicated so that the other party feels no diminution of either respect or significance. Remember, as soon as the other party begins to feel that they are not being treated disrespectfully or that their significance is being diminished, they will fall into a "fight-or-flight" mode of behavior. That is, they will either become more aggressive and entrenched in their position, or they will shut-down, psychologically withdraw, and dis-engage. In either of these conditions, meaningful progress is thwarted.

Engaging in a respectful conflict encounter can be a daunting task. The model presented in Table 5.1 is one way to have this exchange. The model offers a sound approach, but that approach will have to be modified given the idiosyncrasies of the involved parties and the unique demands of the situation.

Outcomes

Your first step actually precedes engaging in the conflict encounter. You should decide what "outcome(s)" you would like to achieve through the encounter. As you will see from the example that follows, be clear and specific in your mind. This will help you focus your communication, and it will keep you from

TABLE 5.1 RESPECTFUL CONFLICT ENCOUNTER

- Identify your desired outcomes
- Clarify the context
- Clarify the facts
- Focus on the behavior
- Share personal impact
- Share "big picture" impact
- Clarify for understanding
- Present your alternatives
- Engage in dialogue
- Summarize
- Set the "next steps"

being thrown off-track by the other party. Further, a good conflict encounter is direct, not meandering and not rambling. Knowing what you hope to achieve, up-front, will keep you from straying off topic.

Context

Your first interactive step in the encounter is to clarify the situation or context for the other party. In short, you want to provide enough context so others know precisely what you wish to discuss.

We emphasize this step for a very practical reason. Once leaders muster the nerve to have a conflict conversation, they have a tendency to jump into the intricacies before the other party is fully aware of the nature of the context. At least for a few seconds (or minutes), the other party is not listening to your message. Rather, they are trying to figure out "where all this is coming from." Provide the context to bring them up-to-speed and assure that you're both on the same page. This will not take long. Yet it is an important step.

Facts

This is a step that's often missed when emotions run high. Check your facts with the other party. Be sure that what you think occurred really did. There is no need to press further when a clarification of facts may shed new light and different meaning on what's going on. We are not talking about interpretations here. Interpretations will always be colored by the parties' feelings and needs. We'll deal with this in a minute. Rather, we need to be sure all parties are clear on the facts. It may be necessary to postpone or delay the encounter if additional information needs to be gathered so the facts can be clarified to the satisfaction of the parties.

Behavior

We must keep our focus on behaviors and not on the individual personalities. Of course, clean differentiations between what we observe and what we infer are quite a challenge, as we are talking about two closely linked cognitive processes. However, we all know that taking the conversation to personal rather than behavioral levels is likely to raise defenses, escalate tensions, and imply disrespect.

The language here may be subtle, but it is important. "When you did not check the report" is replaced by "when the report was not checked." "When you went directly to the customer" becomes "when the decision was made to go directly to the customer." Our focus must be on the behavior and not the person. We're not naïve, the other party knows that they "own" their behavior. Yet, a tone of respect has a better chance of being maintained by emphasizing the behavior.

Personal Impact

We believe in stating how the conflict affects you, personally. Our purpose is not that such declarations, typically, have major effects on the movement of the conflict. Rather, such sharing provides a personal, honest, and core dimension to the exchange. There is also a degree of vulnerability here, and such openness usually is seen as a projection of integrity and trust.

So we say, "When the decision was made to go directly to the customer, I felt like I was completely out of the loop, making it hard for me to carry out my leadership role appropriately." There is no argument, debate, or discussion needed here. You are not deriding the other party. Rather, you are stating how you felt and how the events personally impacted you.

Be careful here not to take the bait of arguing your feelings. Others may counter that it's unrealistic to feel as you do, and they may offer a number of feelings that seem more reasonable from their perspectives. Your response should simply be one of reiteration, "Well, I'm only telling you how I felt."

There is an additional point here. Many emerging leaders believe that they must hide their feelings, perhaps as a badge of emotional strength. There are two problems with this assumption. First, an honest expression of feelings and emotions projects openness, authenticity, self-awareness, and self-assurance. Second, most people are not adept at hiding their feelings anyway. People tend to pick up the cues, often nonverbally, and may conclude that you are disingenuous.

Once again, do not assume that your expression of personal impact will sway the discussion or change outcomes. However, this statement of self-awareness adds perspective and human character to what will follow; quite significant in the midst of an emotional encounter.

Big-Picture Impact

This is, perhaps, the key step. Yet, its impact is best experienced when preceded by the set-up steps noted above. Here you share with the other party what you think is at stake and how the overall needs of the team, unit, or organization may be affected by the present conflict.

It's important here to help the other party see how you think they may be affected. If you can help the other see how their personal self-interests may be adversely affected, motivational seeds have been planted. This must be done carefully and directly, however realize that you are only sharing your perceptions of the situation.

Clarity

It's a good idea to hit the pause button at this point and check for clarity. You want to be sure that the other party is still following you and that there is an understanding of what you have shared. Recognize that you are not asking the other party to accept your assessment. However, you do want them to understand and accept the legitimacy of your feelings and perceptions. This is really the old "what I said and what you heard" check-off. There may be a need to back up and clarify. Again, clarification restates what you have expressed to be sure that it has been recognized and heard.

Preferred Alternatives

This is where you express what you would like to see happen. This is not a demand. It is an honest expression of your preferred outcome(s). These preferences should not come as a surprise given the preceding steps. Remember that clear and specific preferred outcomes are likely to fare better. Also, bear in mind that your statements of preference are not the final word. Instead, these preferred alternatives should be the starting point for a respectful and engaged discussion.

Dialogue

Dialogue will be discussed fully in the next chapter. Hopefully, a deep and rewarding dialogue can ensue. Further, we anticipate that steps toward resolution can be carved, and both parties sense that some level of progress has been advanced through the conflict encounter. Further, dialogue is the best way to thwart the dreaded "negotiator's dilemma," where one's propensity for self-gain trumps any efforts to work, constructively, for mutual gain.

Summary and Next Steps

Never leave the encounter without offering a brief summary and suggesting additional steps that need to be taken. Without detailing and gaining agreement on the "next steps," the encounter becomes an exchange that is easily forgotten and never consequated. It is much better to reinforce and build on any positive momentum that has been established.

Putting It All Together

While the steps of the model are straightforward, an example may help bring the steps together. Recently, one of the authors was negotiating with another leader (at the same level) over how we should deploy resources to accomplish a joint task. We'll call him Frank. Not surprisingly, each of us took a slightly different approach which, not coincidentally, favored the units we were each leading. (You realize that his side of the story probably looks a bit different.) We were charged by our boss to meet and get agreement. There were differing needs and expectations with resulting conflict, and the day of reckoning (a final decision) was rapidly approaching.

Admittedly frustrated at our lack of progress, I marched into Frank's office and announced that we would need to meet sometime that day in order to reach our deadline. Looking up from a pile of work on his desk, he muttered a rather dismissive, "I'll get to it." Feeling the swell of emotion, I said, "OK," and left. The exchange, in my mind, could have hardly gone worse. But I was wrong.

Sitting in my office only minutes later, there was knock on the open door and in entered the boss. He was not bringing good news. "I just got a call from Frank. He's all upset. He says that you're badgering him." There was a brief pause, and the boss continued, "Can't the two of you just work this out?" I'm not overly bright, but I know that there is only one answer to that question. "Sure, we'll figure it out," and the boss left.

It's not hard to explain the rush of emotions I experienced. No sooner had I left Frank's office than he got on the phone, called the boss, and tattled and whined (my interpretation and opinion). To me, this is wrong on so many levels that I was able to escalate this set of behaviors to the category of being an "organizational sin." (Yes, as with some of you, impulse control can be a personal struggle.) I took a little time and tried to settle down, think through the issue, and gain some perspective. Then, I scheduled a 2 pm meeting with Frank for what would be our "conflict encounter."

The "outcome" I was reaching for here may surprise you. It was not to resolve our resource issue. Rather, it was to emphasize my concern about going directly to the boss. I hoped to gain Frank's agreement that this sort of running-to-the-boss action could not be part of our interpersonal exchanges.

Entering Frank's office, I began by establishing "context." "I know earlier today, I came in here and may have caught you off-guard. You were busy. But I'd like to talk to you about that event and what followed." That's all that's probably needed. He understands the situation, and we can now proceed with a common context.

Next are the "facts." "I need to check a few things to be sure that I'm understanding all this properly. It seems to me that no sooner had I left your office than you were on the phone to the boss." I was rolling now, "And I think you told him that I was pushing you too hard—even that I was badgering you. I'm wondering if all this is correct?" I attempted to keep my pace in check and to deliver these comments as points for clarification rather than as accusations. Frank was direct and respectful, simply adding, "Yes, that's what happened." We can now proceed, given acceptance of the facts.

Now, there is the "behavior." I addressed Frank calmly and firmly. "I'd like to talk to you about the decision to go the boss." Remember I have nothing against Frank. He's a good guy who is under a lot of pressure. Yet, the behavior is problematic.

"Personal impact" always looks different based on the personality of the individuals and the openness of the culture. In this case, personal impact was a bit understated. "When the decision was made to go to the boss, I was embarrassed, and I felt undercut." That's it. No need for a response, and no expectation that my honesty would result in a movement from Frank.

Now, we are ready for the "big picture." "Frank, when the decision was made to go the boss, it made me look ineffective in my role. But I also think it made you look ineffective in your role. More critically, we look like two leaders who cannot resolve this matter on our own. I think that we both just lost political points in the eyes of the boss."

Does Frank care now? Most assuredly. Suddenly, the big picture has become relevant for him. His needs have been brought sharply into focus. Indeed, most people are prompted to act on conflict when their needs become central. I asked if that all made sense, seeking "clarity," but Frank was already there.

"Frank, here is what I'd like to see" ("preferred alternatives"). "I'd like you and I to agree that when these differences come up, as they inevitably will, we will sit down and knock it out. Even if it gets tense, this is still our responsibility. Let's agree not to take it to the boss, except as a last resort and only after tipping the other party to the move."

The "dialogue" that followed was brief. Frank agreed. After all, he could see that the preferred alternative was in his best interests too. Incidentally, with the air cleared, we were able to resolve the resource issue in about 15 minutes.

And When It's Not So Easy?

At this point, you are likely thinking—that's all well and good. You and Frank played nice, and it worked out. But what of the situations where the other party takes an aggressive or dismissive approach to your attempt to have a respectful conflict encounter? Fair enough—a reasonable question.

First, the respectful conflict encounter approach is sound communicative behavior. Second, in many situations, it represents all that you can do. Third, the approach assumes that you control your behavior despite what the other party does. In short, you become an "actor" instead of a "reactor."

Engaging in respectful conflict encounters is important for all leaders. However, it holds additional sway for emerging leaders. Make no mistake, people are aware of how you address conflicted interpersonal issues. The conflict encounter model demonstrates pro-action, respect, character, and the courage to take difficult steps for the good of the organization. Even when such efforts fail to reach your desired outcomes, they are not necessarily failures. A tone has been set, and a statement of intention has been demonstrated. Even though the immediate issue may languish, the long-term prospects for more positive exchanges may be enhanced through your efforts.

If you are addressing conflicts with peers or superiors, the respectful encounter is probably the best approach at your disposal. With your reports, the respectful encounter is just that—a respectful first step that takes the high road. Of course, if positive movement does not occur, further approaches may be needed. We will address these in the section on "difficult and problem" people.

We have shared this model with thousands of workshop participants. For some leaders, the approach is natural, and the discussion flows comfortably. For other leaders, especially those with more assertive styles, the model requires some degree of stretch. In either case, leaders who practice the model agree to one key advantage. The model provides a concrete way to approach conflict encounters. This structure provides a plan for encountering and anticipating points that are likely to arise. This tends to help leaders feel more confident in addressing conflict. Those on the receiving end of these encounters also report a positive reaction. In most cases, they indicate that using the model helps hold emotions in check, an outcome that is perceived as functional for resolution.

Perspective Taking

Perspective taking is an important behavior that emerging leaders should nourish. This behavior has to do with being able to put yourself in the other party's position, endeavoring to recognize and understand their point of view. Research indicates that perspective taking is associated with a greater tendency to forgive the other party and greater problem-solving capacity (Rizkalla, Wertheim, & Hodgson, 2008).

Perspective taking begins with assuming that the other party possesses a point of view that has meaning and impact for them. In part, perspective taking involves trying to figure out what that point of view is and why it is held. We prefer direct approaches here, and open-ended questions are usually a solid route. For example, "Help me understand why you are advocating that position?" Remember, our fundamental goal is understanding.

Honest and sincere perspective taking also helps avoid behaviors that are generally inappropriate or ineffective for handling conflict. These so-called destructive behaviors almost always extend or further exacerbate the conflict (Davis, Capobianco, & Kraus, 2004).

For example, behaviors that ridicule or demean the other party (and this could include sarcasm) will generally produce little more than resentment and heightened emotions. Perceptions of disrespect or diminished significance are likely to ensue. Recognize that nonverbal expressions of frustration or disgust are powerful, perhaps even more powerful than verbal responses. Body language, the roll of the eyes, and even the tone of voice can project powerful signals that belie anything that is being verbally expressed. Although demeaning behaviors may generate some immediate wins, they are almost always destructive in the long run. Further, demeaning behaviors stand as character statements that are not easily forgotten.

Dealing with Difficult and Problem People

We conclude this chapter with a special type of conflict situation—the difficult or problem person. The significance of this issue for leaders is highlighted by the explosion of work that has addressed this topic in recent years. Stanford Professor Robert Sutton (2010) argues that employees with hostile behaviors and malicious intentions undermine the work culture and destroy productivity. We now work with organizations who have installed more palatable versions, such as "no jerks allowed" policies. Further, there has been an array of solid research over the past few years, addressing a growing concern over aggressive, "bullying" behavior in organizations (Bartlett & Bartlett, 2011; Heames & Harvey, 2006; Saam, 2010).

Difficult people who exhibit unwanted behaviors certainly do not exist in a social vacuum. The underlying issues generally are a function of the person and the situation, and may be affected by leaders and organizational actions. Yet, problem people drain the leader's time and energy. Accordingly, it is not surprising that leaders have a tendency to avoid addressing problem people. Sometimes this avoidance is born of the conviction that "things will surely get better." Sometimes, avoidance is driven by a concern for not setting off an emotional confrontation and making matters worse. More often, avoidance occurs because leaders do not know how or simply do not want to address these difficult cases.

Handling problem people may be new territory for emerging leaders. You have always known that it was difficult to work with certain people. Maybe you avoided them or even actively sought not to work on projects where they were involved. Now, it is your responsibility to address these people and make efforts to bring them more fully in line with the desired cultural framework.

Nobody relishes the prospect of dealing with problem people. These can be tough encounters. Our minds are spinning with possible twists and turns. What if the difficult person becomes defensive and things actually get worse? What if they threaten some sort of legal action? What if they become harshly defiant or, worse case scenario, go ballistic?

Recall, there is often a nagging hope—won't this situation get better if we just give it a little time? Perhaps, and we do need to be careful to differentiate between temporary problems and persistent problems. From time to time, we all probably exhibit temporary problem-person behaviors, especially when we are under extreme stress from work or home. For example, we can be empathetic toward the employee who is struggling through divorce or health issues while still finding ways to assure meeting performance expectations. Some degree of tolerance and time is warranted here. However, persistent problems are different. They have become enduring and pervasive, indicative of a consistent style of behavior.

One of the great questions we receive from emerging leaders concerns this very issue. When is enough really enough? In essence, we are looking for the line where the problem behavior becomes a persistent issue. There are three cues to use: (1) the impact on overall performance; (2) the way other people are being affected; and (3) the duration of the problem behavior. When performance and people are being affected, we must find some means to remediate the situation

The Types of Problem People

Pervasive problem people emerge along two dimensions: (1) problems with performance; and (2) problems with interpersonal skills. As such, two classic categories of problem people arise—people who have been labeled as "charming but unreliable," and people who fall under the banner of "talented but abrasive" (Singh, 2007, p. 165). Let's look at each of these types.

Charming but unreliable people perform at levels below expectation. Usually, their performance is not terrible. Instead, it manifests in smaller ways. They miss deadlines; their reports are late; their work fails to meet the expected quality standards; or they cannot be counted on to do their part on team projects. However, these folks have wonderful interpersonal skills and warm, charismatic personalities. They are socially adept, and people like them. In many cases, their charm provides cover for their performance deficiencies. No one wants to make a big deal of their performance shortcomings because they are so likeable. At times, other team members may even cover for them and complete some of their work.

The struggle for emerging leaders is that you probably do not have anywhere near the social and interpersonal capital that the performance-challenged charmer has. So, you are cautious about stirring up resentment, especially as it surrounds someone who is popular and well-liked.

But there is an ever-present and escalating issue brewing. These folks become bigger problems when they are allowed to persist. Over time, colleagues become tired of "picking up the slack." Resentment builds as colleagues rightly question the equity or fairness of the leader's refusal to deal with someone who is consistently missing the performance mark. Difficult as it will be, these individuals must be addressed through conflict encounters.

In many ways, the "talented but abrasive" person is even more troubling because they do perform, generally at very high levels. They tend to be extremely bright and are often technical experts in their areas. The problem arises not from performance but in the ways they treat people as they go about performing. Winning at all costs is frequently their focus. They display some combinations of the following characteristics or behavioral styles: (1) impatience with others; (2) inflexibility in their positions; (3) low tolerance for others and their opinions; (4) an aloof, demeaning, and arrogant manner; and (5) aggressive behavior toward others. As such, they beat people up emotionally, running roughshod over others' feelings and sensitivities. Talented but abrasive people are able to perform at high levels, but they leave a river of battered bodies in their wake.

The emerging leader may feel caught and hesitant to deal with this type of problem person. What if the abrasive expert gets upset and decides to leave? What if they get miffed and performance slips? Again, trouble is brewing. If not addressed, other workers will refuse, eventually, to accept the tirades and boorish behavior of the abrasive offender. They will request transfers from teams where the talented but abrasive person has been assigned. They may even refuse to work on projects where close interaction is demanded. They will blanch at every contact, and overall morale will begin to slide. Critically, you will be seen as a young leader who let things get out of control. Once again, you must have a face-to-face conflict encounter.

The Plan

The plan of action for both problem types is outlined in Table 5.2. It begins by carefully defining the performance expectations and interpersonal expectations clearly and unequivocally. You cannot be too precise here—remember you are dealing with a problem situation. Second, you must identify "gaps" where performance and behavior deviate from the expectations. Performance issues will be easier than interpersonal issues because the metrics are more easily defined. Communication should progress so that the problem person can agree that a gap exists and agree that the gap must be closed.

The challenge generally enters because problem people throw us off our well-honed plan by turning to two behaviors—the use of emotions and excuses. They are masters here. Emotions may be aggressive, almost attack-like, or they may arise as expressions of hurt, an almost pouting style. In both cases, these emotions are used because they have been reinforced in the past. Their presence has caused other leaders to back off and push the real issues aside. Excuses take on a similar role. They deflect attention from the real issue (performance or interpersonal behavior) by creating a barrage of diversions. Resist the temptation of debating the merits of these excuses. You will lose the debate, as your problem person counterpart is much more masterful here.

So what do we do? When either emotion or excuse enters into the equation, we encourage two steps. First, listen. Second, return to the expectations. This is the issue, and this must be the focus. Do not get pressured or baited into moving off the expectations. Admittedly, this is hard. It is a character builder.

The final step is to develop a plan of action to address the problem behaviors. Perhaps additional training is needed; perhaps developmental coaching is warranted; perhaps resources need to be augmented; perhaps some activities need to be shifted. In some cases, where motivational issues are at stake, gaining commitment on behaviors that will be used and avoided may be necessary.

A final and practical word is in order. Problem people are notorious backsliders. Your conversation will probably yield some short-term improve-

TABLE 5.2 ADDRESSING PROBLEM PEOPLE

- Define expectations
- Identify gaps
- Agree on gap and need to close
- Commit to plan of action

ments, but, over days or weeks, they will revert to their previous behaviors. This is to be expected. Reinforce the positive moves and clarify where expectations fall short. Progress will be incremental—the proverbial two steps forward and one step back. As such, have regular check-ins to assess progress and make adjustments. Yes, in most cases, problem people need to be on a short leash, which is extended as their behavior improves.

Concluding Thoughts

Drawn from the classic book *Getting to Yes*, we encourage you to keep two thoughts in mind when addressing conflict (Fisher, Ury, & Patton, 1991). First, the other party is not your rival. Your goal is not to win or defeat them. Rather, others are advocating for a point of view, and that view makes sense to them. Second, demands signal that the other party's real interests and needs are not being addressed and met. Finding that point of view and the underlying need is central to successfully providing leadership in the face of conflict.

In his Pulitzer Prize winning epic, *Founding Brothers*, historian Joseph Ellis (2002) writes of the relationship between John Adams and Thomas Jefferson. It's a solid perspective for our consideration.

> On almost all the disputes over domestic and foreign policy in the 1790's, Adams and Jefferson had found themselves on different sides. And each man had made brutally harsh assessments of the other, rooted in their quite different convictions about the proper course the American Revolution should take. Adams was distinctive, however, for his tendency to regard even serious political and ideological differences as eminently negotiable once elemental bonds of personal trust and affection were established.
>
> (p. 179)

Connection

The Language of Understanding

Tom Bower, founder of Mindset Consulting, is a powerful communicator. During his workshops, he'll line up a series of tennis balls at the front table—one for each participant. Turning to each person, he'll toss a tennis ball, encouraging them to be sure to catch it. Moving through the group, he delivers a seemingly simple commentary. "The secret . . . the secret to successful communication is that . . . you've got to pitch it so they can catch it . . . so that they want to catch it . . . so they understand what it means . . . and so they want to do something with it." In many ways, this chapter is about helping you pitch your message so the folks you work with can catch it and do something with it. In the process, you will build connection, understanding, trust, and influence. Arguably, there is no more powerful tool or skill a leader can possess.

Emphasizing the value of our connection theme may be a bit akin to proving the obvious, but a few comments are in order. Because emerging leaders have been such strong individual performers, the significance of building connections can be underplayed. Such a stance does not square with evidence and practice.

Experts have suggested that no skill is more important to overall career success than that of communication (Harrell & Harrell, 1984). A number of studies underscore this point. For example, the Graduate Management Admissions Council recently conducted a broad survey of corporate recruiters. When hiring MBA graduates, what skills would you think were most important—financial acuity, strategic thinking, or perhaps marketing acumen? No—89% of the recruiters ranked communication skills as their number one hiring characteristic (Hamilton, 2010). In a series of in-depth interviews with senior human resource managers, Bambacas and Patrickson (2008) highlighted the importance of interpersonal communication skills, emphasizing the need for clear messages, active listening, and a tone of collaboration. Interestingly, they also found that these were the skill areas where managers were seen as most lacking (Bambacus & Patrickson, 2008).

Lest we think that the effects of connection and communication lack bottom-line impact, realize that we spend about 80% of our typical work day involved in some form of communication (Nellermoe, Weirich, & Reinstein, 1999). And, consider the finding that as much as 14% of every 40-hour workweek may be "wasted" because of communication breakdowns between managers and staff (Calloway-Thomas, Cooper, & Blake, 1999).

We choose to refer to the subject of this chapter as one about building connections. Some may see that as little more than a variation on good communication. To a large extent, this is a chapter about communication. Yet, there is more. Connection is about developing reciprocal understanding through deep listening, open-ended questioning, and engaged dialogue. It is about the give-and-take exchanges that occur between communication partners. We understand and accept that communication depends critically on how parties interpret and assign meaning to the messages that are used, and we recognize that a careful understanding of each party's environment or context is fundamental, as is the choice of messaging channels. Importantly, we view connection as a complex interaction between parties, what communication experts refer to as a transactional approach to communication (Adler, Rosenfeld, & Proctor, 2013). This foundation of connection and reciprocal understanding is the framework from which influence occurs.

The Under-Communication Bias

Emerging leaders may have a bias that favors under-communication. In short, although emerging leaders, conceptually, recognize the importance of communication, you may be cautious, at a day-to-day operational level, about communicating too much with your people. There are reasonable foundations for this tendency.

Here is the first reason. Remember that emerging leaders are achievers and doers, and they are also motivated self-starters. In short, you may not need a lot of guidance. As such, you often assume (frequently erroneously) that others prefer a hands-off, less-is-better-than-more approach to communication. This is part of a broader fallacy where we tend to assume that others' preferences and motivations are similar to ours (Human & Biesanz, 2011).

The second reason is an interesting permutation of the first. The pace of change in today's organizations is high and the rate of acceleration of change is ever-growing. As business demands are escalating, people are working harder. As such, emerging leaders may argue that they do not want to add more stress to others by adding more information. Therefore, the tendency seems to be to communicate less as the pace of change rises (Duck, 1998).

The thinking here is exactly backwards. Under stress, people need more (not less) connection, contact, and communication. We have worked with hundreds of organizations going through a variety of changes, some quite dramatic. We have never heard the people in these organizations say, "Could you please tell the leaders to tone down the communication, as they are just telling us too much." Quite the contrary, people yearn to know what's going on and what they do not know, they will make up.

There is a third and powerful reason for the under-communication bias. Emerging leaders are quite sensitive about being labeled as a "micro-manager." We have noticed that the micro-manager designation takes on a particularly derisive tone for our emerging leader audiences, as we discussed in an earlier chapter.

Consider the following example. In a recent coaching session, a new manager reported that she had restated performance expectations and asked for weekly check-ins from an underperforming direct report. Apparently, the direct report's retort was to defensively charge the manager as "just trying to micro-manage me." The new manager was devastated. Clearly, the direct report had touched a hot-button issue. The manager was so distraught at the hint of being labeled as a micro-manager that she had decided to back away from the check-in meetings. When we asked her why less communication was better than more in this situation and why holding an underperformer accountable was a bad approach, she shrugged and replied, "Well I sure don't want to be a micro-manager."

Let's be clear. Micro-managers drain the creative energy and heart from an organization. Further, the organization can progress no faster than the speed at which the micro-manager operates. We abhor the ego-fragile and narcissistic actions of micro-managers. However, clear, frequent, and open communication that encourages two-way exchanges and dialogue are the antithesis of micro-management.

Fourth, many emerging leaders argue that they simply do not have the time for open, two-way communication. We met Steve in a workshop for high-potential (hi-po) leaders. These young leaders had been hand-picked from their respective organizations, and the talent base was impressive. Even among this group, Steve's comments and ideas soon led us to conclude that Steve was the hi-po of the hi-pos.

During an open discussion, one of his peers asked Steve, "What's the most important thing you do to assure your success as a leader?" Steve did not hesitate, "I meet with each of my six direct reports for a 30-minute one-on-one session each week. In addition, my door is open every day at 4 pm for anything that's going on that they want to discuss." The peer recoiled and asserted that this was just an unrealistic use of limited, precious time. "OK," Steve replied as he accepted the feedback, "But I still meet."

In all likelihood, the beauty here is not the fact of meeting, but what occurs during those meetings. Issues are addressed, future plans and directions are highlighted, questions are asked, and developmental coaching takes place. Steve's people feel that they are "in this together" with him. Steve will even tell you that he feels these meetings actually save him time in the long run and build spirit and trust along the way. The excuse of time is generally just that—an excuse.

Fifth, and finally, many emerging leaders choose to rely on technology rather than in-person, eyeball-to-eyeball interaction. Technology has certainly changed the nature of communication, and younger emerging leaders have grown up being tech-savvy. Impersonal technologies, such as texting and tweeting, are increasingly permeating our communication landscape (Lenhart, 2010; Smith & Brenner, 2012). The key for emerging leaders is to clearly understand the best form and channel to use given the people who are involved and the surrounding context. For example, texting a change in meeting locations is efficient if all intended recipients are focused and attuned to this method.

There is an interesting twist here. Carol Goman (2011), reporting the results of a recent *Harvard Business Review* study, notes that 95% of professionals feel that in-person meetings are essential to successful, long-term business relationships. She further comments that when the communication has any "emotional charge," face-to-face communication is "the only way that others can note the alignment of your verbal and non-verbal messages and be convinced that your motives match your rhetoric" (Goman, 2011, p. 39).

Communicating for Information and Understanding

In simplest terms, communication is a transfer of information and meaning from one person to another. At times, we focus on the first part of that definition and exclude the second part. The first part is relatively easy, while the second requires time, sensitivity, and creativity.

There is some long-standing controversy about whether meaning is really part of communication or whether it is a separate interpretive event that takes place once one receives a communicated message (Berlo, 1960). This point is theoretically sound. However, more pragmatically, we prefer to think of communication as "the process by which people interactively create, sustain, and manage meaning" (Dainton & Zelley, 2005, p. 2). Meaning suggests a deeper level of interaction and connection. It involves a mutual exchange (a give-and-take), where intentions, assumptions, and beliefs can be shared, clarified, and discussed. In short, this process involves all communication parties creating a sense of shared understanding and shared meaning.

Let's not miss the critical distinction we have just noted. With admitted overgeneralization, we have found that young, emerging leaders are very good at transmitting information. After all, that is your language. Here are the facts. Here's what the customer wants. Here's what upper management has prescribed. However, emerging leaders may be much less adept at assuring that messages are fully understood. They sometimes miss that transmitting messages does not lead to action. Rather, it is the understanding, shaping, and meaning that a recipient derives from a message that prompts action. In short, we have no hope of creating influence and getting action if deep and meaningful communication does not occur.

Communication Breakdown: Why It All Falls Apart

There are probably as many answers to the "how does it all fall apart?" question as there are unique people and situations. So what follows is by no means intended to be exhaustive. However, it does represent three key reasons for communication breakdowns.

The Audience and the Under-Story

First, emerging leaders may communicate in ways that make sense and have meaning for them but not their intended audience. We encourage you to start your communication process with the audience firmly in mind. What are their needs? What sort of reaction will they have? Is there likely to be emotion involved in their interpretation? How might this message be perceived (or misperceived) given what you know about the audience?

We recently worked with a leader who was perplexed at what she perceived as a "distant and standoffish attitude" she felt coming from the five members of her team. She commented, "It's almost as if they don't trust me." As we talked through recent events, only one piece seemed to make sense. She had recently dismissed a new team member as the three-month probationary period drew to a close. There was nothing sinister involved, just a decision that the person-job skill set was a mismatch. We asked how the decision was communicated to the rest of the team. Obviously sensitive to privacy issues, the leader noted that there really was no communication—people just knew.

What she missed was the under-story. The new team member was well liked by other team members. The new member was a hard worker who was always available to help out when others asked. Some members of the team even socialized, outside of work, with the new member. Interestingly, all teammates also recognized that the new member did not possess the right skills for the job. Yet, the here-today-and-gone-tomorrow approach left the teammates feeling uncertain. Confidences could have been maintained while providing sensitivity toward the team members. Importantly, the leader made the right business decision. And, at the same time, failed to think through how the decision would impact the audience of remaining team members.

Making the Catch

Communication is a two-way, interactive process. How will you know if your audience has received the message and garnered the understanding and meaning that was originally intended? One key to assuring proper reception lies in the method or channel of communication that is used.

Certainly, communication can falter because leaders choose improper modes or channels of delivery. Let's clarify what works and explore where various methods seem most appropriate. In today's technology-rich world, continual connection and instant reactions are often expected. There are tremendous advantages here. We are never far removed from information and person-to-person access. This makes the choice of channel of delivery even more important.

We encourage you to read the situation, look at the issues and the stakes, and look at the people involved. If we are delivering information whose understanding is clear and non-emotional, then electronic forms of conveyance are fine. Emails and texts work in these situations.

However, when issues are nuanced, personal, emotional, or where depth of understanding must be assured, electronic forms can become risky. In many cases, an eyeball-to-eyeball encounter is needed. Recall the under-communication bias that was noted earlier. We often shun the personal encounter because it takes so much time. Even more likely, you have probably all been involved in email battles, where each successive exchange takes on an increasing risk of misinterpretation and unfavorable assumptions. In short, many situations demand a personal exchange.

An example may be helpful. We worked with a promising young leader who decided that she needed to talk with her boss about her need for expanded duties, greater latitude, and a bump in compensation. Her arguments were compelling. We probably didn't hide our shock as she prepared to leave by saying, "I'll email this request to my boss as soon as I get to my computer." Cringing in disbelief, we asked if "all this might go a bit better with a face-to-face meeting?" Yes, she was busy. The boss was busy. But the sincerity and passion of her case would be lost electronically. The boss would simply miss too much. There was also a reasonable risk that he could misconstrue the tone of her request. On nearly every level, the situation dictated a personal meeting.

Now here is the trick. In deciding what is best, take the other's perspective. How might this information be received? Will there be a need for further clarification? Will emotions come into play? Could the message be misinterpreted? Are you showing the proper degree of respect if a personal meeting is not held? If you are in doubt, opt to meet!

Lack of Cultural Sensitivity

Today's work context is multi-cultural, and we experience this diversity at the interpersonal, team, organizational, and even inter-organizational levels. A number of studies have helped us understand how to explain various dimensions of culture. The most popular sources comes from the work of Geert Hofstede (1980; 2001), and the research that his framework has generated (Kirkman, Lowe, & Gibson, 2006). Five dimensions of culture are provided: (1) power distance; (2) uncertainty avoidance; (3) individualism-collectivism; (4) masculinity-femininity; and (5) long-term-short-term orientation.

A number of cues emerge. Consider, for example, the dimension of power distance. Countries with low power distance (such as Austria, Denmark, and the U.S.) are more egalitarian, seeking to minimize distinctions between traditional bases of power. As such, behaviors aimed at influencing or even challenging the boss are accepted as appropriate. However, countries with high power distance (such as India, Mexico, and the Philippines) emphasize authority, status, and positional power. In comparison to a low power distance context, high power distance employees may be less comfortable and less willing to offer input, and they are more likely to submit to the boss's wishes.

Further, consider the individualism-collectivism dimension. Individualistic countries (such as the U.S., U.K., and Canada) emphasize and reward personal achievement, autonomy, and self-sufficient initiative; whereas collectivistic countries (such as China, Japan, and Indonesia) value duty, tradition, and group decision-making (Adler, Rosenfeld, & Proctor, 2013).

Adler and Elmhorst (2010) have offered an interesting distinction between high-context and low-context communication styles. Countries with high-context communication (such as Germany, Scandinavia, and English-speaking countries) value self-expression, where opinions and needs are openly shared with others. Countries with low-context communication (such as Southern Europe, Asian, Latin American, and Middle Eastern countries) value indirect expressions and even ambiguity so that "no" does not have to be expressed directly and harmony can be upheld.

As you read the rest of this chapter, keep the cultural context in mind. It helps explain why dialogue may be easier with some than others; why feedback may be readily expressed by some but not others; and why some prefer a more active role than others in matters that affect them.

Deep Listening

If given the opportunity to select a single skill that we could give all emerging leaders, we'd choose to make them better listeners. Listening—deep listening—is at the heart and soul of so much of what impactful leaders do (Johnson & Beechler, 1998). And, leaders, at all levels, are notoriously poor listeners. Recall that you process information quickly, and you're driven toward action and results. With paraphrasing apologies to songwriter Paul Simon (1964), emerging leaders are often "hearing without listening," which means, of course, that real listening is not taking place. Listening is a deliberate discipline, and that discipline can be refined and honed. We suggest eleven steps for deep listening, as presented in Table 6.1.

Stop Talking

The first step is for the leader to quite literally "stop talking." We are not trying to be cute or glib here. Leaders have a tendency to prefer talking over listening. One cannot listen while talking.

TABLE 6.1 STEPS FOR DEEP LISTENING

- Stop talking
- Mono-tasking
- Connect early
- Focus
- Tone
- Pace
- Minimal encouragers
- Open-ended questions
- Perception checks and clarifications
- Nonverbal cues and reflections of meaning
- Summarize for understanding

Mono-Tasking

Listening is a mono-tasking activity. It's tempting in a fast-paced world to pride ourselves on our multi-tasking capacities. Whatever place multi-tasking may have, it has *no place* in deep listening. We've all been in meetings where, in the midst of deep discussions, people were checking emails, texting, and sketching plans for the next meeting. Deep listening is hard enough without all these distractions. Further, multi-tasking behavior signals disrespect and minimizes the person who is speaking.

There are occasions, especially during meetings, when people may use multi-tasking behaviors to signal their dissatisfaction with the pace or direction of the meeting. Such passive-aggressive action reduces the chances for empathetic consideration of others' points of view. Further, a statement of dismissiveness, disrespect, and depleted significance has been registered.

While some people may routinely violate our mono-tasking encouragement, such violations are dangerous for emerging leaders. The risks of misperceptions, bruised feelings, and missed content are simply too great.

Connect Early

Listening and communicating have their best chances of flourishing when the parties can make a positive initial connection. It may seem subtle but the tone for listening is established quickly. Eye contact, facial expressions, and even a smile are probably the most noteworthy.

We've all experienced it. We recently met with a young member of a medical leadership team. As he bustled into our meeting, our first point of contact was abrupt and perfunctory. Despite the obligatory handshake, he made no eye contact and his face was expressionless. What was our perception? "It's just one more meeting for this guy. It's clear he doesn't care what I have to say."

Focus

A listener must turn his or her focus toward the person who is speaking. As the listener, concentrate on the speaker's message and concentrate on the needs that are revealed within that message. This means that you must, at least for the moment, turn your attention away from your agenda and toward the speaker's agenda. Daniel Goleman (2006) refers to this process as "attunement" and offers the following: "Attunement is attention that goes beyond momentary empathy to a full, sustained presence that facilitates rapport. We offer a person our total attention and listen fully. We seek to understand the other person rather than just making our own point" (p. 86).

Perhaps an example from the coaching realm will be helpful. In coaching, we are always conscious of focus. We enter the conversation by trying to purge our self-interests and zero in on the other party. We try to screen out everything else than the person and the message.

Tone

We have often commented to leaders, confused why their well-intentioned messages missed the mark, "It's probably not what you said but the way that you said it." By tone, we include both verbal and nonverbal tone. There is little doubt that people read deep meaning from the tone that is projected.

A short, quick, and unemotional tone may signal action and decisiveness. Such a tone may also signal that prolonged conversation and differing opinions are not desired. Tone goes beyond words to suggest affect and sincerity. We've all been in situations where the words expressed said one thing, while the sarcastic tone conveyed a quite different meaning.

Pace

Deep listening often requires the emerging leader to purposefully slow down or, in communication language, to "pace down." Recall that as a hard-charging, successful achiever, you are revved up for action, preferring rapid exchanges and quick processing. That's great and that's fine, but it may not be where your people are.

You may need to slow your rate of speech and even allow some brief gaps of silence (which always seem much longer than they really are). You may need to refrain from the common tendency to rush the other party's form of expression. Further, if you are asking a penetrating question or posing a matter that requires some degree of reflection, give the other party some processing time. There is an old coaching skill that may be relevant. It's called the "silence gap." If you ask a tough question of others, wait . . . wait at least 15 seconds before speaking again. You'll be surprised at the additional depth and meaning that you will garner from just a bit of pacing down.

Minimal Encouragers

Minimal encouragers are brief interjections from the listener that serve to: (1) let the speaker know that you are tracking; and (2) encourage the speaker to continue speaking. Nods of the head and a simple, well-timed "uh huh" may be enough, as long as these flow naturally and do not seem programmed. We also like a bit more. Consider an occasional "OK," or "that makes sense" to accompany your affirmative nod.

Open-Ended Questions

Deep listening places a heavy reliance on open-ended questions. These questions are not only a means of gaining greater clarity but a way to guide the other party toward a greater level of expression. Open-ended questions are those that cannot be answered with a simple response, but require more extensive disclosure.

For example, you might say to a team member, "I understand you have trouble working with Sarah." This comment begs for a short and definitive answer. "Yes." We find out little more than what we already know. The conversation moves to a deeper level when an open-ended question is posed. "Why is it so difficult to work with Sarah?" The other party is obliged to probe further. Even if the other party replies, "I don't know," you can continue with an open-question format, such as, "Tell me about a situation where you and Sarah had difficulty working together."

Perception Checks and Clarifications

Whether you are speaking or listening, these interventions are critical for assuring clarity and understanding. A perception check, just as the term implies, is a verbal check-in to make sure that you are connecting with the other party. As such, perception checks are used to make sure the other party is following and understanding your message. They should be sprinkled into the communication periodically.

When presenting a major point, it is good to stop periodically and check by asking, "Does that make sense?" or "Are you OK with that?" In essence, we are checking in with the other party to be sure we are on the same page—together in our understanding.

Clarifications are used when you are listening to the other party's message. They keep the communication from moving ahead too fast when you are struggling with some part of the message. It could be as simple as, "Could you restate that last point, I did not really pick up on it?" Or, even better, you may try an open-ended question here. "I'm not sure I got the last point. Could you help me understand how it fits in and why it's so important?" Catch the tone here. We seek clarification. We do not demand it.

Nonverbal Cues and Reflections of Meaning

One value of face-to-face communication is that we can attend to nonverbal cues. Although statistics vary, some experts assert that as much as 90% of the communication process comes through nonverbals (Fromkin & Rodman, 1983).

Consider a meeting that occurred between two colleagues, Jen and Lisa. Both entered the meeting with different assumptions, different views of the situation, and quite divergent interests. Yet they plunged ahead in what was a slightly emotional but respectful exchange. It was one of those settings laden with tension, where the wrong word or expression could send emotions escalating. During their discussion, Jen emphasized a key concern and did so rather strongly. Almost immediately, Lisa's eyes shifted downward, she turned slightly in her chair away from Jen, and appeared to become nonverbally disengaged. To ignore this signal and press on could be counter-productive, especially if Lisa truly had disconnected from the conversation.

So what does Jen do? Here is where the "reflection of meaning" skill can be employed. Reflections of meaning involve two things: (1) an awareness of what you have observed; and (2) an open and honest request for understanding about what has occurred. In the case above, Jen stopped presenting her message and took a diversion. "Lisa, I'm not sure what has happened here, but I sense that we're not connecting right now. Perhaps I'm pushing too hard or perhaps I've offended you. Can you help me understand what's going on?" In this case, Lisa responded openly and candidly, "I think your last comment was over-the-top and bullying." OK. Now they can address an issue that would serve as a detriment to any further efforts to connect and communicate.

Two things should be noted. First, everyone may not choose to be as open and direct as Lisa. But at least you have shown some level of awareness and sensitivity to your communication partner. Second, sometimes reflections of meaning can turn in unexpected directions. A colleague once asked a workshop participant, who was sitting arms-crossed with a distressed and defensive look on his face, "I'm thinking you disagree with the points I'm making here?" The participant simply added, "Actually, I'm not feeling well. I'm trying to hold it together until the break." It's interesting that what was perceived as a disrespectful action turned out to be a quite respectful and considerate response. Now, the facilitator knew and could act accordingly—an immediate break, in this case.

Summarize for Understanding

Most of you have heard of (and many of you have read) Stephen Covey's bestseller, *The 7 Habits of Highly Successful People* (1989). Covey's experience-based design does not minimize the impact of the habits and views that he shares. For example, he suggests that we should seek first to understand, then to be understood, imploring us to "diagnose before we prescribe" (p. 237). This is an important guideline that is easier said than done. Even Covey notes that this involves a paradigm shift for people who are programmed to seek first to be understood. Covey's language speaks to emerging leaders who are seriously pursuing activities of influence. "It's a paradox, in a sense, because in order to have influence, you have to be influenced" (Covey, 1989, p. 243).

Summarizing helps assure that you have heard the other party and that you have understood the intent and meaning of the message. Summarizing is done to make sure you have *accurately* captured the message. Further, it allows the other party an opportunity to clarify and add points that need correction or emphasis. However, summarizing is not a time for judgment. In fact, we encourage you to hold your judgment at this point. Judgments, evaluations, and impressions of meaning are part of the dialogue process which comes next.

Dialogue

Dialogue can be a game-changer for emerging leaders. Dialogue alters the nature and tone of interpersonal exchanges, and it provides a framework for creatively discussing important issues so that optimal decisions get made. Among other advantages, dialogue has been shown to help establish common ground and build trust (Hardy, Lawrence, & Grant, 2005). There are a number of excellent sources available on this topic (Bohm, 1996; Patterson, Grenny, McMillan, & Switzler, 2002).

In the most literal sense, the word dialogue means "converse." As such, a dialogue is a conversation. However, the interpersonal skill of dialogue goes deeper. Dialogue is a conversation between parties where one is: (1) willing to present my ideas, views, feelings, interpretations, needs, and concerns on a subject; and (2) listen to and engage other parties so I can understand their ideas, views, feelings, interpretations, needs, and concerns regarding that subject. Quite succinctly, dialogue is "the free flow of meaning between two or more people" (Patterson, Grenny, McMillan, & Switzler, 2002, p. 20). Through dialogue, we are expanding the "pool of shared meaning" by making it safe for everyone to add their meaning to that pool (Patterson, 2002, p. 21).

Leaders set the communication tone for their teams and units. You create the climate or conditions where dialogue can flourish. Unfortunately, you can also create a tone where any hope of dialogue is dashed. A lot of this has to do with how you ask for and receive input from others. As noted above, dialogue demands that all parties feel safe to expand the pool of shared meaning.

Let's envision it this way. A project leader is sitting in a room with three of her senior team leads. Everyone in the room has been with the company much longer than the leader. She knows that her team leads have experiences and viewpoints that are likely to be varied and diverse. Somehow, this team must come together to engage in an open and candid discussion about a staffing gap that is affecting the overall project.

Let's assume that all parties have done their homework (at times, a quite heroic assumption). As such, each person has arrived at certain impressions. Further, as each party has studied the situation, they each have arrived at clear ideas on what needs to be done—ideas that are framed in solid, well-thought-out logic.

The dialogue rolls out in an intriguing manner. The leader enters the discussion with a sense of understanding and meaning, drawn from her analysis, experience, feelings, needs, and concerns. More importantly, she enters the conversation with her own set of ideas.

Even at this juncture, a possible breakdown to effective dialogue may be bubbling just beneath the surface. It is known as the "commitment bias" (also referred to as escalation of commitment) (Staw, 1976). The commitment bias suggests that, because the leader has thought through the issues with care, she enters the collective conversation with some degree of commitment to a course of action. Further, the more deeply and thoroughly she has studied, the deeper is her commitment. Because of this, she will tend to screen out or diminish arguments that stray too far from her commitment—and thus, the bias.

Of course, the team leads are behaving in a similar manner. They enter the conversation with ideas and commitments that are drawn from their own unique experience, analysis, feelings, needs, and concerns. And they too have a solid set of views and ideas on how the team should proceed.

As you can see, the power of dialogue can be thwarted as parties are reluctant to budge from their well-reasoned commitments. Will all this come together or dissipate in a hurry? It's in the leader's hands. The leader must create a setting and tone for dialogue, enabling and encouraging all parties to share their needs and options. One may argue that if mutual trust exists among the parties, then open sharing will occur. Of course, trust is important and necessary, but it's not enough. The leader sets the tone for dialogue. We suggest a practical, five-step process that is outlined in Table 6.2.

Deep Listening

We begin by returning to the elements of deep listening that were framed earlier. Dialogue is grounded in deep and respectful listening by all parties. The difficulty, of course, is to practice attentive listening when you have a point to

TABLE 6.2 STEPS FOR SUCCESSFUL DIALOGUE

- Deep listening
- Openness and disclosure
- Facilitation
- Empathy and validation
- Expansive problem-solving

make and an opinion to express. Consider the proverbial question, "Are you really listening or just getting ready to talk?" Recall that our charge is to listen first; summarize what you have heard to assure clarity and signal other parties that you have been focused on their messages and the needs that are represented; and then offer your opinion.

Openness and Disclosure

Team members may be willing to jump into the discussion and share at the level and depth where their meaning becomes clear. That's great, but often that's not what happens. People hold back. Disclosure is always bounded. We are not naïve. In a politically-charged organizational climate, there is always concern over how much to reveal and when it should be revealed. When this happens, leaders must move the discussion—what is known as "forwarding the action"—and often that means making the first move.

As such, the dialogue process requires that the leader establishes a tone of openness by willingly sharing personal concerns, needs, feelings, and opinions about the issue at hand. Often, leaders are reluctant to take this lead owing to a fear of biasing any resulting discussion. That may happen, but it need not if the leader is careful with tone and demonstrates a sincere willingness to hearing all views to the discussion. Further, by expressing personal views, leaders allow themselves to be vulnerable, signaling the expectation that others will follow a similar course. Through this move, vestiges of uncertain and unknown "hidden agendas" can be minimized.

Facilitation

Leaders must facilitate dialogue by encouraging others to add their concerns, needs, feelings, and opinions. The leader must encourage and enable this sharing by: (1) making it easy for others to share; (2) demonstrating that you are attentively practicing deep listening when they do share; and (3) making it safe for others to share.

The best way to make it easy for others to share is to ask them to do so. If you have already shared, you merely are asking for them to reciprocate. You have modeled the practice already. The process becomes safe when the legitimacy of what is shared is accepted and negative repercussions for sharing are removed. A tone of understanding rather than judging must be present. At this stage, we want to hear and understand, not judge or evaluate. In this manner, the "pool of shared meaning" can be expanded.

Empathy and Validation

Leaders and all team members must demonstrate empathy toward one another. Empathy is generally considered as one of the qualities of emotional intelligence. Cambridge Professor Simon Baron-Cohen (2011) explains that "empathy is the ability to identify what someone else is thinking or feeling and to respond to that person's thoughts and feelings with an appropriate emotion" (p. 10). In the language of dialogue, empathy is our capacity to understand and appreciate the meaning that has been expressed by another (Goleman, 2006).

Empathy is expressed through validation. Here, you share with the other party what you have heard and the meaning you have inferred. Then, you confirm or validate that meaning. This is a statement of understanding and acceptance of another person's "right" to hold their feelings and opinions. It is not a statement of agreement. In essence, you are validating the other party's right to feel what they feel and express what they have shared.

Serving as a university department chair, one of the authors had the following experience. Holly, a bright young woman, was about to graduate. As Holly entered my office, you could sense her emotional intensity. You could also hear it and see it through her quivering voice and her agitated shifting in her chair. As Holly rolled out her concerns, they were aimed at one of our department's professors. Without going into all the issues, Holly felt that the professor had "cost her a letter grade" by not allowing her to make up a missed assignment. She asserted that it was a clear violation of the course syllabus. The more she talked, the more her anger swelled to the point that her hands were now shaking.

I must admit that as I glanced at the syllabus, it appeared to me, quite clearly, that Holly had misunderstood the stated policy. The professor in question had behaved properly. Now there are options. I could tell Holly, as many people like to do, not to get upset. (By the way, people who are upset just love you telling them not to get upset.) Or, I could point out that she was wrong—which would most likely be marginally effective at best, given her emotional state. Instead, empathy and validation seemed the better route. "Holly, I've known you for nearly four years now. You are good student and a fine young woman. I know you are frustrated and concerned. That makes sense. Honestly, if I thought someone had treated me as you think this professor has treated you, I'd be frustrated and upset, and I'd be talking to the department chair too."

Recognize that this is merely empathy and validation of Holly's feelings and her meaning. It is not an acceptance that her argument is correct. It's probably not surprising that Holly began to relax, almost instantly. She knew that there would be no escalating argument and no aggressive pushback. Instead, there was emotional validation. As Holly took some breaths and regained her composure, I asked if she would take another look at the syllabus, and we read it together. Viewing the material with fresh and more objective eyes, Holly commented, "I think I'm wrong, huh."

There is no assurance that empathy and validation will produce a Holly-like response. In fact, it's unrealistic to think things will be wrapped that neatly across all situations. However, the tone that is achieved through empathy and validation allows us to proceed to the final step with an enhanced probability of success.

Expansive Problem-Solving

Some may argue that expansive problem-solving that focuses on workable solutions really extends beyond the framework of dialogue. However, problem-solving is the logical outcome we should expect from dialogue.

Understandably, some emerging leaders dread getting embroiled in tough interpersonal exchanges, especially when final responsibility for action rests on their shoulders. This can also be part of the excitement of being a leader. Now, with all the issues on the table, how can we sift through all sides and find workable solutions?

First, there is almost always a solution within an atmosphere of open dialogue and collaboration. There are some guidelines to consider. Initially, start by affirming the common purpose that everyone is working toward. Next, identify areas of agreement. Finally, brainstorm new ways to merge options—what are often known as bridge-solutions.

Let's consider one more example. We coached a young sales manager who was struggling between the demands of one of his most important customers and the adamant rejection of those demands from his immediate boss. Following the absolute letter of the contract, the boss was on solid legal footing. Yet, the young manager sensed, quite intuitively, that such a position could threaten long-term relations with a needed customer. Together, we talked, and the manager decided to have a candid conversation with his customer contact to try to figure out what was going on, what had changed, and most importantly, to understand more deeply what the customer was experiencing. In short, what was the customer's meaning?

Not surprisingly, the customer's side of the story was different. Facing a forceful and metric-driven new boss of his own, the customer contact was responding to escalating pressure to perform. Importantly, the new manager learned that the real issue had little to do with the current delivery but with the customer's need to get a better deal down the line.

Everything is now different. In fact, they were able to strike a deal that increased the number of pieces purchased while slightly decreasing the price, a figure that was mutually beneficial and maintained a key relationship.

Leading Up

Emerging leaders must be adept at leading up. Leading up is a connection and communication theme, as the goal is to create influence with the boss. Increasingly, as organizations recognize the significance of leadership throughout the organization, the value of lower-level leaders who can affect and influence their bosses for the good of the organization is gaining attention and traction. At times, you may be making the case for additional resources. At times, you may question a decision by noting its effect on your team or unit. At times, you may simply need to offer a different perspective given the unique experiences that your team faces. In any event, such efforts at leading up should be undertaken with clarity and confidence.

In recent years, the leadership literature has provided some excellent insights in this arena (Feiner, 2004; Gabarro & Kotter, 2005; Maruca & Milhaven, 2000). In the following sections, we offer some key points to keep in mind when interacting and influencing the boss, and we offer a model for influential upward communication.

Know the Boss

Let's examine some key considerations for influencing the boss. The first and most important point is to "know the boss." Know the boss's needs and pressure points. Know the agenda and focus that the boss is pursuing. Arguments that enhance or forward the boss's agenda are likely to receive favorable consideration.

In addition, get to know the boss's style and preferences. If the boss is cautious and analytic, structure your presentation accordingly. Cover the facts and provide written documentation. If the boss is direct and decisive, be time-conscious and thoroughly prepared. Keep in mind, you will be most influential when you can show the boss, in a logical and rational way, how your request "contributes" to the agenda that he or she is pursuing.

A lot of this depends on your relationship with the boss. And a lot depends on how the boss chooses to connect with junior leaders. Some bosses foster an open style that invites questions and respectful pushback. They see that as the basis for creativity and growth. Others are more reserved and distant. One of the best cues you can gather here is how the boss has responded to your requests (or those of others) in the past.

The Go or No-Go Decision

You must carefully consider whether the matter or issue at hand warrants an exchange with the boss. It's the classic "go or no-go decision." We always ask our emerging leaders to consider four points at this stage. First, is the issue really important enough to go to the boss? Second, what might the fallout be from this conversation? This is clearly a subjective risk assessment. Third, are you and the boss in an acceptable emotional state for this exchange? Fourth, is this battle worth the fight? "Pick your battles." You can't go to the boss too often.

Think in terms of impact and long-term needs. For example, do you really want to use your social capital with the boss on this immediate issue? Although we never have complete clarity on any of these points, the process of con-sidering and assessing each point will help you reach the go or no-go determination.

The Point of Entry

Choose the proper "point of entry." This is largely a matter of timing. If the boss is facing a critical deadline by the end of the week, you may be judicious to wait until next week to meet and make a request. Seemingly small matters, such as the time of day, can have important point of entry impact. One young leader shared that her boss was a meticulous planner with a nervous need to work through his daily agenda. She noted that she would never go to the boss early in the day because he was caught up in his own schedule. However, she had learned that toward the end of the day, with his own to-do list in check, the boss was much more likely to take time and be open. Apparently, the magic time was 4 pm, and everybody knew it.

An additional and obvious item about the point of entry must be noted. Never publically criticize the boss or engage in action that could cause the boss to lose face. Bosses will always respond negatively when embarrassed or blindsided. Never go there.

The Boss's Language

You've got to "speak the boss's language." Bosses have limited amounts of time. Further, they generally deal with and process requests in terms of financials and metrics. Tight, to-the-point presentations with clear metrics or evidence of bottom-line considerations are almost always received more favorably than emotionally-laden presentations that take too long to get to the point. Bosses deal with results-oriented impact. Frame your requests, as best you can, in terms of the impact for your team and, when possible, the overall unit.

Be Realistic

Be "realistic." Never ask the boss to take an action that you would not take if you were sitting in his or her chair. This is a matter of good sense, but it also speaks to your integrity and character. Leadership author Michael Feiner (2004) provides additional advice, imploring leaders to ask the boss for what you need but to be willing to accept the reality of "no".

Deliver Quality Results

Be good at what you do. Consistently, deliver quality results. Be known as someone who gets the job done and exceeds expectations. The plain and simple bottom-line—bosses are more likely to be influenced by people who are top-notch performers than those who are not.

A Model of Influence

There is a way to approach the boss which follows closely our model for respectful conflict encounters. As noted above, our goal is create influence with the boss. Our model is presented in Table 6.3.

TABLE 6.3 APPROACHING THE BOSS

- Explain your motives
- Explain the situation
- Explain the impact
- Come with alternatives
- Maintain self-control
- Review the next steps

The first step is to "explain your motives" for meeting with the boss. Be clear and specific, removing any question of hidden agendas or lack of loyalty concerns. Most bosses appreciate such candor, thus creating a more relaxed encounter.

Second, "explain the situation" as you see it. Frame your comments in terms such as, "This is what our team is facing," or "This is the situation as we are experiencing it." It's important that the boss sees the situation from your perspective. However, it's also important that you signal the boss that you understand that your perspective is not the only perspective. Once again, you are showing maturity and breadth and a willingness to be part of the bigger game. It's entirely possible that the boss may share his or her view of the situation, which may put a different twist on matters.

Third, explain how the situation "impacts your team," and how you feel it "impacts the big picture." Remember, if you can frame the big-picture impact so that it speaks to the boss's agenda and is backed with metrics, you will build a stronger case.

Fourth, be prepared to come forward with a "suggested plan or alternative." Wait for the boss's cue. In most cases, the boss will ask for your suggestions. If not, frame your request in terms of a need. For example, "This is what we need to in order to complete the project on schedule."

Fifth, "maintain self-control." At some point, the boss may engage in a political response or even an emotional response. In other cases, you may get little more than "I'll think about it." You have a few steps to take here. Listen and seek clarification. Ask some open-ended questions to gain better clarity. Work the process and remain respectful. And, be sensitive to know when it's time to fold and move on. Remember there will be another day and another issue.

Sixth, "review what has been concluded." This may include next steps, conveyance of additional information, and points of accountability. Be clear.

"Let me be sure about our next steps. You want more documentation on my proposed alternative. Is that right? I'll get that to you, in written form, by the end of the week. Is that OK?" Successful influence with your boss is often a series of steps—a process—rather than a one-stop activity. Thank the boss for the time and consideration, even if your attempt at influence has been unsuccessful.

Responsible Delegation

At some point, all emerging leaders face the need for and challenge of delegation. Without hyperbole, the leader who is unable to delegate will not succeed. Delegation allows you to accomplish more and develop your people, thereby enhancing both performance outcomes and the individual motivation of those who work for you.

The struggle that we face with delegation arises because we know that we are still responsible for what happens. If our people do not provide quality, high-level performance, we are on the line. Therefore, delegation must be approached carefully and with proper developmental perspective. There are six keys to responsible delegation: (1) teaching; (2) clarity; (3) preconditions; (4) incremental steps; (5) adjustment; and (6) ego-orientation.

First, delegation must be approached as a teaching or coaching activity. Rarely is delegation a carte blanche, turn-them-lose activity. Instead, it is an opportunity to shape and work with people, helping them become ready to assume larger roles.

Second, when delegating, clarity of expectations and outcomes must be direct and unequivocal. Let your people know exactly what is expected and needed.

Third, there are certain preconditions that must be considered before delegation becomes viable. People must possess the task-related skills necessary to do the job. They must possess the motivation, drive, and confidence to do the job. In short, you must have assurance that there is an acceptable probability of success once delegation has taken place. If any of these concerns are not sufficiently in place, more teaching and coaching may be needed.

Fourth, delegation often must proceed in incremental steps, increased steadily as an employee's skills and confidence increase. Expanding an employee's role too quickly (except for rather mundane assignments) may lead to frustration and lowered motivation.

Fifth, you should meet with your people and review how they are progressing with the delegated task. Again, you are teaching and shaping, offer ideas and needed points of correction. Mistakes will happen, perhaps. We want people to learn from and avoid further occurrences of those mistakes.

Let's assume that you want to shift negotiations with one of your suppliers from you to one of your people. Start by taking the employee with you to one of the meetings. Discuss what's going on. Review and discuss what has been learned once the initial meeting has concluded. During the next meeting, allow the employee to play a role, increasing that role as the employee's experience grows. Between sessions, there is discussion and coaching. Incrementally, the employee is being empowered, in both skills and confidence, to take over the negotiations.

Finally, in order to be an effective delegator, you will need to check your ego. You must understand and accept that desired outcomes can be achieved in different ways. This is challenging because most of us are pretty sure that our way of doing things is the best. Here, outcomes are invariant; behaviors and approaches are not, as long as they are conducted within the standards and character of your unit.

Concluding Thoughts: The 80/20 Feedback Rule

Management wisdom is replete with a broad selection of so-called 80/20 rules. Yet, this time-honored version provides a sound perspective for new leaders. Let's distinguish between two types of feedback—affirming and improvement-focused. While the positive and negative feedback monikers are often used, the terms are misleading. For example, "negative" carries a punitive tone that we wish to avoid. The goal of all feedback is the same—to assure consistent, successful behaviors from your people.

Affirming feedback provides encouragement, reinforcement, appreciation, and recognition for the good work that has been done. It is used to underscore and highlight the accomplishments, as well as provide encouragement to continue what have been successful actions. Improvement-focused feedback draws attention to behavior that needs to be adjusted or modified, and its intent is to foster behavioral change that will lead to future success.

There are certainly times when improvements and corrections need to be made and need to be made quickly and decisively. However, the 80/20 rule offers an important perspective. It purports that as we interact with people over time, the preponderance of our feedback (80%) should be affirming and a much smaller proportion (perhaps no more than 20%) should be improvement-focused.

Imagine what transpires when this theme is ignored or even reversed. We've seen leaders eschew affirming feedback, arguing that "I don't have time to pat my people on the head for doing what they are getting paid to do." Such leaders provide a strong dose of improvement-focused directives with limited affirmation. Consequently, team members learn to become cautious and defensive as their leaders approach, knowing they are about to be corrected.

A different atmosphere and cultural emphasis arises when workers know their leaders are primarily supporters. In fact, this approach enhances the salience of improvements and corrections when such feedback needs to be delivered. Our encouragement for emerging leaders could not be stronger. Focus on affirming. Correct sparingly. The impact will be more dramatic.

Commitment

The Strength of Performance through People

It is exciting to interact with people who are playing at the top of their game, and it's depleting and frustrating to encounter those who are not. Some people just seem to go through the motions, merely "task-involved," performing the minimum that is required and absolutely nothing more. In today's highly competitive climate, such behavior is insufficient. We need more. We need people who care—those who feel a sense of connection, passion, and ownership in their work. We need people who are "psychologically-involved"— a workforce who engage their work with a sense of commitment.

How does this happen? To a large extent, it's a matter of motivation. There is no topic in the management and leadership field that has received more attention. Thousands of research studies have explored the nuances of organizational motivation, and excellent compilations have provided summaries of our more popular and accepted research models (Latham, 2012; Locke & Latham, 2004; Porter, Steers, & Bigley, 2002; Steers, Mowday, & Shapiro, 2004).

Motivation can be seen as an individual's willingness to exert high levels of effort toward organizational goals. Of course, motivation is a complex process, involving "a set of energetic forces that originate both within as well as beyond an individual's being" (Pinder, 1998, p. 11). Therein we encounter the "paradox of motivation." Although organizational demands necessitate high levels of employee commitment, no leader, regardless of position or power, can make someone "become motivated." Motivation is a personal, individualized action (LePine, LePine, & Jackson, 2004). As leaders, we attempt to affect motivation by creating an environment—a set of conditions—that help our people decide to engage their work with focus, dedication, and energy.

Fundamentally, we are concerned with three motivational issues: (1) "energizing" our people; (2) "directing and channeling" the behavior of our people; and (3) "maintaining and sustaining" desired behaviors (Steers, Porter, & Bigley, 1996, p. 8). We possess an amazing capacity to create opportunities for commitment. Evidence has suggested that "leaders who were skilled at inspiring and motivating others tended to have direct reports who were more satisfied and committed overall . . . positively affect[ing] the productivity of the team and the willingness of less motivated employees to work hard" (Zenger, Folkman, & Edinger, 2009, pp. 20–22).

The purpose of this chapter is to unfold some key studies, models, and practical ideas that will help you with this critical process. A little theory? Yes. However, with paraphrasing apologies to Kurt Lewin, there often isn't anything quite as practical as a solid theory.

Ability, Motivation, and Performance

We generally believe that performance is a function of ability and motivation (Anderson & Butzin, 1974; Heider, 1958). This is a powerful formula that deserves closer attention. Both parts of the equation are essential. Without ability—that right mix of talent—even the most powerful motivational efforts will fail to achieve desired results. By the same token, even the most talented and gifted employee will fall short without the energy and drive that comes from motivation.

Let's explore the first part of this equation. Ability is drawn from three sources: (1) aptitude—that right mix of skills, talent, and intelligence; (2) training—the developmental efforts we use to make sure that skills are always evolving and relevant; and (3) resources—making sure that our people have the human, technological, and financial support they need to do their jobs and to do them well. The ability factor is one reason why organizations are so careful with their selection and placement processes. As Jim Collins so aptly reminds us, we have to get the right people on the bus (Collins, 2001). This is also why organizations spend so much time and money enhancing abilities through training, coaching, and other developmental efforts.

There are some key lessons for the emerging leader at this point. First, assess and make sure that you have the right people in the right roles—what is known as "person-job fit" (Kristof-Brown, Zimmerman, & Johnson, 2005). While it is unlikely that you will get to select your team, you will have some latitude in assigning tasks. Try to match the talents of your people to the specific challenges you face. An argument could be made that, if we get the right people into the right jobs, there is probably little need to motivate one toward engaged and committed work. You may even be able, at times, to engage in "job shaping," where you adjust aspects of the job to more fully capitalize on the talents of your people (Buckingham, 2005).

Second, keep offering developmental opportunities so that your people are growing and learning. Third, do what you can to secure the resources needed to maximize performance. Discretion is needed. Request resources judiciously and build a compelling case when making a request of your boss.

The motivation side of the equation comes from three sources: (1) direction; (2) energy; and (3) persistence. Here leaders assure direction through the agenda that we set and the expectations we convey. We help assure that our people pursue their tasks with energy by providing physical and psychological support, and we do it by providing valued rewards for meeting expectations. Persistence is encouraged as we offer understanding and genuine concern, remove barriers when we can, and demonstrate an optimistic and resilient attitude in our own behavior.

Pragmatically, one of the issues that you face is that you probably hold limited formal reward power over those you are trying to motivate. How do you lead co-workers whom you may not be able to reward with a bonus or a bump in salary? In many cases, you may have limited power to reprimand and discipline.

There is help and insight from a number of well-researched motivational theories and models. Although the models presented here are limited and evolving, they provide excellent frameworks to better understand why people do what they do (or don't).

The Impact of Equity

We have addressed the issue of equity and equity theory in an earlier chapter. Recall that equity is a perception—a perception of fairness, built on the logic that those who demonstrate the highest levels of desired outcomes should receive rewards that are commensurate. Generally, if people believe that they are being rewarded fairly for their efforts, they feel motivated and choose to maintain or enhance their performance. However, if they experience feelings of unfairness or inequity, motivation falters and effort lags (Adams, 1963; 1965; Mowday, 1996).

Rewards should be viewed broadly, as anything a worker values. The most tangible reward that we have is compensation. However, other forms persist: including work assignments that provide variety and challenge, opportunities for growth, recognition, status symbols, honest and earned statements of appreciation, and other situationally-valued considerations. These non-compensatory factors become even more critical when our capacity to extend meaningful differentiations in compensation is limited or non-existent.

Part of the interesting and practical nuance of equity theory is the insight into how people draw their perceptions of fairness. The theory states that people determine the fairness of a reward by: (1) assessing the personal effort that was required to obtain their reward (their effort-reward ratio); and (2) comparing their personal effort-reward ratio to their perception of the effort-reward ratio of some other person who is similar to them—a referent other.

A simple example will suffice. Suppose you had a great year at work. As a team leader, you worked long hours, traveled extensively, always went the extra mile, and saw your team exceed its goals in all areas. A colleague, who was hired at the same time, had a disappointing year by all accounts. His team missed its targets in many areas, and you were asked to bail him out of a couple of high-profile projects. Now, you have just learned that he received the same salary increase as you. In all likelihood, a sense of unfairness and inequity will arise.

When we experience such inequity, we respond in one of six fundamental ways: (1) adjusting our effort (in most cases, reducing effort); (2) attempting to change the outcome (for example, asking for more money); (3) leaving the situation (for example, seeking a reassignment project or even leaving the organization); (4) changing the referent other (for example, comparing yourself to someone who seems more appropriate); (5) cognitively altering the inputs of others (for example, assuming that the referent must be doing much more than what we know); and (6) cognitively altering your evaluation of the reward (for example, reasoning that, although the compensation was low, important and valued experience was gained).

What are the implications for the emerging leader? First, perceptions of equity can have far-reaching effects. Fairness must always be a center-stage issue. You want to be sure that rewards are distributed as fairly and equitably as possible—a view known as distributive justice (Homans, 1961; Nowakowski & Conlon, 2005). People can easily feel slighted and quickly assess that perks are not being distributed fairly. The key is to be sensitive here.

Beyond this, communication is important. People will accept decisions, even those that may not appear equitable on the surface, if you can explain the reasoning or rationale for the way the decision was made. This is known as procedural justice (Colquitt, Conlon, Wesson, Porter, & Ng, 2001; Lind & Tyler, 1988; Nowakowski & Conlon, 2005). Procedural justice is enhanced when you clearly explain the process, procedures, and line of reasoning you used when making a decision; listen to the perspectives of those who feel inequity; and maintain the highest levels of dignity and respect (Bies & Moag, 1986; Bies & Shapiro, 1987; Phillips, Douthitt, & Hyland , 2001; Tyler, 1987).

Further, equity requires that you are consistent when dealing with different people in similar situations, and that you are consistent over time (Leventhal, 1980). Be sure decisions are based on accurate information and are free of bias (Steers, Porter, & Bigley, 1996). Of course, trust is a key factor. When people feel that you are trustworthy and credible, they are more likely to accept the logic and fairness of the procedures and reasoning you employed (Tyler, 1989).

Applying the Expectancy Model

Although criticisms of this model have been offered, expectancy theory is also one of our more useful and practical approaches to motivation, as you will soon see (Isaac, Zerbe, & Pitt, 2001; Porter & Lawler, 1968; Roberts & Glick, 1981; Vroom, 1964). In short, the model suggests that three decisions affect whether we are motivated to perform a given task: (1) we must feel that our efforts will result in reaching the goal that is set; (2) we must value the rewards that are offered for goal attainment; and (3) we must feel that reaching the assigned goal will result in promised rewards. Further, we assume that, if any of these factors is low, one's overall motivation is diminished. Part of the insight of this model draws from pinpointing cognitive actions or decision points that people process.

We apply this model diagnostically. That is, if motivation appears problematic, the model offers considerations of what might be occurring. Initially, we are reminded, once again, of the importance of having crystal-clear performance expectations and goals. Logically, one cannot be expected to exert effort toward a goal if they are unsure of exactly what that goal is. As leaders, we may err at this very point. Sometimes, we assume that "under-defined" goals are appropriate, as they give people more latitude and discretion. Recall, from our earlier discussions of goal-setting theory, such thinking runs counter to the evidence (Locke, Shaw, Saari, & Latham, 1981). Instead, we opt for clear, specific, and challenging goals (Locke & Latham, 1990). Further, if you have any doubt about whether your people have the right level of clarity, we'd suggest specifying and clarifying the expectations and goals again.

Next, we know that motivation can break down if an individual perceives or believes that there is a low probability (expectancy) that their efforts will result in reaching the designated goals or performance outcomes. There may be many reasons for this belief. People may feel that the goals are too lofty. They may feel that they lack the talents, skills, resources, or time to reach the goal. And, we must never minimize the impact of low confidence; that is, our people may possess the needed capacity but don't feel like they do.

As a leader, you may consider a few avenues in an attempt to facilitate a positive perception of this expectancy (Stewart-Williams & Podd, 2004). First, make sure that the performance outcomes that are desired are, indeed, attainable. Next, make sure that you have the "right" person for the right job. That is, make sure that your people have the necessary skills, knowledge, and abilities. Consider whether some level of training is needed. Additionally, you may need to help build the follower's self-efficacy or self-confidence, perhaps using the ideas we suggested in Chapter 3 (Bandura, 1977). You may need to give people additional resources or time, or shift some of an employee's current responsibilities to others. Finally, you may need to break the task down into smaller tasks so that there are multiple, easier goals that incrementally build to the original assigned goal. Remember, if a person honestly believes that they lack the capacity to meet outcomes or that their efforts are unlikely to reach performance expectations, their motivation will be negatively affected.

Next, motivation may falter if individuals feel as though the rewards offered for performance are of limited value to them. In short, they may not feel like the rewards help fulfill personal needs that are most central at this time. To the extent that you can, align rewards with the needs of the workers. Remember that the needs of a follower may not be the same as yours or others, and they will change over time (Human & Biesanz, 2011).

The perceived value of rewards is set against a context that includes tradeoffs. For example, an employee may highly value the promotion being offered as it brings more responsibility, challenge, and status. Simultaneously, the same worker may reason that the promotion means less time with his or her family, a dimension of life that he or she highly values. Therefore, the promotion carries both positive and negative value. The lesson here is to recognize the complexities that are involved and to understand how different people may assign differing values to similar rewards.

Following the model, motivation may be adversely affected if a person feels there is a likelihood or probability that even if they reach the goal, the promised rewards will not be forthcoming. Largely, this is an issue of trust, based on assumptions of fairness and justice. For example, people may see other employees who were promised rewards that were never delivered. They may even feel that you are offering rewards that you do not have the capacity to deliver (new project assignments, raises, time off, or promotions). As you can see, this perception is drawn from impressions of your credibility and the organization's likelihood of delivering on promises.

There is a caution to note at this point. At times, emerging leaders promise valued reward outcomes to followers during informal conversation. Leaders may knowingly make promises with the best intention of honoring them, yet be blocked by external constraints. Both of these mistakes can lead to a breakdown in the follower's expectancy that the leader will deliver on espoused promises. We disagree with the adage that leaders should "under-promise and over-deliver." Instead, don't promise what you cannot deliver, and deliver on what you promise. This means "acting" with integrity—actually doing what you say you are going to do to the best of your ability; and it means "thinking" with integrity—realistically analyzing your ability or capacity to do what you say you are going to do. If you think with integrity and act with integrity consistently over time, your credibility will flourish with your followers.

Job Characteristics Model of Intrinsic Motivation

This model offers specific help for leaders who possess limited capacity to offer formal compensatory rewards. This model has gained recent momentum, as its applications appear to be especially relevant for today's highly talented knowledge workers (Pink, 2011).

This model looks at the nature of the job itself, as a source of intrinsic motivation, providing energizing impact through the work that is done. The job characteristics model contends that individuals will be more motivated if their work provides: (1) skill variety; (2) task identity; (3) task significance; (4) autonomy; and (5) feedback (Hackman & Oldham, 1976; 1980).

Skill variety occurs when work provides people with the opportunity to use different skills. This may reduce boredom; it may increase one's sense of mastery; and may even increase task identity and significance. It also fights the depleting stress of underutilization—the feeling that we have talents and skills but are not given the opportunities to use them.

Task identity is being able to see what one has accomplished, that is, being able to identify with a final product or outcome. Task significance is being able to see that one's accomplishments play a part in helping the team or organization succeed. Significance comes from a person's perception that what they do is important; makes a meaningful contribution; and truly makes a difference.

Autonomy occurs when you provide your people with more latitude in how they perform their work. Research suggests that autonomy is one of the keys to increasing creativity in the workplace (Amabile, 1998; Coelho & Augusto, 2010).

Leaders often have opportunities to build and enhance these factors, but it does take some time and sensitivity. A few years ago, we met a CEO for an early morning meeting. As we walked toward his office, we passed by a custodian doing some work before the masses arrived for the day. The CEO stopped, "Larry, when the Board met here yesterday, this place was spotless. I was so proud. It's due to you and your people. Thanks." There is a clear statement of identity and a powerful commentary about significance. Do you have any doubt that the place looked just as good for the next meeting?

Research on creativity has noted that high task significance is also a key to creativity (Amabile, Conti, Coon, Lazenby, & Herron, 1996). If individuals feel that their work effort has a transcendent purpose or has a critical, positive impact, creativity is positively affected.

Our people gain feedback when they have the chance to see the results of their work. For example, part of the excitement of working with technology is that we often get clear and direct feedback about whether or not our efforts have been successful.

Organizational Behavior Modification

Organizational behavior modification (OB Mod) is an "intervention to encourage desired performance behavior and discourage undesired behavior," built on providing feedback and positive reinforcement (Luthans, Maciag, & Rosenkrantz, 1983, p. 28). We use the tenets of OB Mod regularly, and this model is the basis of most compensation systems. OB Mod is drawn from the conceptual principle that we are motivated to seek pleasure states and avoid pain states (Freud, Dufresne, & Richter, 2011). Helpful theoretical and practical applications are readily available (Babb & Kopp, 1978; Kazdin, 2008; Komaki, Coombs, & Shepman, 1990).

We offer a fundamental, five-step process (Stajkovic & Luthans, 1997). In step 1, we must "identify the behavior" we want to change. For instance, if we have a sales staff, we may desire our people to increase sales. Thus, sales is the behavior that we wish to change (to increase).

In step 2, we measure the "baseline" of the current behavior, that is, the levels of sales that are currently being achieved for each salesperson. This step allows us to later assess the modification system; to see if behavior has actually changed as a result of our intervention.

In step 3, we identify possible "consequences" (at times "unforeseen consequences"). This is an important and often overlooked step. For instance, if we reward sales quantity, are we likely to experience an unforeseen consequence of decreased time, attention, and responsiveness toward customers— in essence, a lower quality customer interaction? Or, if we start a commission pay system to increase sales, is there a risk that our salespeople will engage in undesired or skeptical behaviors (such as exaggerating claims about product benefits) to increase sales? In other words, we need to look at our OB Mod system from a holistic perspective.

In step 4, "reinforcement" is applied to solicit the desired behaviors. These reinforcements may come in one of two forms: (1) positive reinforcement; or (2) negative reinforcement. Positive reinforcement is applying something positive, such as a reward, to elicit a desirable behavior. Negative reinforcement is removing an unpleasant condition, such as a probationary period, to elicit a desirable behavior.

In step 5, we "measure" behavior again to see if the desired change has occurred. If it has, then no corrective action is needed. If the behavior has not changed in the desired manner, adjustments are needed.

We must be careful to distinguish reinforcement from punishment. Punishment is the application of something negative to eliminate an undesirable behavior. As such, no new desired behavior is produced. There is considerable discussion about the overall efficacy and effect of punishment, and its use has considerable potential for long-term negative consequences (Luthans & Kreitner, 1985). We have all seen examples of this, such as employees responding to disciplinary action by temporarily complying, yet building resentment over the long run.

It is also important that you are aware of the principle of extinction in the context of OB Mod. Extinction notes that, when reinforcement is removed, the behavior will return to the baseline. Because of this, it is important to reinforce consistently and quickly while people are in the learning phase. However, once a desired behavior becomes routine, a variable payout is more important. That is, the reinforcement should still be given, but can be given randomly when the behavior occurs.

Although a brief overview of OB Mod, this model offers some important insights. The model recognizes that if behaviors are going to be systematically changed, we need to approach the task systematically. We can't just haphazardly attempt to change behaviors without a clear method and a way to determine if our intervention was a success.

Next, the model emphasizes that individuals are sensitive to OB Mod— maybe a little too sensitive. Consequently, you must think about behaviors that are being rewarded unintentionally. At times, we may even desire one behavior while rewarding another—what has become classically known as "the folly of rewarding A, while hoping for B" (Kerr, 1975). For example, we work with some companies that extol their desire for creativity from their leaders. Yet, creativity is not formally rewarded. New contracts are rewarded. And, perhaps most critical, mistakes (a by-product of innovative creative inquiry) are dealt with harshly (punishment). Or, as mentioned earlier, the quality of output may go down as the quantity of output is rewarded.

The Psychology of Flow

Psychologist Mihaly Csikszentmihalyi (1990) has done some wonderfully creative and pioneering work that centers on the "psychology of flow." Let's take a deeper dive into this popular concept. Csikszentmihalyi believes that, when our talents, skills, values, experiences, and passions are aligned with the challenges and demands of our work, we are "in the flow." When we are in the flow, we're firing on all cylinders. Our skills and talents are being fully utilized.

In the flow, we perform at our highest levels, and we tend to derive our greatest sense of meaning and significance from our work. In the flow, we also tend to lose ourselves in the task at hand. Time slips by as we are locked-in on the immediate challenge. Our energies are focused on the task and the task alone.

By contrast, when our work stifles or restricts our ability to use "all we are," we feel underutilized and experience boredom. And, when work demands and challenges push us beyond our skills and capacity, we will live with anxiety and stress.

Those of you with athletic backgrounds will be familiar with being "in the flow" or "in the zone." Consider the example of the mountain biker. When conditions are just right, you are flying through the woods, completely focused on going as fast as you can without crashing. You're focused on moving through the tress without hitting them, moving over logs and rocks, all the while pushing yourself physically to stay on pace. All of a sudden you realize that the last few minutes are a blur; that all your thoughts about the stress of the days are gone; that the only thing you have been focused on was riding the bike. This is a flow state.

We often ask workshop participants to assess whether they are currently experiencing "flow" at work, and, if not, what they must do to attain flow. It is an insightful activity. Those experiencing flow for a preponderance of their work time express feeling energized and excited by their work; work time seems to "stand still"; personal contentment with work prevails; and performance levels are remarkably high. Emerging leaders typically report that flow occurs when they are challenged and stretched by their assignments. Once tasks are mastered and challenge dissipates, they feel a bit of boredom and long for new challenges.

There is an additional point of significance for emerging leaders. We not only hope that you experience flow states in your work, we want you to help create work environments where your people can experience their own flow states on a regular and on-going basis. So, what can we do to help our people here?

First, in order to experience a state of flow, we need a clear sense of purpose, and we need clear goals and expectations. In turn, our people need the same things. However, in developing and projecting a sense of purpose, we must help our people see beyond vague statements of hope and even broadly-framed mission and vision statements. We want our people to believe that their work has impact and meaning (Izzo & Withers, 2001). We are not suggesting any over-the-top or feigned sense of emphasis here. However, we do want to convey to our people the cause to which they are contributing and the way their work affects that cause.

A couple of examples may help. One of our young leaders was a bank officer whose duties included working with and overseeing a group of tellers. He built the sense of impact and meaning through a consistent message. "We want people to feel confident that we care about them and will take care of their money. The first line of contact, the first impression of our bank that customers experience comes from their initial contact with you." Simple and direct, yet a powerful message.

We heard the message from employees of a small catering business, telling us that they had the privilege of being part of some of the most important events in people's lives—weddings, anniversaries, birthdays, memorials, and other celebrations. Where did that line of thinking originate? Or, consider the purchasing manager for a large international company. She asserted that, if she did do her job well, the impact rippled and affected the whole line of business. Someone—some leader, no doubt—made her feel that sense of meaning.

Second, in order for your people to experience their flow state, the task at hand has to challenge them. In short, they must have opportunities to use their unique array of skills, talents, and abilities. However, if they feel like their tasks are too easy, they become bored, and flow and subsequent motivation are unlikely. On the other hand, if they feel like their tasks are too hard, frustration, anxiety, and stress will ensue. In both cases, your people will not experience the positive mental energies and performance that come from flow.

The psychology of flow provides a few paradoxes. First, individuals may not actually be aware that they are in flow states until they have come out of them. Second, the challenges that put individuals in flow states may not be tasks that they necessarily enjoy or look forward to doing. Finally, every job is multi-faceted, with certain necessary activities that are mundane and routine. Although you will not create work settings that ensure continual flow, look for opportunities; allow your people to feel the challenge of stretch assignments; learn their unique skills; and give them the chance to do what they do best as often as you can.

Attribution of Causality

Heider (1958) argued that when individuals face unexpected outcomes, they become "naïve psychologists" and attempt to determine the cause. Usually, this cognitive process is sparked by failure. When individuals succeed, they take less time to figure out why they had the outcome because they achieved their goal in the manner that was consistent with their original intentions.

Typically, when we experience failure, we seek to determine if the failure was due to internal causes (we have control) or external causes (beyond our control) (Weiner, 1985). Further, as we examine our failures, we strive to determine if they are stable or unstable; that is, if you attempted the task again, would you anticipate failing again (stable) or not (unstable)?

Let's use you as the target person. If you attribute your failure to internal causes and that failure is perceived to be stable, you'll probably conclude it's due to a lack of ability. If you attribute your failure to internal causes and that failure is perceived to be unstable, you'll probably attribute the failure to a lack of effort.

However, if you attribute your failure to external causes and believe that failure is stable, you tend to attribute the failure to the difficulty of the task or the lack of resources. Finally, if you attribute your failure to external causes and that failure is unstable, generally you will attribute your failure to luck, chance, or fate (see Table 7.1).

TABLE 7.1 ATTRIBUTIONAL CONSIDERATIONS

	Failure is perceived to be: Stable	*Failure is perceived to be:* Unstable
Failure is perceived to be due to: *Internal Causes*	Ability	Effort
Failure is perceived to be due to: *External Causes*	Task Difficulty	Luck

Of course, our employees do not say, "I attribute my stable failure to internal causes." Instead, they come at it in practical terms, saying, "I just don't get it. It doesn't seem to matter what I do, I just can't seem to perform up to my boss's expectations. I just don't think that I have what it takes to succeed at this job." In essence, what they are saying is, "I lack the ability to do my job." If you are able to understand their likely attribution for failure, you can help more readily facilitate future performance.

For instance, let's assume that we want to help others see that a recent failure was due to misfortune or uncontrollable influences. As such, we may have to show them that their failure is not stable. Remind them of times when they have succeeded. Or we may show them that the failure is due to external causes. Perhaps we need to remind them that there are larger forces at play, such as a bad economy.

There are situations where we are convinced that the right person is assigned to the right job. That is, their skills, knowledge, and abilities are adequate to successfully perform their assigned task. Here, in most cases, we would like for our people to be able to attribute their failure to a lack of effort (or wrong direction of effort). If people attribute their failure to a lack of effort, they are likely to believe that they are able to perform and thus, will try again. However, if they attribute their failure to some other cause, and we feel it is due to a lack of effort, then to assist in successful performance, we must offer clear and specific feedback.

If an individual attributes their failure to a lack of ability, they are essentially saying, "I'm not capable of performing my job." Remember, we assume that the person does actually have the ability, but is just lacking the belief that they can. We suggest that you can influence the person's self-efficacy, helping them believe that they can do the job.

If the person attributes their failure to the task being too difficult, they are saying that the failure is stable and external. That is, they always expect failure, and it's because of factors out of their control. If you disagree with them and want to move them to attributions of effort, then we suggest breaking the task into smaller tasks that, when sequentially completed, ensure that the original task is completed.

If the person attributes their failure to misfortune or luck, they are saying that the failure is unstable yet is caused by something outside of their control. We may need to help them see how they have some control over their results. Perhaps, you can remind them of times when they have performed and how that applies here.

There is another powerful twist here. It's known as the self-serving bias (Miller & Ross, 1975). This bias suggests that most people tend to attribute their successes to internal factors (such as talent, hard work, and wonderful personal ingenuity). However, they tend to attribute their failures to external factors (such as an unclear assignment, a lack of resources, an impossible task, or bad luck). In short, when your people assess themselves, they tend to feel they succeed because of what they do and fail because of factors beyond their control.

However, you may not see it that way. When you evaluate the failure of one of your people, you come at it differently. You fall prey to a different form of bias, what is known as the fundamental attribution error (Ross, 1977). Your tendency is to attribute another person's failure to internal factors (such as a lack of ability or a lack of effort). As such, you may underestimate the impact that external or situational factors may have had.

You can see the set-up here. You and your people are coming at the attributional process quite differently. Our hope is that this awareness will raise some cautionary flags, thereby improving understanding, communication, remedial actions, and eventual outcomes.

There are times when individuals attribute their failures as we do. For example, we may assess the person's talents, the situations where they are asked to perform, and conclude: (1) they do not have the ability to succeed; (2) the task is too difficult; or (3) that their failure is the result of randomness. Here, we may choose to invest in training so that abilities and skills coincide with job demands. Of course, we may choose to remove the person from the task. We have to help people see that although things did not work out this time, they probably will in the future. It may help to reassure them that they did nothing wrong.

Addressing Employee Expectations and Needs:
Building a Culture of Commitment

Even if you are unfamiliar with the Great Place to Work Institute, you know their work. These are the folks who produce the annual list of the "100 best companies to work for" that appears each February in *Fortune* magazine. Researchers from the Institute analyzed these "best" companies and determined the practices they have in common (Burchell & Robin, 2011). Five dimensions emerged: (1) credibility; (2) respect; (3) fairness; (4) pride; and (5) camaraderie. These are interesting and important themes, many of which we have discussed throughout this book. These should be ongoing, front-burner issues for the emerging leader. As we ask our workshop audiences, "How are your practices contributing to these dimensions?"

We gain additional clarity from the studies of "engagement" that have originated with the Gallup organization. Among other keys, this work underscores the motivational impact of: (1) giving your people the opportunity to do what they do best; (2) providing sincere recognition and praise; (3) providing opportunities for growth and development; (4) giving people the chance to offer opinions that will be considered; and (5) showing your people that you care about them as people (Buckingham & Coffman, 1999).

As we have stated, each of your people is idiosyncratic, and blanket motivational approaches will affect people in different ways. Some may be challenged and activated by a given outcome or reward, and some may not. Armed with this caveat, we summarize (in Table 7.2) thirteen key employee needs that today's employees seem to expect and desire. Note that each of these is non-compensatory.

We have discussed most of these, but a couple points of emphasis are in order. The issue of being able to trust the boss has received considerable attention, and there is evidence of a clear link between trust and retention. Namely, "the more employees trust their boss, the greater their intention to remain with the organization," a factor that appears to be even more dramatic for women than men (Stawiski, Deal, & Ruderman, 2010, p. 5).

Recent research emphasizes that providing employees with opportunities to build new skills and improve existing skills is fundamental to motivating and retaining top talent (Donohue, 2007). These opportunities include developmental assignments and opportunities to receive mentoring and coaching (Herman, Deal, Lopez, Gentry, Shively, Ruderman, & Zukin, 2011).

Finally, we should never underestimate the power of affirming recognition. It costs nothing but time and takes nothing more than an authentic statement

TABLE 7.2 EMPLOYEE EXPECTATIONS AND NEEDS

- Trust in the boss
- Exciting, interesting, and challenging work
- Sense of making meaningful contributions
- Personal significance; feeling that the job is important
- Freedom and discretion
- Dignity and respect
- Equitable treatment
- Feeling of achievement and accomplishment
- Being part of a well-functioning team
- Being part of success
- Personal growth and development
- Work-life balance
- Earned praise and recognition

---

of appreciation. Many leaders tend to minimize or even forget the power that a well-timed statement of earned praise and recognition can produce.

Building Teams

Increasingly, you are being asked to lead and build commitment within teams, and this has been the subject of consideration for emerging leaders (Hill, 2003; Hill & Lineback, 2011; Zenger & Folkman, 2009). You must align teams in the right direction and keep them motivated and moving as needed.

Trust is fundamental to effective team collaboration and functioning (Carson, Madhok, Varman, & John, 2003). In fact, when discussing small group resiliency, Weick (1993) suggested that, in order to create new, more informed perceptions of reality, team members must trust that, when others share their perceptions, honesty and candor will prevail (that is, there is no undertone of manipulation). Here, we focus on what is known as collective trust, a shared belief among team members that each member will meet commitments, negotiate honestly with other members, and abstain from taking advantage of other members (Cummings & Brimley, 1996).

Of course, this requires careful and rich communication. As such, communication and trust are foundational for team commitment and effectiveness, and these factors seem to be even more critical for virtual teams (Sarker, Ajuja, Sarker, & Kirkeby, 2011).

Be clear with team members about their roles, understanding what they must do; how their performance supports what the team is trying to accomplish; and how their work relates to and affects others on the team (Hill & Lineback, 2011). In addition, team decisions and subsequent commitments must be indisputably clear. Research on teams has noted that when team members had an "accurate" and "shared understanding" of the preferred strategy, they outperformed other teams (Marks & Mathieu, 2000). By accurate, we mean that there is an understanding of the proper strategy, a strategy that works and will yield the best results.

You may have to help your team be accountable and improvement-focused. Here, we suggest a four-step process (Druskat & Pescosolido, 2002; Hackman & Oldham, 1976) that can become part of your standard operating procedure. First, before performing a task, the team members need to be told that one of their goals will be to diagnose and learn how their performance strategies can be improved.

Second, after performance has occurred, a discussion among all team members should take place. The discussion should include asking each person to diagnose the positive outcomes, why they occurred, and how they can be maintained in the future. And it includes asking members to discuss and diagnose negatives outcomes and areas of improvement. Of course, the need for a climate of trust is paramount.

Third, through these discussions, team members develop new performance strategies for the next time it works together. Fourth, and finally, the process is repeated, becoming a common process of team interaction. If this four-step process is followed, a team should become more effective as each team member develops and internalizes a more accurate understanding of successful team strategies.

One of the unfortunate side effects of working in teams can be "social loafing." Social loafing is the tendency for one member to withhold effort. This happens if someone believes they can "free ride" on the efforts of others. If one team member feels like another member is a free rider, the first member may actually reduce his or her efforts in an attempt to restore equity. Or, even more likely, those who feel they are covering for social loafers will, over time, become resentful.

By carefully attending to the group, you can help minimize social loafing. One thing you can do is to help build and ensure trust among team members. When individuals work with others that they trust, they can more easily and accurately predict other group members' effort.

You may also provide challenging performance standards. Here, team members will have to take on specific roles and perform in order for the overall task to be completed. This increases accountability of each member so they are not able to "hide" their lack of effort. Further, by reducing redundancies (having multiple people doing the same task), you increase accountability and reduce the "free-rider effect." You may apply a form of expectancy theory called the collective effort model (Karau & Kipling, 2001) Here, you show each group member how their specific role plays a part in the completion of the overall team goals.

As a team leader, you will need to: (1) establish communication patterns in the team and keep members involved (who talks to whom); (2) decide the topics that are appropriate for discussion (is it appropriate to share feelings and emotions?); and (3) manage conflicts (making sure members are not bullied or pressured toward conformity) (Hill, 2003). As such, you set the agenda and to a large extent, establish the culture of the team. Hill (2003) notes that you must foster both "support and confrontation among team members" (p. 298). This can be a challenge, as you must encourage frank exchanges while being sensitive to the egos that are around the table.

In many ways, you are learning how to coach your team, providing guidance, direction, sensitivity, and the capacity for growth. Recognize that effective teams must spend time together, a consideration often thwarted by today's time-pressured context.

Young Dogs and Old Dogs

Over the past decade, we have experienced a transition in traditional reporting structures, as younger people are being promoted and charged with leading their more senior colleagues. In part, this shift is born of demographic necessity. Increasingly, however, it appears that organizations are "valuing competence over tenure and age" (Deal, Peterson, & Gailor-Loflin, 2001, p. 6). Like most transitions, fresh opportunities coincide with perplexing challenges.

One of the most frequently asked questions that we encounter speaks to this theme. "How do I motivate people who are older and have more experience with the organization?" In short, how does the talented younger dog effectively motivate the more seasoned older dog? To a large extent, the research and models of this chapter have addressed this issue, at least in part. Here, we want to offer four specific ideas that should be helpful.

First, as you will recall from our discussion of generational issues in Chapter 4, Baby Boomers tend to value and place high personal priorities on their work. As such, they generally have high work-role salience, suggesting that work is key to their sense of identity (Ruch, 2012; Twenge, 2006). Accordingly, these workers must feel that their work and their overall contributions are needed and appreciated. They need affirmation, as it reinforces their focus on work.

Second, keep your senior people in the loop by letting them be collaborators on critical decisions. There are a number of important motivational and performance advantages to this approach. Asking senior employees for their input and participation signals that you understand, value, and appreciate their experiences and perspectives. This is also a statement of trust and respect. In addition, it is likely that they will offer views that will enhance the quality of the ultimate decision. Additionally, seeking participation helps assure their commitment to your success, as most people feel more affinity toward actions where they have been involved.

There is a caution here. You are seeking input. You are thoughtfully reflecting on and considering this input. Consensus may become apparent. But it may not. In those cases, you must be the final decision-maker. If you move in a direction that differs from the advice you received, make sure that your people know: (1) that their input was important; (2) that you actively considered the input when making your decision; and (3) the rationale you used to reach your final decision—yes, the value of procedural justice once again. Although there may be information that cannot be shared, don't minimize the impact and importance of what can be shared.

Third, continue to provide training, development, and growth opportunities to your more senior employees. This will not only provide challenge to your people but will sharpen the skills that are needed in our rapidly changing jobs. Be careful of labels and stereotyping. For example, while more senior employees may be less comfortable or less adept at new technologies, opportunities to learn and adjust should be encouraged, not dismissed. You can teach an old dog new tricks, and, in the process, they may help teach the new dog some of their old tricks.

Fourth, be willing to provide necessary developmental feedback. At times, emerging leaders are reluctant to address issues with senior employees. At the same time, it is probably not surprising that more senior employees have reported experiencing frustration when younger leaders provide feedback, especially corrective feedback (Woodward, 1999). Keep in mind that key performance and behavioral gaps must be addressed. Don't shy from this responsibility. The key is to be clear, direct, and respectful.

Concluding Thoughts

To a large extent, everything we have discussed in this book is a motivational topic. In this chapter, we have offered specific models as aids for you to consider when building and sustaining the drive and effort of your people.

In reality, we can only talk about themes and possibilities. Motivation is nuanced, as are our people. Our challenge, as leaders, is to be on the cutting edge of possibilities, always alert to and thinking about ways to enhance our motivational climate. We have to be ready for new turns and twists, and we have to be bold enough to initiate some of our own.

A young leader recently shared one of his motivational efforts. Somewhat apologetically, he commented that all he was doing differently was going to the break room and having coffee with his people at the start of the day. He had no agenda—a small and inconsequential act. But he heard his people's stories. He learned of some of their struggles—their kids, aging parents, a nagging ailment. His sensitivities were heightened. He learned that leaving a few minutes early to pick up her kids at a day care was a huge deal to one person. And simply asking about her Alzheimer-stricken mother meant the world to another. He learned that pitching in to help ease the workload of another, over two months ago, had not been forgotten.

And, they knew he was there too. They sensed he cared. They sensed he was real and genuine, a person who could be trusted. Was performance affected? After all, that is the key metric. He wasn't sure—a candid response.

What does all of this mean? It's pretty simple. Once all the incentive systems and grand plans have been enacted, motivation is, at its heart and core, really a relational process.

With this in mind, we end with a story of unexpected outcomes in unexpected places. It occurred at a rest stop along a busy highway.

The restaurant's fast-food line weaved and curved in a perfect Disney-world-style queue. The operation was an intriguing study of efficiency. The line moved with surprising speed. Behind the counter, the employees worked with diligence and cordiality. Folks darted about filling orders, but with a sense of mission and intensity that differed from the obligatory actions that often characterize such establishments.

The manager, a woman in her late thirties, moved through the operation, helping where needed and generally assuring that no bottleneck would cripple the speed or accuracy or quality that was taking place. There was a sense of action but not a sense of confusion. It just seemed like a well-run place.

And then, we noticed him. At the end of the counter was a young man named Bob, an employee probably in his early twenties. By his stilted actions and the delivery of his speech, one could surmise that he was a person with some degree of intellectual disability. Customers would bring their receipts to Bob who would check the items noted on the receipt and then check to be sure that the contents of the bags that had been placed before him corresponded. Only when he was sure that the order was correct would he release the bag to the customer. Bob was good at his job. He worked hard; he was focused; he concentrated; and he never forgot to issue the same comments to each customer, "Thank you. Have a good day." Bob worked with what appeared to be pride and dedication.

And then it happened. The manager, bustling along the counter, moved behind Bob and paused for only a moment. Bob turned slightly, addressed his boss, and shared, "I'm doing a good job." We fixed on the manager, hustling amid the full-court press of customers. She stopped. She walked over to Bob, completely unhurried and undistracted. She looked at Bob and the orders he was sending on their way. And she simply said, "You are doing a real good job, Bob. I'm so glad you work here. Thanks." She was then on her way to the next station. The encounter, the entire encounter, took perhaps 15 seconds.

This is a simple story, but critical motivational lessons abound. For starters, there was respect. Next, the manager offered affirmation. We sometimes fool ourselves into believing that our people really do not need affirmation, or at least, need it infrequently. The long and short—most leaders offer affirmation far too infrequently. The example also shows how the manager built up Bob's sense of importance and significance. She contributed to his growing self-confidence. She showed she understood and cared. In that short exchange, an array of motivational insights, drawn from years of accepted theory, were demonstrated.

And there is something else. It may be the most important lesson. The manager stopped! Although she was incredibly busy, she did not miss the opportunity to reach out to her employee, address his needs, and create "motivational impact." She had a "point of entry," born of Bob's needs, and she took it. Motivational impact will always be greatest when our people are ready; when they ask for it; when they need it. Yes, a simple story indeed.

8

Change

The Call to Opportunity and Possibility

Transition and growth are essential components of a healthy existence. We experience this reality in our personal lives, in our relationships, and in our organizations. At work, change permits us to pursue new opportunities, adapt to the shifting needs of customers and employees, embrace new technologies, expand our array of possibilities, and refine our competitive positions. In all dynamic and competitive situations, those who fail to change will stall and eventually decline.

We live in an era where organizational change is accelerating into a swirl of turbulence—turbulence that is replete with heightened uncertainty, instability, and volatility (Reeves & Deimler, 2011). In many cases, we face changes that are broad and even radical, entailing substantial shifts to new priorities, new strategic directions, and a rash of new initiatives (Gioia, Thomas, Clark, & Chittipeddi, 1994). Of course, these changes are disruptive and, as such, they are laden with the likelihood of resistance.

Against this backdrop, it is disappointing but perhaps not overly surprising that planned organizational change efforts have a rather unimpressive track record. Evidence indicates that the majority of change initiatives fail, and up to 90% fall short of being declared complete successes (Beer & Nohria, 2000; IBM Business Consulting Services, 2004; Karp & Helgo, 2009).

As an emerging leader, you are an agent of change in your organization, and your influence is paramount. Research indicates that the way leaders like you treat their people during change dramatically affects how people deal with change (Brockner, Konovsky, Cooper-Schneider, Folger, Martin, & Bies, 1994; Lind & Tyler, 1988). Although you may have played a limited role (or even no role) in developing a given change initiative, you are charged with its execution. You are the direct link to the people who must implement change (the recipients of change), and the criticality of this responsibility cannot be overstated. No change initiative stands a chance of succeeding unless you and your peer leaders make it happen. As we will see in this chapter, the stumbling block for most change is generally not in the plan but in the execution of the plan.

Recent research on change has focused on the theme of commitment and the leader's role in building followers' commitment to change initiatives (Fedor, Caldwell, & Herold, 2006; Hersovitch & Meyer, 2002). The argument here asserts that "commitment goes beyond just positive attitudes toward change to include the intention to support it as well as a willingness to work on behalf of its successful implementation" (Herold, Fedor, Caldwell, & Liu, 2008, p. 347). Although many systemic factors affect commitment (not the least of which is the reward system), your actions and interactions play a dramatic role.

Emerging leaders also face the subtle and problematic issue of sustainability. It is common for enacted change to lose its impact (often rapidly) and for new approaches and behaviors to be lost and abandoned—a process known as "initiative decay" (Doyle, Claydon, & Buchanan, 2000). You are asked to help guard against this phenomenon and ensure that "new working methods and performance levels persist" for an appropriate period and become part of the norm (Buchanan, Fitzgerald, Ketley, Gollop, Jones, Lamont, Neath, & Whitby, 2005, p. 190; NHS Modernisation Agency, 2002).

Change brings added complexity to your role. On one hand, you are a facilitator, guiding your people to enact desired changes. Concurrently, you are charged with ensuring continued delivery of day-to-day results that are essential to performance outcomes. As one leader succinctly commented, "I have to help my people move toward tomorrow, while being sure that we win today."

In this chapter, we will explore some key perspectives and actions that will help you lead and assure change that brings the best chances for commitment and sustainability. Like all themes in this book, we draw from solid research and models. And, we will offer positions and actions that will be both relevant and helpful to you in your leader role.

The Two Sides of Change

Two processes impact our confrontations with change (Heath & Heath, 2010). The first is "rational"—that reflective and analytical side of our thinking that underscores in careful, logical detail the competitive business case for change and the action steps needed for implementing the change initiative. This rational view or approach to change has dominated the change literature (Burke, Lake, & Paine, 2009). Intellectually and rationally, most people understand that yesterday's approaches and strategies will no longer suffice, and that change is essential to success.

In many cases, this process is activated by crisis (Kanter, 1983). We see an erosion of our customer base; competitors grab increasing levels of market share; our people bring more loyalty to the table than cutting-edge skills; and our products seem stodgy and unappealing. The sacred bottom line, the ultimate measure of rationality, is affected, and everyone takes notice.

The second process is different. It is "emotional"—that instinctive and deeply personal side that is always struggling to figure out, "How does all this affect me?" As such, what we accept, intellectually and rationally, we may resist as it confuses us, disrupts us, threatens us, and generates an array of fears. Rationally, we may grasp the importance and the need. Emotionally, at a more visceral level, the status quo looks pretty good.

Of course, both processes—rational and emotional—are essential to successful change. Both must coincide and be carefully addressed. If either is missing, change can be "short-circuited," and meaningful change can be "limited and sometimes self-defeating" (Van de Ven & Sun, 2011, p. 59).

While understanding this duality, research and practical experience underscore that the emotional side of change often overwhelms and derails the rational side, resulting in rigid resistance and failed initiatives (Heath & Heath, 2010; Kotter & Cohen, 2002; Labianca, Gray, & Brass, 2000). As such, we are challenged to underscore the rational business case for change, while displaying active sensitivity to the personal and emotional nuances that are at play. Let's take a deeper look at the emotional side and the resistance that accompanies even the most rationally accepted change.

The Logic of Resistance

It is natural that individuals resist change. In fact, resistance is a normal, psychologically healthy response to the ambiguity, confusion, disruption, and fear that people experience when confronted with change. To some extent or at some time, nearly everyone feels the pangs of resistance. Resistance is not limited by position, talent, experience, or intelligence. Rather, resistance results from the human tendency to want to hold onto what is known, familiar, and comfortable—what we commonly refer to as the status quo.

As an emerging leader, it is important for you to recognize why resistance occurs, and it is critical to understand how you can help people move beyond resistance. There is a duality here, another paradoxical theme. You must provide understanding and sensitivity toward those who demonstrate resistance. However, you cannot allow resistance to immobilize your capacity to change. Let's dig beneath the surface and take a careful look at the nature of change and resistance.

Endings

A few years ago, we decided to move from the city to a home in the country. Sitting on four acres, surrounded by woods, and with neighbors out of sight, the new home was an introvert's dream. My wife shared that she absolutely loved the new house and couldn't wait to settle in.

On our last weekend at the old house, we sat on the couch, watching a movie. As I glanced over, she was crying. Of course, I did what most guys would do. I apologized. (I wasn't sure what I'd done, but was sure it was probably my fault.) She cried and asked if I was upset. (Although I really wasn't, I feared that soon I would be.) When I asked what was wrong, she said it was the move—a response that appeared as illogical and off-base as one could imagine. Then she pointed across the room to the oak molding that framed the doorway to the next room.

And, I saw it. Along the vertical edge of the oak frame were a series of marks, all in pencil, at successively higher levels. If you guessed that this was our measure of our children's height as they grew, you'd be right. "That's my boys." She sobbed. "That's my boys growing up. And after tomorrow, I'll never, ever see that again." She had to leave it behind, and she grieved.

It's a funny, offbeat, and personal story, but it's one that's typically shared with our leader audiences who are facing change. When you ask people to change, there is something that they leave behind; something that will never, ever be the same again; and it hurts; and they grieve; and they fight; and they resist.

What is left behind varies. It may be status or position. It may be colleagues who had become close friends. It may be a job that they loved and where they excelled. It could even be where their office is located. But, make no mistake, regardless of all the positive outcomes that change may hold, something is left behind, and it hurts.

Disruption and Stress

Recipients of change are affected, at a personal and emotional level, by the magnitude of change—the extent to which change creates disruption from the status quo (Fedor, Caldwell, & Herold, 2006). Some changes are relatively benign. They occur gradually, produce minimal disruption, and in reality, are barely perceived. Generally, under these conditions, we adapt without much concern or consternation (Greve, 1998; Hulin & Judge, 2003).

However, disruptive change creates ambiguity and uncertainty, and, as such, results in stress (Holmes & Rahe, 1967). The discomforting impact of this stress moves in a number of directions, and it raises serious, personal questions. Can we handle the stress of change? Will we be successful in our new roles and new job? Will we lose status, power, and key relationships as a result of change? And looming beneath the surface, what happens to who we are and what we've accomplished—in essence, our personal identities? Clarity has been shattered; ambiguity takes center stage. Our sense of order and our natural need for control are in flux. But there is even more going on.

Here we turn to a research model that is particularly relevant for our understanding of stress and its relationship to change and resistance to change—the transactional theory of stress (Lazurus & Folkman, 1987). In general, this theory indicates that we experience stress when we believe that we are unable to cope with a new situation—in essence when we believe that we are unable to cope with change.

According to the transactional model, when we encounter a demand for change, we determine (often subconsciously) if the demand is: (1) benign; (2) a challenge; or (3) a threat. As noted above, if the change is perceived as benign, minimal stress is experienced, and we readily adjust.

Interestingly, if we perceive the change to be a challenge, we typically mobilize our resources to rise to the challenge. What results is known as "eustress," the positive stress that motivates individuals to higher levels of activity and outcome. We have all experienced this. It's the stress that brings extra energy and focus as we rise to deliver a report to the management team. It's the motivating drive that comes from the stress to reach a key project deadline. We have long known and accepted that some level of increased stress can actually enhance our performance (Leung, Huang, Su, & Lu, 2011; Yerkes & Dodson, 1908).

However, if the change is perceived to be a threat, a different processing set arises. Follow the logic that unfolds. Initially, we determine if we are able to cope. If we feel that we have the capacity to cope, our challenge response, as noted above, is activated. However, if we believe that we are unable to cope, "distress," that dysfunctional or so-called "bad" stress, is experienced (Barling, Kelloway, & Frone, 2005; Selye, 1978). Here, stress can become overwhelming and dysfunctional outcomes, including performance declines, may be experienced (Jex, 1998).

It is interesting and important to understand that these judgments are always framed in the eye of the beholder. From your perspective, asking three of your people to change offices to a different floor is no big deal—benign in every sense. However, to those affected, a different picture may be in play. They may perceive a major disruption—a threat—and a threat over which they lack control. Is it surprising that resistance follows?

The lack of control theme is important to acknowledge. Your current change initiative, in all likelihood, comes on the heels of other recent changes. Accordingly, people may be uneasily pondering the "what's next?" question. In addition, if recent changes have brought reductions in staff, added anxiety and stress may be felt through a phenomenon known as "layoff survivor syndrome" (Noer, 2009). Although people may be assured that their jobs are safe, they remain in fear, positing that they have little control of their destinies. After all, in many cases, those who were dismissed had been solid colleagues prior to the latest restructuring.

For a leader, the presence of resistance can be disarming and frustrating. This can especially be the case when those who resist take a passive-aggressive stance. Here, people are not actively rebellious. Their responses are more subtle. They may be sullen, resentful, and stubbornly cautious about even the most minor adjustments. Negativity and pessimism may take center stage. At times, a sulking attitude of victimization may be projected. Resistance is being played out at an emotional level.

The leader's temptation may be to respond to this display of emotional manifestations with our own burst of emotion—often projecting our frustration, impatience, and disappointment. While all these emotions may be understandable, they do little to ameliorate resistance or advance a change initiative. Here, as in most cases, the leader is better being an actor rather than a reactor.

Armed with this understanding, we are ready to move forward and consider how to be a positive actor for change. In the following sections we will detail five specific areas of action that should help you lead change. In sequence, these are: (1) expressing the need for change; (2) creating new meanings and avenues of adaptation; (3) building communication and connection; (4) involving people in the process; and (5) reinforcing the momentum.

Expressing the Need for Change

Creating and articulating the need for change is the underpinning of our most successful change models and arguably, the most critical step in the process of change (Hiatt, 2006; Kotter, 1996). It is also the step that is most often minimized or glossed over (Kotter, 1996; Kotter, 2008). To do so is almost always an error. We generally believe that even the best change initiatives are likely to fail if leaders are unable to instill a clear and dramatic sense of need in those who will be affected, those who are the recipients of change (Hiatt, 2006; Kotter & Schlesinger, 1979).

Originally conceived through the pioneering work of Kurt Lewin (1947) as a process "unfreezing," the goal was to call older, traditional, and accepted ways of doing things, the so-called "status quo," into question. Today, we drive more deeply. For example, Kotter (2008) argues that we must illustrate to our people, with unmistakable clarity, that there is a driving need for a change to happen—what he refers to as a "sense of urgency" or its popular corollary, the "burning platform." Here recipients must be convinced that change must occur. Put another way, we want our people to understand and accept, at a deep attitudinal and belief level, that maintaining the status quo is not only untenable and unacceptable but ultimately disastrous.

Noted scholar Edgar Schein (2010), in his book, *Organizational Culture and Leadership*, addressed this theme. Schein argued that leaders must be "creating a motivation to change" by instilling a sense of disruption and disequilibrium through what he called "disconfirmation" (p. 301). Here, disconfirmation is "any information that shows to the organization that some of its goals are not being met or that some of its processes are not accomplishing what they are supposed to" (Schein, 2010, p. 301). Schein notes that the presence of disconfirmation information often leads to "survival anxiety" among change recipients, a sense of urgency that change must happen or "something bad will happen" (Schein, 2010, p. 301).

Creating and articulating a clear and compelling need for change serves at least two critical purposes. First, as noted above, it provides the fundamental motivating prompt to embark on change. Second, and more subtle, it helps fight against initiative decay, that tendency to backslide and lose the momentum of change.

We are trying to create influence by appealing to the rational side of change through the use of rational persuasion (Fable & Yukl, 1992). Here we rely on facts and logic to explain the need for change and the potential consequences of not changing.

Consider the following example. We worked with a unit of a large organization, attempting to reignite what had been a failed change initiative. Here is how it failed and how it was resurrected.

The unit's manager was an entrepreneurially-oriented thinker—a bit brash, but clearly brilliant. Always taking a fresh and innovative stance, he had identified a major new market opportunity—a new initiative that had to be exploited. In fact, as he studied and researched the competitive field, he became more and more assured that this initiative would position his unit for rapid growth and unprecedented competitive success. In retrospect, he was probably right.

His ideas were brilliantly conceived and a few, select, top leaders were consulted. Mostly, however, he held his ideas close. He had the facts, figures, models, and conviction to drive the initiative into action. With limited explanation, but with undeterred personal passion, he thrust the change on his unit. Six months later, the plan was scrapped, and the leader's luster was badly tarnished. He was moved to a different location.

Enter a new leader. Interestingly, he too believed in the initiative. But he came at it differently. He brought his people together. He shared facts; he discussed the competitive landscape; and he asked for input. He asked "what if" questions, such as, "What will happen if we don't move on this initiative and our major competitor does?" He helped his people see what was at stake, and he helped them see that the status quo was laden with threats—real threats. Perhaps most significant, he helped the unit's people understand and accept the rippling, negative impact of doing nothing.

In all fairness, the new initiative was little different from the original. And, yes, the second manager had the luxury of time and the clarity it brings. However, the key was that the second manager met with people, and he took the time to build the need—the sense of urgency. As one member of the unit shared, "I was not sure what we would do exactly, but I knew doing nothing was a formula for disaster."

Keep in mind that your people are more likely to perceive urgency when three conditions are revealed: (1) a current crisis; (2) an impending crisis; or (3) a timely opportunity (Kotter, 1995). Through careful and consistent communication, leaders must champion the need for change. Kotter offers remarkable clarity here, noting that leader communication must be so convincing and thorough that at least 75% of the people accept that the status quo must change. Only then will the change initiative have high potential for success.

As an emerging leader, you may, or you may not be involved in developing the original case for the sense of urgency. However, you will be charged with articulating and explaining the case in clear, direct, relevant, and meaningful terms to your people. And you will have to remind your people from time to time of this compelling case. You are helping your people understand that there is a reason for change and a reason why we cannot return to the status quo. With an acute eye on your people and their needs, you are reminding them and underscoring for them the "case for change."

What your people want and need are not continual repeats of the complex and fact-laden case. Instead, they need, from you, a briefer "rallying case." For example, "We've all seen the numbers, and we know how customer tastes are changing. This is our best path for growth and new jobs." Or, "Our industry is changing and we must adapt. We must bring in new technologies and offer new products." Note that we are not attempting to suggest that the changes being experienced will be void of disruption and stress. Instead, we are reaffirming why these changes make sense and must be undertaken.

Meaning and Adaptation

The recipients of change are immersed in an ongoing and rather constant process of trying to make sense of their new work situation (Weick, 1995). An increasingly accepted view of organizational change argues that the most challenging aspect of change deals with the way recipients interpret what is going on (Schein, 1996). As change presents new directions, new strategies, and new policies and values, people may experience "meaning voids," as they are trying to make sense of what is going on (Ravasi & Schultz, 2006). In short, their established frameworks for understanding the organization have been broken, and they are struggling to create new beliefs and meanings (Mantere, Schildt, & Sillince, 2012). We believe that change recipients experience resistance when they encounter major shifts in meaning (Labianca, Gray, & Brass, 2000).

As a consequence, leaders are encouraged to engage in "sensegiving," carefully communicating new beliefs and new meanings to help recipients in their interpretation of change (Gioia, Thomas, Clark, & Chittipeddi, 1994; Maitlis & Lawrence, 2007; Smith, Plowman, & Duchon, 2010; Vuori & Virtaharju,

2012). Although we may provide sensegiving in a number of ways, we will emphasize three specific actions.

First, make sure that your people understand, as clearly and vividly as possible, the vision and the purpose of the change (Gioia & Chittipeddi, 1991). As noted earlier, your people may ask over and over again for the explanation and reasoning behind the change. In most cases, they are also asking for clarification of the vision. As such, you should be able to articulate the vision clearly and concisely. Once again, a 15-minute oration will not work. You want, and your people need, "the elevator speech." It must be crisp, relevant, expressed in practical terms, and no more than a couple minutes long. If it takes five minutes to deliver, tighten it up! In these few minutes you should do three things: (1) remind them of the sense of urgency; (2) remind them, concisely, of the basic vision; and (3) remind them of the benefits.

We know that change initiatives often fail because the basic vision is not clearly articulated and communicated (Kotter, 1995). So, you can anticipate these inquiries. You may need to use a variety of communication mediums. Stopping by to talk, one-on-one may be important; sending out clarifying memos may help; providing opportunities for open discussions may make sense. Remember, a one-shot approach is probably doomed.

Many organizations today are carefully focusing on "messaging the change," that is, considering in detail how the message should be presented to unique audiences. While all leaders need to speak and share the same thematic message, your specific "message points" will be geared toward your audience and their needs.

Second, part of dealing with new meanings is to define for people "what will not change." We worked with one young leader, whose people understood the logic of change but responded with hesitancy and apprehension. He asserted to his team that the company's key values of respect, integrity, trust, and belief in its people were unwavering constants. While one may dismiss such actions as "just words," these words are part of building cultural symbols that reinforce and legitimize the change.

There is a very practical third point that must be addressed. It seems that "survival anxiety" (bad things will happen if we do not change) is often accompanied by "learning anxiety." Learning anxiety is "the feeling that I cannot learn the new behaviors or adopt new attitudes without losing a feeling of self-esteem or group membership" (Schein, 2010, p. 302). Insightfully, Schein (2010) contended that, in order for change to occur, learning anxiety must not exceed survival anxiety.

You play a role in reducing the learning anxiety of your people. Let's look at this more closely. We generally believe that people experience learning anxiety for five reasons.

First, learning anxiety arises if people fear a loss of their legitimate power—power that has been gained during their organizational tenure. Second, learning anxiety occurs if people fear they will lose competency, even temporarily—that is, with change they will not feel or be competent while learning new ways of completing job tasks. Third, learning anxiety comes because people fear that they will not perform adequately. Here, they may even surmise that they will be punished by management for not adapting quickly enough. Fourth, individuals may experience learning anxiety because they fear a loss of identity as a member of the organization. Fifth and finally, individuals may experience learning anxiety because they fear they will no longer be a member of a certain group.

Let's look at an example. We were recently asked to help facilitate a change effort for a division of a mid-sized company. In planning meetings with the divisional vice president, certain individuals were tagged as "resisters" and "foot-draggers." For the most part, these were senior managers who stood to lose some status and comfort. However, two young men, both barely 30 years old, were highlighted as "go-to guys." In fact, the VP referred to them as his "young comers."

During lunch on our first day, one of the young comers took us aside, assumed a serious tone, lowered his voice, and shared, "I'm one of those resisters you've been talking about." Fighting the temptation to inform him that he was wrong, we asked if he knew why. He did, indeed.

It seems that, for the past two years, he had been a corporate troubleshooter. If the company had a problem in a facility in another state, he packed his bags and handled it. He was on the road with regularity, sometimes for a month or more at a time. He was good, and he was successful. "I've performed. My stock could not be higher." Then, came his frank assessment, "With all this change, I'm moving to a new area with a new boss. I've got to prove myself all over. I'm just not sure that I have the desire or energy to make all those sacrifices again." It's not hard to understand and appreciate what he was experiencing.

Fortunately, we do have some useful guidance (Schein, 2010). Learning anxiety can be minimized through on-going training and development efforts, thereby helping our people understand that we have every intention of helping them develop the new skills that are needed to adequately perform their realigned duties.

Support groups can have an important impact. These groups can facilitate a form of psychological safety by allowing change recipients a platform to air their frustrations during the learning process. Hopefully, this helps people get a better feel about what's going on, and it offers them a chance to express some of their concerns. By sharing their concerns and frustrations with others in a similar situation, possible solutions may arise (in the group), and methods or approaches for overcoming learning obstacles may be developed. This venting should not be regressive, given that a strong sense of urgency has been established.

Finally, we must ensure that reward systems are properly aligned with the new change requirements. Remember that people do what they are rewarded for doing. If we expect new behaviors, but reward old behaviors, we will get old behaviors (Kerr, 1975).

Building Communication and Connection

Not surprisingly, communication is a key. It is generally accepted that on-going communication during the change process is fundamental for successful change (Allen, Jimmieson, Bordia, & Irmer, 2007; Fiss & Zaja, 2006; Klein, 1996; Salem, 2008). Most leaders undercommunicate during change. Remember, when people do not know or understand what is occurring, they create explanations to fill in the gaps. They make it up. Rumors mount, and the emerging story may differ greatly from reality. During change, the communication faucet needs to be wide open. Unfortunately, in many organizations, the faucet produces little more than an occasional drip.

There is a reason for this. Leaders, particularly those at higher levels, are often so immersed in the dynamics of change that taking time to communicate becomes a back burner issue. Further, top leaders have planned and discussed the change for months. For them, the themes have become well-discussed, even common. As such, leaders may fail to understand that everything is new and potentially threatening to the recipients of change. What may seem obvious at an executive level is neither clear nor obvious to recipients deep in the organization. Recipients experience threats. And they are unsure if they have the capacity to cope.

While top leadership will articulate the vision and unfold the evolving structure of change, you are the key source of on-going communication. You have the most contact with the people being asked to change. They know you. They understand you. They trust you. And, most critical, they have access to you.

Your careful, on-going communication will serve at least three functions: (1) clarifying information; (2) soliciting input; and (3) providing relevant feedback to address issues and reduce the miscommunication of rumors.

Giving your people a voice—the opportunity to share their concerns, their dissatisfactions, and even their fears—can be powerful and constructive (Hirschman, 1970). In fact, we encourage leaders to listen to the resistance. If you think most leaders balk at the prospect of openly listening to resistance, you are, of course, right.

But, let's think about what is going on. Should we assume that there is no resistance? Should we assume that if we do not hear about it, it does not exist? No, that would be naïve and foolish.

However, we can, through either demands or inaction, press our people into "suppressing" their resistance. It happens all the time, as people sense that "the boss just doesn't want to hear about problems." Of course, when people suppress their resistance, it does not go away. It simmers, just beneath the surface, breeding frustration, resentment, and deeper resistance.

It seems more prudent to give people opportunities to "express" their resistance rather than forcing them to "suppress" it. More information is almost always better than less. In addition, we gain other advantages.

By listening, we demonstrate to our people that we care about them and empathize with what they are experiencing. This draws on a behavioral theme known as interactional justice (Bies & Moag, 1986; Tyler & Bies, 1990). As Leung, Su, and Morris (2001) note, "Employees often give primary focus to interpersonal issues such as whether the authority considered their particular needs and concerns, treated them with respect and dignity, and attempted to avoid bias" (p. 1156). In fact, we believe that interactional justice elicits higher levels of acceptance (Greenberg, 1994; Leung, Su, & Morris, 2001; Lind, Kulik, Ambrose, & de Vera Park, 1993).

In part, people gain a cathartic effect by sharing, getting their concerns off their chest and into the open. Will there be some complaining, carping, and whining? Yes. We're reminded of the wonderful imagery provided by Jeanie Duck (1998), noting that it's OK to let people visit "pity city" (p. 68), you just can't let them move in. This is where the sense of urgency comes back in play. People can complain, but we cannot go back. The status quo is unacceptable and must change. We already agreed to that.

There is an added subtlety here. By "resisting" change, by questioning and having probing conversations, change recipients are actually acknowledging that the change is occurring (Ford & Ford, 2009). Through these conversations, change recipients are mentally engaged in the change and thoughtfully thinking about the benefits and potential risks of the change rather than just, blindly and without commitment, accepting the change. Questioning and challenging the change actually strengthens the potential of change success because, after questioning and committing to change, individuals are less likely to engage in backsliding (resorting to the old ways of doing things) than individuals who blindly accept the change—helping mitigate the chances of initiative decay.

As people express their views, you will find that some (perhaps quite a few) of their concerns are simply incorrect. They are based on rumors and worse-case scenarios that are highly unlikely. You should also use this opportunity to provide information that may be missing from the followers' sense-making process. And, you have an opportunity to help clarify reality, deflect rumors, and ease the emotional uproar.

Further, as you listen, you will find that there are probably some legitimate concerns that can be handled with relative ease and little cost—the so-called "low-hanging fruit." You may be able to address some of these, and in other cases you may have to take them to upper management.

Finally, if you listen, openly and thoughtfully, you will find that your people are often quite insightful in pointing out obstacles and problems that management had not previously considered. In some cases, they will raise concerns that are credible stumbling blocks that must be addressed. In short, your people see problems where no one else did simply because they are closer to the action. Obviously, this input becomes critical new information that you will need to consider and share with your boss.

There is an obvious caveat, but it must be expressed. Remember that all of your recipient's concerns are, indeed, legitimate. That is, if they are sharing their concerns, they are sharing their perceptions of reality. This is their reality, and they are going to react and behave in a manner that reflects this reality. We have seen leaders dismiss follower concerns as "silly" or "wrong." Keep in mind that, during change, people may be particularly fragile, fearful, and they may even be pushing the bounds of logic. Yet, they deserve to be treated with respect.

Remember that resistance and open expressions of that resistance are not bad (Ford & Ford, 2009; Ford, Ford, & D'Amelio, 2008). In fact, discourse is part of the process of change. Leaders who dismiss this point and try to either ignore or minimize discourse run the risk of setting an undertone in the organization that will establish routines that run counter to the change initiative. Ford, Ford, and D'Amelio (2008) noted that the resistance to change literature takes an unreasonable "change agent-centric" view. They noted that the basic motives and underlying "question" that individuals asked about change was different depending on whether one was a change agent or a change recipient. Change agents asked the question, "How will this get accomplished?" while change recipients asked the question, "What will happen to me?" (Gioia, Thomas, Clark, & Chittipeddi, 1994).

There are many strategies that you may use to foster connection during change. However, our more successful emerging leaders commit to increase the number and frequency of contacts with their people during change. Paradoxically, although your people need more time with us, there is less time available. You are consumed by dealing with change, and time to connect with your people is reduced. You are moving as quickly as you can, handling all sorts of new and often unexpected demands. There is considerable firefighting that takes place.

At the same time, your people—the recipients of change—are unsure, worried, confused, and stressed. Remember, people generally need more and deeper connection and more touch points as they deal with change. You must build these "avenues of connection."

The methods you use can vary and be original; whatever seems relevant for your people and your situation. For example, one leader had twice weekly breakfast meetings with her staff. The meetings generally lasted only about 20–30 minutes, and there was no set agenda. Instead the leader encouraged her people to just talk, ask questions, and dialogue. Regularly, the leader would clarify vision and direction, but mostly she listened.

The key here is to stay on top of the change. As in the example above, the connections need be neither lengthy nor formal. In addition, it is also important to stay in touch with your peer leaders. Have regular check-ins, support one another, and work to build an atmosphere of supportive and consultative exchange.

Involving People

Providing mechanisms of participation and involvement of change recipients can be important. Certainly, this strategy is most effective when the change agent does not have all the relevant and needed information to design a successful change initiative (Kotter, 1996). Additionally, this strategy is also useful when the recipients have enough power that they can resist the change and disrupt the change process.

There are two main advantages of this strategy. First, with the additional relevant information, a better change initiative is designed, thus, hopefully, increasing the likelihood that the change will provide the intended positive results. Second, as we have noted elsewhere in this book, when individuals participate, they become more accepting of the initiative. It is interesting that when individuals are asked to give input into a change initiative, and they feel that their input is valued, they are more likely to accept the change. This acceptance tends to occur even if their opinions are not actually used. The main disadvantage to this strategy is that it is time consuming.

Reinforcing the Momentum

Once change begins to show positive outcomes, it must be reinforced. You are a key player here, as the reinforcement is best when it is timely, personal, and sincere. You want to follow the psychological principle of the law of successive approximations, which holds that, when new behaviors are being learned, it's beneficial to reinforce as we progressively get closer to (or approximate) the desired behavior. Kotter (1996) calls these short-term wins, and he emphasizes that we need to create and celebrate these short-term wins.

Early reinforcements need not be overly complicated or costly. Sincere appreciation may be enough. We've seen leaders bring their teams together; pinpoint the behaviors and people for recognition; and then have a celebratory cake for everyone to share. The important theme is to recognize individuals and teams who are putting the desired changes in place and are experiencing some positive results. By focusing on desired behaviors and reinforcing them, we are sending clear signals to all our people of the acceptance and efficacy of the change. Further, by reinforcing desired behaviors, we are helping to combat the risk of initiative decay.

As change evolves, you will have opportunities to reinforce change through broader, systemic measures, most notably through the compensation and advancement systems. Those who are on-board and producing desired results must be provided with tangible rewards in order for momentum to continue and equity to be maintained.

I'm Just Not Sure

Sooner or later, the question always arises. Over and over again, we're asked by emerging leaders how they can support a change they either do not understand or find to be disagreeable, inappropriate, or strategically flawed. We may even hear the bravado of higher-level, more senior managers who openly speak out and voice their opposition to anyone who will listen, an approach laden with danger for emerging leaders.

It's a double-edged sword. If you support a change you oppose, won't your people see through the charade? What happens to your character; what happens to trust; and what happens to your standing as a leader? However, as an emerging leader, you are an agent of change, and you must be a team player. Wouldn't it be a statement of foolishness and insubordination to oppose upper management? Wouldn't it be political suicide?

There are no easy answers here. As with most tough issues, a lot depends on the people and the stakes. We are always careful to understand the situational dynamics before offering prescriptive advice. But, we will not duck this issue.

First, if the change does not make sense to you, seek understanding. Ask for clarification. In all likelihood, you will have the chance, perhaps only with your immediate boss, to voice your concerns. This is the avenue to pursue. If you are asked for input, offer it in objective, outcome-focused, and respectful terms. It is perfectly reasonable to share concerns about your people and how they will be affected. In other words, when you are asked for input (the point of entry again), this is the time to be frank and candid.

Second, if it appears that things are up in the air and lack definition and direction, quite frankly that might be the case. Remember, those at the top have engaged in considerable study and analysis, but they may be unable to delineate all the details.

Third, it is possible that you may have some role in shaping and rolling out the change as it evolves. Accordingly, it is likely that you will gain more clarity as the process and time proceeds. Don't expect all the pieces to fall in place overnight.

Fourth, explain to your people what you know and what you do understand. Take the next best step, and let your people know that this is how we will proceed. Things are in flux and may change, but convey the direction that will be pursued—for now. Do not share more than you know or promise what you cannot deliver. There is a temptation to do both. Succumbing to this temptation, you only add fuel to the rumor mill and expose yourself as shallow and non-credible.

Fifth, never denigrate upper management and their decisions, even if you disagree. By the same token, you need not be a disingenuous cheerleader. The best course is to be clear with your people regarding expectations. Let them know that, "This is the course that's been set, and this is what we will do." Be clear. If you project a tone of vacillation, you may expect your people to waver and expectations to fall short. You look bad. They look bad. And the consequences for you and your people are likely to be undesirable.

An Attitude Toward Change

There is an old backpacker's story that some of us have experienced. Deep in the woods, after a few hours of hiking, one hiker turns to his friend and meekly says, "I think we're lost." The friend shakes his head in disagreement, proclaiming that they cannot possibly be lost. "It's true that I don't know where we are, but I know how to get back," he proudly proclaims. Pulling from his pocket his trusty compass, he sets a course that will take them to their camp. "We go northeast; head toward that tall bank of trees on the hill in the distance."

Soon they come to a cliff and the complaints start. "You never said anything about a cliff," the first hiker grimly comments. "Well, I didn't know it was here. All I know is this is the right direction." Soon, they encounter a stream and further down the trail, a steep and rocky incline. Again, the only explanation the compass-holder can offer is, "I know where we are headed but I do not know the obstacles along the way."

A few years ago, on an early morning run in the dark in a strange city, one of the authors and a colleague paused after about 30 minutes of running. Apologetically, I admitted having no idea of how to get back to the hotel. My colleague just smiled, showing me a small GPS that he wore on his wrist. The GPS showed in remarkable detail every street and every turn of our return trip!

There is a basic point to sharing these stories. When going through change, our people dearly want the GPS. In reality, all we generally have is the compass. As leaders, we do not and we cannot be expected to know every blip and every obstacle that will appear as we move along the path of change. All we have is the compass. However, the impact of the compass should not be minimized. We must help our people know that we do have a sense of direction, vision, and focus, even as we admit being unable to predict every snare along the way.

Concluding Thoughts

Your organization will undoubtedly change. As an emerging leader, you will scan your work environment for change initiatives. You will use these opportunities, champion change, and in the process, showcase your leadership skills. Look for these opportunities.

Embrace change. Underscore the urgency and herald the benefits on the horizon. Support your people. Expect some pushback. Clarify and communicate. Establish clear expectations. Don't sacrifice standards of excellence—not one bit. Celebrate wins—even small wins. Reinforce and reward success as best you can—even if it's only a heart-felt "Nice job." Show gratitude and appreciation for the moves that are made. Remind people that we are always changing—that we must be always changing. Make sure they know who is holding the compass!

9

Crisis

Developing Through the Cauldron of Adversity

Kay Redfield Jamison is Professor of Psychiatry at the Johns Hopkins University School of Medicine and co-author of the standard medical text on manic-depressive illness. Manic-depressive illness or bi-polar disease is the crushing state where people experience periods of euphoric "highs" followed by maddening periods of depleting "lows." Not only is Jamison one of the world's foremost authorities on the subject, she has suffered with the illness throughout her life. Her memoir, *An Unquiet Mind* (1995), is a riveting revelation of her personal quest for health and inner-peace. During her manic states, Jamison's energy, creativity, and intellect were so intensified that she performed at amazing levels. However, during her depressive states, she sank to such depths of madness that she attempted suicide.

Jamison struggled with the confusing prospects of her inner challenge—her personal crisis. In fact, the most striking dilemma she faced was in her answer—the drug lithium. Lithium was her life-line, enabling her to stave off the draining impact of her depressive condition. However, taking lithium also dulled the intensity of her experiences and diminished her consuming drive to work and perform at unbelievably outstanding levels. In short, she could not quite reach her peak while using the drug. Listen to her images:

> Depressed, I have crawled on my hands and knees in order to get across a room and have done it for month after month. But, normal or manic, I have run faster, thought faster, and loved faster than most I know.
>
> (Jamison, 1995, p. 218)

Her decision is complex. With one choice, she will sacrifice unparalleled, remarkable performance. With another choice, she can mitigate the consequences of agonizing through deep dives of depression. Her choice guarantees mixed consequences.

Herein lies the message for our emerging leaders. The decisions that create real anxiety, real tension, and even panic are always in the gray zone, where all choices seem to carry some degree of mixed consequence. These will be your defining decisions.

These nuanced, multi-faceted decisions define the nature of leadership. They are tests of intellect, character, and courage. Many leadership decisions are rather routine, almost programmable. Any member of your staff can follow the rubric and make the call. However, these mixed decisions demand more. And this is where leadership is earned and proved.

Many people, sitting in the chair of leadership—your chair—are not up to the challenge. They wilt; they vacillate; they anguish; and they wait. Credibility is tested and shattered. Successful leaders grasp the challenge; they study the issues; and they weigh the impacts. And they decide, with a full sense of accountability.

Importantly, successful leaders learn to "come alive" and even thrive in this decision context. There is a sense of challenge and accomplishment in knowing that everyone simply is not able to work through such demanding decisions. That realization is not meant to demean others. Rather, it becomes part of your framework of confidence for the unique opportunities and challenges that you will face.

Confrontations with Adversity

Despite our hopes, the path of leadership and life is rife with challenges and roadblocks. Research has suggested that dealing with the experiences of hardships, obstacles, traumatic events, and adversities are important developmental events for leaders (Bennis & Thomas, 2002a; 2002b; McCall & Hollenbeck, 2002; McCall, Lombardo, & Morrison, 1988; McCauley, Ruderman, Ohlett, & Morrow, 1994). Critical lessons are learned through these disrupting events, supporting the popular claim that leadership is forged in the cauldron of adversity. The authors of *The Lessons of Experience* go so far as to suggest that "nearly all developmental events involve a confrontation with adverse circumstances—obstacles that must be overcome" (McCall, Lombardo, & Morrison, 1988, p. 87).

Of course, caution must be raised. Asserting that adversity breeds development assumes that one can and will learn through the sting of crisis. We are reminded that while one person may develop from twenty years of experience, others simply have the experiences over and over again for twenty years.

Leadership scholar Morgan McCall (2010) wryly reminds us, "Experience is said to be 'the best teacher,' yet the number of years of experience does not predict expert performance, executive effectiveness, or, ironically, teaching ratings" (p. 679). Further, recognizing the developmental nature of adversity and crisis is of little comfort to those battling the disarming impact of such events.

In the previous chapter, we discussed change. Although change brings uncertainty and anxiety, it is but one of many personal and business challenges of adversity with which leaders must struggle. Previous work has categorized the most powerful developmental experiences that leaders encounter, experiences that include how we handle obstacles and job transitions (McCauley, Ruderman, Ohlett, & Morrow, 1994). Particularly relevant for emerging leaders are "job transitions," where we are pushed into unfamiliar territory, requiring that we prove to ourselves and others that we can handle new sets of responsibilities. As your responsibilities continue to grow and expand, you will encounter this transition with some frequency.

We have mentioned adversities and obstacles previously in our sections on character and confidence. Obstacles can range from dealing with difficult people (which may include the boss) to confronting adverse business conditions. Some obstacles can be subtle and tough to put your finger on, such as feeling that the workload is growing while management support is withering. Others, such as getting passed over for a promotion, are direct and obvious. And, in today's business climate, some of you will face termination, a major disrupting transition that may be prompted more by external events and business conditions than by individual performance.

In this chapter, we want to accomplish three major objectives. First, we want to help you understand the nature of adversity and why it occurs to all of us. If nothing else, this will help you establish reasonable expectations and help you not feel "singled out" when the inevitable pangs of crisis touch you. Second, we hope that you will be able to step back and see some of the powerful lessons that may arise as you address and deal with adversity. Third, we want to help you develop and demonstrate resilience—the ability to bounce back, stronger, more experienced, and more effective because of what you have experienced.

A Crisis

It's important to provide some definitional structure to our topic of inquiry. Differentiating a "problem" from an "adversity" or even a "crisis" is largely a matter of perception—driven by the intensity of the situation, how closely or personally the situation touches us, and the level of disruption that arises. For example, when unemployment levels within a society escalate, we all experience the rippling impact of some level of discomfort. But for those individuals and families that are displaced, each week of unsuccessful job searching plunges them closer and closer toward crisis.

Like any stressor, two people can face the same events and emerge with dramatically different experiences and effects. What one person views as a slight problem, another sees as a crisis. On many occasions, we have listened to emerging leaders describe their "crisis event." Assessing these situations, we know that senior leaders may find it tempting to dismiss them as "much ado about very little," given the bigger picture playing out. Indeed, five years from now, with the buffer of experience, these events would be little more than fleeting blips on the young leaders' radar screen. In short, today's crisis may be tomorrow's routine. However, we live in the moment, not the future. Therefore, such dismissal would be insensitive, counter-developmental, and inconsistent with the emerging leaders' reality.

When a leader says, "I've got a crisis," we assume that this is precisely how the leader feels. A year from now, this issue may simply be a "bother." Two years from now, the intensity may be so insignificant that minimal dissonance ensues. However, right now, a crisis exists.

Emerging leaders must learn a process for addressing and working through crises. In fact, one of the best measures of a leader's potential comes from how they assess, understand, and deal with the crises they confront. In general, we tend to be less concerned with the emotional intensity leaders face and more concerned with the process of assessment and action they pursue. Additionally, it's not much of a leap to suggest that, as you become comfortable with a process for dealing with the crises and adversities that arise, your confidence and resolve will grow, and, in all likelihood, subsequent events will appear just a bit less crisis-like.

Bennis and Thomas (2002a; 2002b) speak of adversities and crises as being "crucible events"—personal trials which prompt deep introspection. There is much at stake. People are watching, generally assuming that your true character and leadership acumen will be revealed under pressure. Will you respond to a tough interpersonal crisis with hot-headed impulse? Will you vacillate and twist in the winds of indecision? Will you demonstrate composure and firmness? Will others understand, accept, and trust that you've "got your arms" around the issues? Well, let's see.

Categories of Adversity

Leaders, like everyone else in the organization, are whole people. The various domains of our lives cannot be segmented and compartmentalized, regardless of how hard we try. The research is clear. We all fall prey to what is known as the "spillover" effect (Friedman & Greenhaus, 2000). What happens in one area affects other areas. Family affects work. Work affects family. Health affects everything else.

This spillover can be positive and integrative (Bailyn, Drago, & Kochan, 2001; Greenhaus & Powell, 2005). For example, a great day at work buoys our spirit, leading to positive interactions with our loved ones at home. But the spillover can take on a more negative tone. An argument with the boss affects our attitude, creating pessimism and depleting subsequent interactions with our team members, our family, and our friends. Try as we might, we cannot create neat and independent segmentation.

In many cases, leaders strive to mask the presence of spillover, and in some cases such efforts are noble and necessary. For example, we worked on a not-for-profit board with a highly regarded CEO of a local business. He arrived a few minutes late for one of our board meetings, although his report was the key item on the agenda. His presentation was solid, thorough, and analytically strong—consistent with his style. However, knowing him pretty well, we could not help but feel that he was distant and disconnected. He just seemed less engaged than normal.

We chatted briefly as the meeting ended. He had spent his afternoon dealing with an emergency—true crisis management, if you will. His company had experienced an industrial accident earlier in the day, and there was a loss of life. Recognizing he had done all he could for the moment, he opted to attend the board meeting. He felt it was inappropriate and unnecessary to share this information with the board. So, he pressed on. Is it any wonder that he was just a bit distracted?

Within this context, we need to look more carefully at the nature of adversity. Previous studies help us understand the variety of adversities that emerging leaders are likely to encounter (McCall, Lombardo, & Morrison,

1988; McCall & Hollenbeck, 2002; Moxley, 1998). We summarize these adversities into two rather broad categories: (1) business adversities; and (2) personal adversities. Let's look at each of these categories.

Business Adversities

Business adversities, generally, arise from one of four sources: (1) the stress of leadership; (2) mistakes; (3) the business environment; and (4) interpersonal issues. Let's briefly examine each of these.

The leader role brings you excitement, challenge, and opportunities for personal and career growth. Yet, the leader role also brings high levels of stress. Linda Hill (2003), in her study of new managers, noted that it was common to experience anxiety, stress, and emotions that far exceeded what was originally anticipated when stepping into the job. Her choice of descriptors included such powerful images as "emotional upheaval," "debilitating" stress, and an array of "uncomfortable" psychological and physical symptoms (Hill, 2003, p. 175). Unfortunately, but perhaps not surprisingly, she also found that new leaders were often reluctant to share these concerns, even with those closest to them.

As we have discussed throughout this book, the stress of leadership is intensified by the novelty of your role, the evolving nature of your self-confidence, and the changes in skills and perspective that you are facing. There is an added dimension to this stress. You are now responsible for other people, and your decisions affect others in dramatic ways. You affect others' feelings about their work, themselves, and their overall well-being. This is a daunting challenge, laden with elements of stress.

Second are the ordinary mistakes and missteps that all leaders make from time to time. In a way, these are self-created issues. But they are part of the normal pattern of a leader's life. It's the simple reality that leader decision-making is often blurred and thorough analysis still leaves room for uncertainty and less than 100% assurance of the proper action. In short, no one is smart enough or insightful enough to make the right call all the time. There is merit to the sentiment that leaders who do not err are playing it so safely that they have already abdicated their leadership.

The third source of business adversity comes from the dynamic and imprecise nature of the business environment. Here we turn to sage advice, "Sometimes good decisions have bad results." We make the best decisions possible, given the information available. But there are often unforeseen twists and turns. The economy takes a downturn; customers are fickle; suppliers unexpectedly miss deadlines; and corporate directives seem to come "out of left field." We are pushed off-stride by the unexpected. When they arise, these unscripted emergencies bring periods of confusion and anxiety—and at times, even panic.

The fourth source of business adversity comes from interpersonal issues. In all likelihood, the strongest and most anxiety-laden sources of stress you encounter come from the myriad of interpersonal issues that you deal with on a day-to-day basis (Manzoni & Barsoux, 2009).

The majority of our coaching encounters, for example, center on tricky people issues that may, without deft handling, explode into full-blown interpersonal crises. Of course, these adversities are draining because of the time, energy, and emotional toll they take, as well as the risks of fractured interactions in the future.

It is important to keep in mind that every leader struggles with these concerns. For example, in earlier research, we asked organizational Presidents and CEOs to note the issues they found most perplexing and troublesome—the proverbial "what keeps you up at night" question. People problems were always at the top of the list (Stoner & Gilligan, 2002). This realization may not provide comfort and solace, but it does assure you that what you are experiencing is not atypical.

There is an additional reality check. Add to all of this the likelihood that your networks of social support may now be in flux. Co-workers, who were friends and sources of emotional release, are now subordinates. As such, you are understandably tenuous about the appropriate level of contact and sharing. Friends who were sources of diversion and relaxation may be affected. While they are still your friends, limitations of time may have wedged between you and them. For many emerging leaders, job demands make it more and more difficult to carve out time to spend with friends.

Personal Adversities

The second broad category—personal adversities—covers a range of items that deal with both work and non-work issues. On one level, we may encounter career disruptions and adjustments. Generally, these are adversities when the expected or desired career moves do not take place. Perhaps an anticipated promotion does not come through. Or a plum assignment goes to a colleague instead of you. Or a wonderful and opportunistic project does not come your way. Perhaps, a performance appraisal falls well short of your expectations and hopes. Perhaps, you reach a point of transition where a change in careers is contemplated or enacted. And, in some cases, you may even have to deal with a termination. Regardless of how these career events are construed, they do pose adversity, although the level and extent varies.

Of course, personal adversities extend beyond work. They may include personal and family health issues. And they may include family relationship issues. Further, emerging leaders often have young families. As job and family demands collide, you are likely to struggle with work-life balance concerns.

In short, adversity is part of life, and leaders are certainly not impervious to the vagaries of life. The way these adversities are understood and addressed becomes the more critical concern.

Building Resilience

It is not reasonable in a few short pages to provide a thorough statement of how one perseveres through adversity. Every situation, every struggle, and every person is different. Yet this much we do know, all leaders must trudge along this path. And, of course, emerging leaders do not have the tempering luxury of time and experience.

We have known for a long time that successful leaders have the ability to be resilient—to bounce back when faced with problems and adversities (Maddi & Kobasa, 1984). In this section, we offer practical thoughts—provisions for the journey.

We start with some research and theory. Martin Seligman, recognized as the father of positive psychology, has provided groundbreaking work that is relevant and helpful. In one of his experiments, research subjects were randomly placed into one of three groups. In the first group, subjects were bombarded by a loud and bothersome noise. However, by pushing a button in front of them, the noise stopped. In the second group, subjects were exposed to the same noise. However, despite their efforts and attempts, they were unable to make the noise stop. Subjects in the third group served as the control and were not exposed to the noise.

In a subsequent experiment the following day, all subjects were exposed to a loud and annoying noise. Subjects in groups one and three rather easily found a lever that enabled them to stop the noise. However, subjects in group two typically did not even try to stop the noise. As Seligman explained, "In phase one they failed, realized they had no control, and became passive. In phase two, expecting more failure, they don't even try to escape. They have learned helplessness" (Seligman, 2011, p. 102).

The concept of "learned helplessness" has a broad range of applications. One of the more interesting lessons from Seligman's work is how readily people can move from disappointment and failure to helplessness. Harvard Professor Tal Ben-Shahar (2007) offers, "When we fail to attain a desired outcome, we often extrapolate from that experience the belief that we have no control over our lives or certain parts of it" (p. 24). That can be a discouraging and dangerous mindset, to say the least.

Importantly, everyone does not display this tendency toward learned helplessness. Even Seligman found that about a third of the people in his experiments did not yield to the learned helplessness path (Seligman, 2011). It seems a lot has to do with our expectations. In fact, experts argue that our expectations of success or failure are often so powerful that they become self-fulfilling prophecies (Rosenthal & Jacobson, 1992).

Seligman (2006) believes that we can, indeed, develop "learned optimism"— expectations that we will succeed rather than fail—and he argues that this optimistic mood contributes to success and happiness. Schulman (1999), in applying these foundations to a sales environment, noted that a "belief that one will succeed produces over-achievement and the belief that one will fail produces underachievement" (p. 31).

In unpacking this phenomenon, experts highlight our "explanatory style," the established and rather habitual way that we go about explaining the failures and disappointments that we encounter (Abramson, Seligman, & Teasdale, 1978; Seligman, Abramson, Semmel, & von Bacyer, 1979). Optimists, as opposed to pessimists, are more likely to: (1) reframe adversity into a challenge; (2) view roadblocks as opportunities; (3) persevere to find meaningful solutions to the problems they encounter; and (4) maintain self-confidence throughout the process (Schulman, 1999).

Logically, optimistic expectations can be important for emerging leaders as you traverse the obstacles and adversities that will arise. In addition, people want their leaders to project optimism and optimistic expectations. We have all experienced those with a pessimistic tone and felt the mood they generate. It is a wallowing mood that drains and depletes the energy from those around them.

Of course, we must be realistic. Even extremely seasoned, optimistic leaders experience periods of confusion and doubt when confronted with deep adversity. However, in part due to their optimistic reframes, they seem to be able to work quickly through this stage and move toward a process of solutions (Stoner & Gilligan, 2002). This progression is not easy. Six steps are important: (1) reframing the adversity context; (2) permitting adversity to be a revealing experience; (3) reframing adversity into challenge; (4) appreciating the control reframe; (5) having the courage to make adjustments; and (6) engaging in next-best-step thinking. Let's examine each of these steps in more depth.

Reframing the Adversity Context

Successful leaders view adversity as an "interruption"—a blip on the screen—and are able to view adversity as part of a broader context. In short, they "reframe the adversity context," taking a big picture view of what is occurring. We all know the experience of being enmeshed in adversity, feeling somewhat overwhelmed, and allowing our focus to center on the immediate events rather than the broader picture of success. It is important to remind ourselves that our path of success has never been linear. There are always steps of progress and periods of developmental questioning.

Of course, this reframe may be more challenging for you than your more senior counterparts. Because you have less experience, you have likely dealt with fewer setbacks and roadblocks in your career so far. We must be diligent in reminding ourselves that we are not defined by the events of adversity. Adversities are the proverbial "bumps in the road," and they will always be there, throwing us temporarily off course. Those bumps do not define the road, and the two cannot be confused.

Realistically, most leaders do experience a period of disillusionment and confusion in the face of adversity. This may include a range of emotions spanning the spectrum from embarrassment to fear to anger. After all, we are whole people with natural emotions and strong egos. However, successful leaders understand this flow of emotion and its temporary nature. They understand the wisdom of a colleague who once shared, "There are two kinds of people in the world—those who have grappled with the disrupting pain of crisis, and those who will."

Permitting Adversity to be a Revealing Experience

Second, adversity can be a "revealing experience." Leaders can realize that adversity is a time for reflection, careful examination, and honest questioning;

resulting in new insights and critical learning. It is safe to say that, without such reflection, the developmental value of adversity is strongly diminished.

While the immediate impact of adversity is always emotionally disorienting, successful leaders refuse to sink into prolonged periods of self-pity or submit to the numbing inaction of self-doubt. Instead, they quickly assess what happened and what was learned. This reflective capacity is, no doubt, enhanced as one surmounts various adversities over time.

Ask yourself three questions. What is being revealed about me—my character? What has been revealed about others—their needs, concerns, sensitivities, and passions? What have I learned about my behavior in this circumstance? The answers will form the basis for your adjustments.

Reflecting on adversity as a revealing experience will allow you deeper insights into your core foundations. As such, you can rediscover what brings you significance and what really counts in your career and life. In the process, you will reaffirm your personal core values. In addition, you will begin to identify and accept your limits, recognizing what you can and cannot control.

Reframing Adversity into Challenge

As we have noted previously, it's not a stretch to presume that most emerging leaders have strong needs for achievement and are motivated by new challenges. In a sense, you are probably energized by challenge and the process of mastering the challenge. You strive for significance—that feeling that you count and are an important part of making a difference for your organization. Responding to adversity, in turn, can generate a deep sense of lessened significance.

Reframing adversity is a matter of mindset, looking at the situation differently. It is generally accepted that successful leaders (and subsequently their organizations) can envision and delineate creative opportunities in situations where others see only problems (Weinzimmer, 2001). In short, resilient leaders are able to see the positive dimensions in adverse situations (Jackson & Daly, 2011).We encourage you to accept and apply this mindset.

Here, it is important to remember that everybody cannot do what leaders do. Everyone in the organization cannot set an agenda, build connections, respond decisively and constructively in the face of conflict, create a climate of commitment, and move the organization through essential change. And everyone does not have the ability to envision opportunities and realistic challenges in the face of adversity. As a leader, this is where your uniqueness shines through.

Appreciating the Control Reframe

Whether personal or business, adversity creates some loss of control. Leaders relish control—being able to get our arms around the situation. Accordingly, dissipated control can be quite a struggle. During adversity, there is a tendency to recognize, with blazing clarity, all the factors that we are unable to control. It's probably natural to focus on those factors, lamenting our condition of lost control.

Successful leaders turn from this trap. Rather than focusing and emphasizing what cannot be controlled, they center on what can. In short, they determine to put their energies and efforts into what they can affect rather than engage in destructive anxiety over factors beyond their control. Admittedly, this reframe is easier said than done.

There is a deeper dimension here. Thinking through this reframe, you will begin to honestly and objectively understand your limits. Rather than being a depressing insight, you may find that this insight, once recognized and accepted, has a liberating quality. This insight provides an opportunity to turn loose of what is beyond your realm of influence. It's great advice to tell people to not worry about things they can't do anything about. However, that advice is based on the assumption that people know what they are unable to control. Importantly, remember that you are developing through your experiences. Current limits should not be entrenched restrictions that exist into the future. They are simply today's reality.

Making Adjustments

One learning that is prompted by crisis and adversity is the ability to adapt. Adaptation is the capacity to resist swaying in the wind, shifting toward the latest whim or fad or posturing toward the loudest or most powerful voice. Rather, adaptation is the intentional behavioral decision that one reaches after carefully reflecting upon and moving past adversity. Adaptation draws from a realization that what worked in the past will no longer suffice.

The ability to responsively adapt is certainly one of the most important qualities an emerging leader can possess in today's volatile and fast-paced world (Hamel, 2012). Further, the pace of adaptation will surely increase, and the need to be a "quick study" will become only stronger.

Adversity and crisis are the impetus for adaptation because in both cases status quo thinking has proven to be dangerous and unproductive. Yet, it's still amazing how often well-intentioned leaders fall under the oft-stated definition of insanity—"doing the same things but expecting different outcomes."

Next-Best-Step Thinking

There is no special magic here. Rarely do we have a perfect strategy for handling adversity, and waiting for all the pieces to fall in place is usually not viable. Don't search for perfection, search for the next best step. That is what people need and that is often the only reasonable way to adjust to adversity. Is this approach laden with uncertainty? Yes. Does this approach enhance your vulnerability? Yes. Is this approach the only realistic path for a leader to pursue? Yes.

We realize that it is impractical, in some cases, to expect to reach a single optimal decision outcome. The cost of gaining the essential information is too high; the time needed to wade through the data and options is problematic; and the energy and stress on everyone is too onerous. Thus, we make the best call we can—we provide a decision that is "acceptable." We recognize that our natural drive for perfection must be replaced by "next-best-step" thinking. Largely, this perspective accepts that "a good decision today is better than a perfect decision six months from now." Opportunity costs abound, and perfection is too uncertain.

This next-best-step approach is neither cavalier nor uneducated. It is reasoned, analyzed, and judged for risks and consequences. It may not be the defining step, but it is the best we have available right now. There is enough going on with adversity, don't allow vacillation and indecision to further exacerbate the situation.

Perseverance

While the value of perseverance may seem rather obvious, a series of research studies has taken a fresh look at the quality of perseverance through the concept of "grit." Here, grit was defined as "perseverance and passion for long-term goals . . . working strenuously toward challenges, maintaining effort and interest over years despite failure, adversity, and plateaus in progress" (Duckworth, Peterson, Matthews, & Kelly, 2007, pp. 1087–1088). The authors noted that people with grit "stay the course," and they pointed to grit as an essential factor in high achievement.

Of course, the concept of grit does not exactly plow new ground. Previous work has highlighted the "intensity" and "persistence" that successful leaders possess (McCall, Lombardo, & Morrison, 1988). Here, we also think of the motivational theme of "drive," the capacity to exert energy, initiative, and tenacity. Research suggests that, while drive alone is not sufficient for success, the presence of high levels of drive certainly contributes to leader success (Kirkpatrick & Locke, 1991).

We are also reminded of the work of Jim Collins (2001). Recall that Collins's "level-5 leader" possessed both humility and an uncompromising professional will. This force of will created an intense drive to succeed, an unwavering resolve to achieve great results. In short, intentional perseverance toward important outcome metrics is being noted.

The significance of perseverance may also be underscored by looking at what happens when it is missing. We may look for scapegoats. We may attribute our plight to external factors, thus easing our pain and disappointment. More likely, however, we take on the role of being a "victim"—a plight that is about as far from difference-making leadership as we can get.

The Role of Mentors

Mentors or trusted colleagues can be invaluable when facing the uncertainties of crisis. We have written in earlier chapters about the value of mentors. Mentors offer a form of support that differs from what others can offer during crisis. Mentors help you put the adversity in a proper perspective. Mentors help you talk through the issues and find meaning and needed adjustments. Mentors can offer advice from their repertoire of experiences.

Understandably, people turn to family members and close friends when confronted with adversities. These individuals generally offer "emotional support," and, in that role, they are indispensable. However, family and friends generally do not have the background to provide a solid source of "advisory support" regarding business adversities and crises.

Advisory support comes from close colleagues. These must be colleagues that you trust, implicitly and without reservation. Only then can an open sharing and discussion of the adversity situation take place without concern about privacy or repercussions. Baring one's soul is a fragile and potentially dangerous activity. Move carefully and judiciously. Sharing with a peer may not be best. Turning to a boss can also be politically charged. Accordingly, we prefer senior, non-boss mentors. Look for someone whom you respect, and look for someone whose sole benefit from the exchange is clearly to help you develop and progress.

Helping Others Deal with Adversity

Adversities are likely to throw our people and our teams into "anxiety-land." So, the penetrating question becomes, how can we respond and lead our people through the trauma of business uncertainties and other dramatic change? Two points are certain: (1) impressions of our leadership are drawn most strongly from how we handle these inevitable situations of adversity; and (2) there are no easy answers. That being said, we offer six key steps for you to consider.

Focus and Clarity

Remember that adversity creates uncertainty and fear. Providing your people with focus and clarity is critical. Although you will not be able to provide the laser-sharp focus that people desire, provide as much as you can. Importantly, performance expectations cannot slip, and standards cannot be bent.

During times of uncertainty, it may be important to focus on the short run. As noted above, this is what we call "next-best-step" thinking.

Communicate

Share information when you can. During tough times of change, leaders have a tendency to turn the communication faucet down to a slow drip, rationalizing that they'll fill their people in when they've got it all figured out. This is a practice that's understandable but dangerously wrong. Indeed, as noted in the previous chapter, the metaphoric faucet of communication needs to be wide open.

Remember, it is virtually impossible to overcommunicate with your people during times of change and adversity. In fact, what people do not know, they make up. Rumors, with worst-case scenarios, fill in the gaps of misunderstanding.

Touch

Touch is an encompassing term for being present and reaching out to connect with your people during difficult times. Sometimes, touch simply means being present and available to your people.

Politics aside, most people agree that one of the most heroic acts of leadership in the last twenty-five years came from Rudy Giuliani immediately following the 9/11 attacks at New York City in 2001. We often forget that Giuliani was vilified in the press in the months preceding 9/11, with public problems that included a widespread garbage strike and personal issues that centered on an extra-marital affair.

Yet, in the hours and days immediately following the attacks, images of Giuliani at Ground Zero, handing out coffee, comforting people, and encouraging rescue workers were impressive. Most notable, perhaps, was that Giuliani was there, at the center of the fray. During times of adversity, even small acts of encouragement and appreciation take on extra importance.

Remove Barriers

We always encourage leaders to see what stumbling blocks and common irritants and barriers can be taken off team members' plates. This is a bit of a balancing act. We cannot allow performance to slip. Neither can we take on responsibilities that must remain with our people. Getting the job done by solving problems is what we expect of team members, and those expectations cannot be mitigated. Yet, if we can remove barriers and obstacles for others, we ease their paths through troubled times.

Equity Takes Center Stage

We have talked earlier about the importance of equity. Recall that equity is a perception of being treated fairly. It is played out by considering how we are being dealt with and treated in comparison to others with whom we work (Adams, 1963; 1965).

During times of crisis, replete with tension and stress, equity considerations take center stage. Fundamentally, people are generally willing to take on extra burdens, make concessions, and extend themselves as long as the pain of doing so is being shared in a fair and equitable way by everyone.

It's not surprising that the first place your team members are likely to extend their gaze of equity is toward leadership. Nothing will destroy morale and subsequent performance more quickly than when workers believe that they are sacrificing but their leaders are not.

You are the important role model here. Frankly, most workers feel that it's largely a symbolic move when the CEO concedes to work for a hugely reduced salary—some for only a dollar a year. Yet, when you pitch-in to help out, put in extra effort, and extend yourself for your people during times of crisis, they see it as a clear statement of you sharing in the pain—thus engaging in equity-clarifying behavior. In short, your people need to know that you are doing what you can for them.

Projecting What You May Not Feel

Jackson and Daly (2011) have noted that "resilient leaders are not only able to survive in difficulty, but they are also able to model behavior that will enhance constituents' ability to thrive" (p. 22). In this regard, it is entirely likely that you will, from time to time, project resilience before you really feel it. Through this progression, you are being neither disingenuous nor being a cheerleading Pollyanna. Instead, you are "putting your game face on" and moving forward.

Recognize that this is what your people need. Further, you build resilience through this projection. You are ensuring your people that we have previously faced adversity and persevered. You are also assuring them that we will once again persevere and succeed.

A Case for Balance

Concerns about work-life balance are particularly critical for our emerging leaders. This concern arises from what has been described as a "perfect storm of competing time commitments" (Stoner, Stephens, & McGowan, 2009, p. 68). Specifically, your leadership roles are demanding increased time, while the responsibilities that come with young families create demanding family obligations. As such, struggles between work and other areas of life are common.

Evidence suggests that leaders in their twenties and thirties are more concerned about maintaining work-life balance than their more senior counterparts. Indeed, within your age cohort, family is generally a top priority, and attaining and maintaining work-life balance emerges as a top-rated career value (Lockwood, 2003; Whitehead, 1999). Interestingly, these concerns and intentions do not necessarily translate into action. When the demands of the job rise, most of us tend to hunker down and work harder (Stoner, Robin, & Russell-Chapin, 2005).

There are logical reasons for our decisions to extend our work. At least four of these are personal. These personal reasons include: (1) we tend to enjoy and find meaning in our work; (2) working harder and longer is often perceived as necessary to achieve desired success; (3) connectivity makes it easier to work without regard for time or place; and (4) work can be a means of escape from the confusion and disappointments in other arenas of life (Hochchild, 1997; Stoner & Robin, 2006).

At least three reasons for our decisions to extend work are external to us, largely drawn from the context of organizational demands. These external reasons include: (1) increasingly competitive business demands that have necessitated a push to expect more from everyone; (2) longer hours that are generally associated with the territory of leadership; and (3) working more is generally reinforced by businesses and organizations. We see these themes daily, and they are supported by research suggesting that the modern work-place reliance on fewer people to do more work implies inevitable increases in workload (Lewis & Dyer, 2002).

Most experts agree that there are five key domains to our lives. Generally, work and family are the most important. The other domains include friends, community, and self. We like to break the self domain into three sub-areas—personal time, health and fitness time, and spiritual time. Because we are whole people, these domains cannot exist independently. What happens in one area affects others—the well-studied "spillover" effect that we mentioned earlier. As noted previously, this spillover can be negative, such as problems at home bleeding over and disrupting work efforts. But, the spillover is often positive. For example, when we feel success and satisfaction at work, it can easily lead to a more positive affect toward other areas (Friedman & Greenhaus, 2000; Greenhaus & Powell, 2005).

The attention given to each domain will fluctuate over the course of your life, but leaving any domain depleted can be problematic. For example, friends provide support and serve as a diversion from many of the pressures of work. Personal time is essential for maintaining healthy responses to the stresses that are part of life. Community time (working with volunteer groups and serving on not-for-profit boards, for example) may be of lower priority at this stage of your career than it will be later. We encourage emerging leaders to choose a limited number (perhaps one or two) of community projects. Although these take time, they often add meaning to your efforts and become wonderful sources for expanding your network of contacts.

Our intent here is not to present an extensive foray into the field of work-life balance. However, we will emphasize the two factors that are probably most critical for emerging leaders: (1) reflective understanding of what is happening to your need for balance; and (2) the need to prioritize.

Reflective Understanding

Reflective understanding helps us recognize when one domain is dominating and excluding other domains. Normally, for emerging leaders, it is the work domain that begins to edge into the others.

It is fascinating how this tendency emerges. It is not unusual that younger workers are committed to maintaining work-life balance, a lack of which they have seen among their parents and more senior colleagues. For example, in one study of young college graduates, an overwhelming majority reported that they would never allow work to become more important than family and friends. Yet, tasting early career success and yearning for more, they soon found themselves working increasingly long hours and feeling the unwelcomed pangs of work-life imbalance (Sturges & Guest, 2004).

Of course, career advancement and success is not the only reason we work longer and harder. Frankly, as high achievers, we enjoy our work and can easily become engrossed by it. Yet, a more dangerous theme may be at work. Researcher Joanne Ciulla (2002) has referred to it as a work ethic of fear. In essence, we are afraid not to work as hard as the next person for fear of the impressions that others (bosses) may draw, and the negative outcomes that may ensue (not getting key assignments or not receiving advancement opportunities). In short, we may be working more—not to attain greater positive consequences—but to avoid negative consequences.

Of course, as we all know, connectivity has exacerbated our tendency toward work overload. We can literally be connected to our work, pretty much irrespective of location or time, if we so choose. The temptation to just put in a little "electronic overtime" is omnipresent. There is an even more insidious culprit here. Consistent with the work ethic of fear, many young managers feel "emotionally tethered," in essence feeling guilty when they decide to refrain from a connectivity check-in. In short, it's hard not to check emails constantly when you think that everyone else is doing so. Researchers have suggested that this leads to a feeling of "cognitive intrusion," an ever-present sense that you should be thinking about work (Ezzedeen & Swiercz, 2002).

Prioritization

The need for prioritization assumes that one has engaged in some personal reflection, knows what is truly important, and has created a base or anchor-level of time and energy that must be devoted to each arena of life. There is no easy path to balance, and all paths lead through intentional prioritization.

Importantly, leaders set the tone here. Lauding the organization as being "family friendly" and espousing the virtues of work-life balance mean nothing when the leader models contradictory behavior. When everyone knows that you work 80-hour weeks, answering emails at 2 am, what message do they receive?

Concluding Thoughts: Time and Memory

In today's chaotic and volatile environment, replete with adversity and crisis, people dearly need leaders who provide hope. Hope asks for neither naïveté nor the cheerleading of hype. Hope is centered, and it is realistic. Hope demands an honest appraisal of reality. And it requires a vision of possibility.

We have chosen, in this chapter, to not provide a model of organizational crisis management. In most cases, this is not the purview of new, emerging leaders. We have chosen to focus on the personal sense that adversity and crisis creates for you and those you lead. Amidst the swirl of obstacles and trouble, your people need a steady, firm, and consistent rudder. Be the calm in the storm!

10

Codas and Continuations

It is a difficult time to be a leader. As we write these final pages, the headlines toll an all-too-familiar tone. Tech giant Hewlett-Packard has just announced that it plans to cut 27,000 jobs over the next two years—the largest reduction in personnel in the company's 73-year history. Some perspective is helpful here. If we round up a dozen HP employees, one of them will be gone. On the same day in our little city, a mid-sized logistics company announced that 189 employees will lose their jobs over the next three months. Although this number dwarfs by comparison, the magnitude of impact is no less for those affected.

These were strategic decisions, crafted by top executives and their teams. In all likelihood, these were painful moves taken in the name of long-term organizational success. As such, we seek neither to question these decisions nor their underlying strategic logic. Yet, we must wonder, what happens next? That question and the inevitable complexity of the response rests on leaders; leaders who are deep in the organization; leaders who feel the impact and see the faces and must help people move forward. Like so many organizational outcomes, what happens next depends on leaders like you.

Facing noble crises such as those above or carrying out every day routines, leaders make a difference—a difference that affects lives. Kets de Vries and Engellau (2010) cogently profess that true leaders are "merchants of hope . . . inspiring people to move beyond personal, egoistic motives—to transcend themselves . . . and as a result, they get the best from their people" (p. 192).

This book has been about growth and development. Our goal has been facilitative—to help you grow into your leadership role and engage the challenges of your position with heightened levels of competence, confidence, credibility, and effectiveness.

Your development as a leader, like most forms of adult development, does not follow a linear and continuous path. Instead, development involves periods of growth and change; followed by periods of stability and plateau;

repeated with further iterations of the growth-stability pattern (Kegan & Lahey, 2009).

Logically, your organization seeks to support your growth. In all likelihood, you will have openings into an array of developmental opportunities as you progress. These opportunities take many forms. Some are job-specific, including new responsibilities and assignments, challenging projects, exposure to key leaders, and the chance to participate in critical decisions. Some opportunities are focused and quite personal, such as mentoring and coaching, participating in leadership workshops, and other educational and training efforts.

Yet, you must assume control. Indeed, your most dramatic growth will probably occur when you are able to "recognize, manage, and even direct" your own learning and change, through a process that may be referred to as your personal "learning agenda" (Boyatzis & McKee, 2006, pp. 49–50). The learning agenda demands that you have an accurate and honest assessment of your areas of strength and the areas where you need to develop. As an emerging leader, you should be building on and leveraging your strengths. Concurrently, you should always have one or two developmental areas where you are working to close the gap between where you are and where you want and need to be.

Leadership has always been about courage—the courage to make the right decisions even as popularity is at risk. You also need courage to assess and address your developmental gaps. Awareness can be gleaned through performance reviews, 360-degree feedback assessments, and careful personal reflection. Realistically, most people know, through experience, where they need to grow. For example, we generally begin our workshops by asking people to share responses to two questions: (1) As leader, what are you really good at doing?; and (2) As a leader, where do you need to get better? We are generally pleased with how candid and on-the-mark folks tend to be. We also tend to see an uncanny consistency between these early expressions and what is formally revealed through 360-degree assessments a few days later. Our call is clear—keep learning.

Like any new activity, some of the needed skills, behaviors, and perspectives will be a stretch. They may seem to expand beyond the well-honed confines of your comfort zone. You will be engaged in making adjustments as you explore and practice your leader role. We love a quote from Eleanor Roosevelt: "The purpose of life is to live it, to taste experience to the utmost, to reach out eagerly and without fear for new and richer experience" (Morin, 2010, p. 27). Keep growing.

This has also been a book about transitions, most notably the transition from doer to leader—a leader who gets things done by marshaling the collective power of others. In a career that will be marked by a series of transitions, this initial transition into the world of leadership will be one of the more dramatic and challenging. We have talked candidly about the struggles and temptations emerging leaders face during their leadership transition. We have also, hopefully, shared the excitement and energy you will experience in your leader role.

A few years ago, Robert Goffee and Gareth Jones (2000) authored an intriguing article built around the question, "Why should anyone want to be led by you?" (p. 63). It's a good question; an intriguingly reflective question; an important question. The answer to this question requires some depth. Parker Palmer (2011) offers a probing call to leadership, encouraging us to find a way to connect with something larger than our own ego. Richard Brown, former CEO of EDS, reminds us that "bad leadership happens when leaders put their personal desires ahead of their good judgment" (Collingwood, 2001, p. 20).

In an organizational world where metrics dominate, the measure of your success has generally come from what you have done; how you have achieved; and what you have accomplished. In leadership, an additional and different set of metrics becomes prominent. Now, the measure of your success rests not so much on what you do; it rests on what your people do because of your presence. You set the tone, and you clarify the direction. You set challenging expectations and ensure outcomes. You communicate, address tough issues, and build connections. You guide and help facilitate action. You lead people through change while maintaining clarity and commitment. Stay true; never compromise your vales; and keep being a difference-maker.

References

1 Challenge: The Playing Field Has Changed

Bass, B. M. (1991). *Bass and Stogdill's handbook of leadership: Theory, research, and managerial applications.* New York: Free Press.

Bass, B. M., Avolio, B. J., Jung, D. I., & Berson, Y. (2003). Predicting unit performance by assessing transformational and transactional leadership. *Journal of Applied Psychology, 88*(2), 207–218.

Benjamin, B., & O'Reilly, C. (2011). Becoming a leader: Early career challenges faced by MBA graduates. *Academy of Management Learning and Education, 10*(3), 452–472.

Bennis, W., & Goldsmith, J. (1997). *Learning to lead: A workbook on becoming a leader.* New York: Perseus Books.

Bennis, W. G., & Thomas, R. J. (2002). *Geeks and geezers: How era, values, and defining moments shape leadership.* Boston: Harvard Business School Press.

Borg, M. J. (1997). *The God we never knew: Beyond dogmatic religion to a more authentic contemporary faith.* New York: HarperCollins.

Bridges, W. (1991). Managing transitions: Making the most out of change. Cambridge, MA: DaCapo Press.

Chabris, C., & Simons, D. (2010). *The invisible gorilla: And other ways our intuitions deceive us.* New York: Crown.

Chatman, J. A., & Kennedy, J. A. (2010). Psychological perspectives on leadership. In N. Nohria & R. Khurana (Eds.). *Handbook of leadership theory and practice* (pp. 159–181). Boston: Harvard Business Press.

Deal, J. J., Peterson, K., & Gailor-Loflin, H. (2001). *Emerging leaders: An annotated bibliography.* Greensboro, NC: Center for Creative Leadership.

DePree, M. (1989). *Leadership is an art.* New York: Dell.

Ellis, C. (2004). *Management skills for new managers.* New York: AMACOM.

Gabarra, J. J. (1987). *The dynamics of taking charge.* Boston: Harvard Business School Press.

Gardner, H. (1995). *Leading minds: An anatomy of leadership.* New York: Basic Books.

Goldsmith, M., & Reiter, M. (2007). *What got you here won't get you there.* New York: Hyperion.

Goleman, D. (2006). *Social intelligence: The new science of human relationships.* New York: Bantam.

Goleman, D., Boyatzis, R., & McKee, A. (2002). *Primal leadership: Realizing the power of emotional intelligence.* Cambridge, MA: Harvard Business School Press.

Harrison, A. J. (2011). *Google's management rules.* Retrieved from http://andrew johnharrison.com/.

Hill, L. A. (2003). *Becoming a manager: How new managers master the challenges of leadership.* Boston: Harvard Business School Press.

Ibarra, H., Snook, S., & Ramo, L. G. (2010). Identity-based leader development. In N. Nohria & R. Khurana (Eds.). *Handbook of leadership theory and practice* (pp. 657–678). Boston: Harvard Business Press.

Judge, T. A., Piccolo, R. F., & Illies, R. (2004). The forgotten one? The validity of consideration and initiating structure in leadership research. *Journal of Applied Psychology, 89*(1), 36–51.

Katz, R. L. (1955). Skills of an effective administrator. *Harvard Business Review, 33*(1), 33–42.

Kotter, J. P. (2001). What leaders really do. *Harvard Business Review, 79*(11), 85–96.

Kouzes, J. M. (1998). Finding your voice. In L. C. Spears (Ed.). *Insights on leadership: Service, stewardship, spirit, and servant-leadership* (pp. 322–325). New York: John Wiley & Sons.

Kouzes, J. M., & Posner, B. Z. (2002). *The leadership challenge.* San Francisco: Jossey-Bass.

Martin, J., & Schmidt, C. (2010). How to keep your top talent. *Harvard Business Review, 88*(5), 54–61.

McCall Jr., M. W., Lombardo, M. M., & Morrison, A. M. (1998). *Lessons of experience: How successful executives develop on the job.* Lexington, MA: Lexington Books.

Mumford, M. D., Zaccaro, S. J., Harding, F. D., Jacobs, T. O., & Fleishman, E. A. (2000). Leadership skills for a changing world: Solving complex social problems. *Leadership Quarterly, 11*(1), 11–35.

Nohria, N., & Khurana, R. (Eds.). (2010). *Handbook of leadership theory and practice.* Boston: Harvard Business Press.

Pfeffer, J. (1977). The ambiguity of leadership. *Academy of Management Review, 2*(1), 104–112.

Reichard, J., & Avolio, B. J. (2005). Where are we? The status of leadership intervention research: A meta-analytic summary. In W. L. Gardner, B. J. Avolio, & F. O. Walumbwa (Eds.). *Authentic leadership theory and practice: Origins, effects, and development* (pp. 203–226). Amsterdam: Elsevier Press.

Senge, P. M. (2006). *The fifth discipline: The art and practice of the learning organization.* New York: Knopf.

Thomas, A. B. (1988). Does leadership make a difference to organizational performance? *Administrative Science Quarterly, 33*, 388–400.

Useem, M. (2010). Decision making as a leadership function. In N. Nohria & R. Khurana (Eds.). *Handbook of leadership theory and practice* (pp. 507–525). Boston: Harvard Business Press.

Van Buren, M., & Safferstone, T. (2009). The quick wins paradox. *Harvard Business Review,* 87(1), 54–61.

Watkins, M. (2003). *The first 90 days: Critical success strategies for new leaders at all levels.* Boston: Harvard Business School Publishing.

Williams, R. (2010, May 2). CEO failures: How on-boarding can help [Blog]. Retrieved from www.psychologytoday.com/blog/wired-success/201005/ceo-failures-how-boarding-can-help.

Wilson, M. S., & Hoole, E. (2011). Developing leaders: India at the crossroads. *Vikalpa: The Journal of Decision Makers, 36*(3), 1–8.

2   Character: The Inside Game of Leadership

Adams, J. S. (1965). Inequity in social exchange. In L. Berkowitz (Ed.), *Advances in experimental social psychology* (Vol. 2, pp. 267–299). New York: Academic Press.

Avolio, B. J. (2010). Pursuing authentic leadership development. In N. Nohria & R. Khurana (Eds.). *Handbook of leadership theory and practice* (pp. 739–768). Boston: Harvard Business Press.

Avolio, B. J., & Gardner, W. L. (2005). Authentic leadership development: Getting to the root of positive forms of leadership. *The Leadership Quarterly, 16*, 315–338.

Barlow, C. B., Jordan, M., & Hendrix, W. H. (2003). Character assessment: An examination of leadership levels. *Journal of Business and Psychology, 17*, 563–584.

Beeson, J. (2009). Why didn't you get that promotion? *Harvard Business Review, 37*, 101–105.

Bennis, W. (2003). *On becoming a leader.* Cambridge, MA: Perseus Publishing.

Burchell, M., & Robin, J. (2011). *The great workplace: How to build it, how to keep it, and why it matters.* San Francisco: Jossey-Bass.

Christensen, C. M. (2010). How will you measure your life? *Harvard Business Review, 88*(7/8), 46–51.

Collins, J. (2001). *Good to great: Why some companies make the leap . . . and others don't.* New York: HarperCollins.

Cooper, C. (2008). *Extraordinary circumstances.* Hoboken, NJ: John Wiley & Sons.

Covey, S. R. (1989). *The 7 habits of highly effective people: Powerful lessons in personal change.* New York: Free Press.

Cropanzano, R., & Folger, R. (1987). Interactional fairness judgments: The influence of causal accounts. *Social Justice Research, 1*, 199–218.

Cropanzano, R., & Folger, R. (1996). Procedural justice and worker motivation. In R. M. Steers, L. W. Porter, & G. A. Bigley (Eds.). *Motivation and leadership at work* (6th ed., pp. 72–83). New York: McGraw-Hill.

Deloitte (2010). 2010 Ethics and Workplace Survey. Retrieved from http://www. deloitte.com/view/en_US/us/About/Ethics-Independence/8aa3cb51ed812210 VgnVCM100000ba42f00aRCRD.

Fortune. (2011). 100 best companies to work for. Retrieved from http://money.cnn. com/magazines/fortune/best.

Freiberg, K., & Freiberg, J. (1996). *Nuts! Southwest Airlines' crazy recipe for business and personal success.* Austin, TX: Bard Books.

Galford, R., & Drapeau, A. S. (2003). The enemies of trust. *Harvard Business Review, 81*(2), 88–95.

George, W. W. (2003). *Authentic leadership: Rediscovering the secrets to creating lasting value.* San Francisco: Jossey-Bass.

Gilbert, J. A., & Tang, T. L-P. (1998). An examination of organizational trust antecedents. *Public Personnel Management, 27*(3), 321–338.

Graen, G. B., & Uhl-Bien, M. (1995). The relationship-based approach to leadership: Development of LMX theory over 25 years. *Leadership Quarterly, 6*(2), 219–247.

Hill, L. A. (2003). *Becoming a manager: How new managers master the challenges of leadership.* Boston: Harvard Business School Press.

Hoy, W. K., & Tschannen-Moran, M. (1999). Five faces of trust: An empirical confirmation in urban elementary schools. *Journal of School Leadership, 9,* 184–208.

Keohane, N. O. (2010). *Thinking about leadership.* Princeton, NJ: Princeton University Press.

Kouzes, J. M., & Posner, B. Z. (2002). *The leadership challenge* (3rd ed.). San Francisco: Jossey-Bass.

McCall, M. W., Lombardo, M. M., & Morrison, A. M. (1988). *The lessons of experience: How successful executives develop on the job.* Lexington, MA: Lexington Books.

McCauley, C. D., Moxley, R. S., & Van Velsor, E. (Eds.). 1998. *The handbook of leadership development.* San Francisco: Jossey-Bass.

Milgram, S. (1963). Behavioral study of obedience. *Journal of Abnormal and Social Psychology, 67*(4), 371–378.

Milgram, S. (1974). *Obedience to authority: An experimental view.* New York: HarperCollins.

Mulholland, M. R. (1993). *Invitation to a journey: A road map for spiritual formation.* Downers Grove, IL: IVP Books.

Perry, R. W., & Mankin, L. D. (2004). Understanding employee trust in management: Conceptual clarification and correlates. *Public Personnel Management, 33*(3), 277–290.

Philippe, T. W., & Koehler, J. W. (2005). A factor analytic study of perceived organizational hypocrisy. *SAM Advanced Management Journal, 70*(2), 13–20.

Posner, B. (2010). Values and the American manager: A three-decade perspective. *Journal of Business Ethics, 91*(4), 457–465.

Reina, D. S., & Reina, M. L. (2006). *Trust and betrayal in the workplace.* San Francisco: Berrett-Koehler.

Roethlisberger, F. J. (1989). The hawthorne experiments. In J. S. Ott (Ed.). *Classic readings in organizational behaviour* (pp. 36–47). Pacific Grove, CA: Brooks/Cole.

Sarros, J. C., & Cooper, B. K. (2006). Building character: A leadership essential. *Journal of Business and Psychology, 21*(1), 1–22.

Walker, B. (2010, June 3). Selig won't overturn call that cost perfect game. *NBC Sports.* Retrieved from http://www.nbcsports.msnbc.com/id/37479309/ns/sports-baseball.

Walster, E., Bercheid, E., & Walster, G. W. (1976). New directions in equity research. In L. Berkowitz & E. Walster (Eds.). *Advances in experimental social psychology* (Vol. 9, pp. 1–42). New York: Academic Press.

Walumba, F. O., Avolio, B., Gardner, W., Wernsing, T., & Peterson, S. (2008). Authentic leadership: Development of a theory-based measure. *Journal of Management, 34*(1), 89–126.

Weick, K. E. (1967). The concept of equity in the perception of pay. *Administrative Science Quarterly, 2,* 414–439.

Zenger, J. H., & Folkman, J. R. (2009). *The extraordinary leader: Turning good managers into great leaders.* New York: McGraw-Hill.

3   Confidence: The Capacity to Lead with Assurance

Atkinson, J. S., & Feather, N. T. (1966). *A theory of achievement motivation.* New York: John Wiley & Sons.

Bandura, A. (1982). Self-efficacy mechanism in human agency. *American Psychologist, 37*(2), 122–147.

Bandura, A. (1986). *Social foundations of thought and action: A social cognitive theory.* Englewood Cliffs, NJ: Prentice Hall.

Bandura, A., & Locke, E. A. (2003). Negative self-efficacy and goal effects revisited. *Journal of Applied Psychology, 88,* 87–99.

Benabou, R., & Tirole, J. (2002). Self-confidence and personal motivation. *Quarterly Journal of Economics, 17*(3), 871–915.

Brown, L. H., & Beckett, K. S. (2007). *Building community in an alternative school: The perspective of an African American principal.* New York: Peter Lang Publishing.

Clance, P. R., & Imes, S. (1978). The imposter phenomenon in high achieving women: Dynamics and therapeutic interaction. *Psychotherapy Theory, Research and Practice, 15*(3), 241–247.

Conger, J. A., & Kanungo, R. (1987). Toward a behavioral theory of charismatic leadership in organizational settings. *Academy of Management Review, 12,* 637–647.

DeCremer, D., & van Knippenberg, D. (2004). Leader self-sacrifice and leader effectiveness: The moderating role of leader self-confidence. *Organizational Behavior and Human Decision Processes, 95*, 140–155.

DePree, M., & Wright, Jr., W. C. (2006). *Mentoring: Two voices.* Pasadena, CA: Max DePree Center for Leadership.

Gist, M. E. (1987). Self-efficacy: Implications for organizational behavior and human resource management. *Academy of Management Review, 12(3)*, 472–485.

Gist, M. E., & Mitchell, T. R. (1992). Self-efficacy: A theoretical analysis of its determinants and malleability. *Academy of Management Review, 17(2)*, 183–211.

Goldsmith, M. (2010). Leader confidence. *Leadership Excellence, 27(1)*, 8–9.

Goleman, D. (2006). *Social intelligence: The new science of human relationships.* New York: Bantam Dell.

Grant, A. M., & Schwartz, B. (2011). Too much of a good thing: The challenge and opportunity of the inverted U. *Perspectives on Psychological Science, 6(1)*, 61–76.

Hollenbeck, G. P., & Hall, D. T. (2004). Self confidence and leader performance. *Organizational Dynamics, 33(3)*, 254–269.

Kahneman, D., & Tversky, A. (1984). Choices, values, and frames. *American Psychologist, 39*, 341–350.

Kets de Vries, M., & Engellau, E. (2010). A clinical approach to the dynamics of leadership and executive transformation. In N. Nohria & R. Khurana (Eds). *Handbook of leadership theory and practice* (pp. 183–222). Boston: Harvard Business Press.

Khurana, R. (2002). The curse of the superstar. *Harvard Business Review, 30*, 60–66.

Kirkpatrick, S. A., & Locke, E. A. (1996). Leadership: Do traits matter? In R. M. Steers, L. W. Porter, & G. A. Bigley (Eds.). *Motivation and leadership at work* (pp. 186–199). New York: McGraw-Hill.

Luthans, F., & Youssef, C. M. (2004). Human, social, and now positive psychological capital management. *Organizational Dynamics, 33(2)*, 143–160.

Luthans, F., Youssef, C. M., & Avolio, B. J. (2007). *Psychological capital: Developing the human competitive edge.* Oxford: Oxford University Press.

Maddi, S. R., & Kobasa, S. C. (1984). *The hardy executive: Health under stress.* Homewood, IL: Dow Jones-Irwin.

McClelland, D. C. (1967). *The achieving society.* New York: Free Press.

McClelland, D. C. (1976). *The achievement motive.* New York: Irvington.

Orth, U., Trzesniewski, K. H., & Robins, R. W. (2010). Self-esteem development from young adulthood to old age: A cohort-sequential longitudinal study. *Journal of Personality and Social Psychology, 98(4)*, 645–658.

Ready, D. A., Conger, J. A., & Hill, L. A. (2010). Are you a high potential? *Harvard Business Review, 88(6)*, 78–84.

Stajkovic, A. D., & Luthans, F. (1998). Self-efficacy and work-related performance: A meta-analysis. *Psychological Bulletin, 124*, 240–261.

Stolz, P. G. (1997). *The adversity quotient.* New York: John Wiley & Sons.

Stoner, C. R., & Gilligan, J. F. (2002). *The adversity challenge: How successful leaders bounce back from setbacks.* Provo, UT: Executive Excellence Publishing.

Vaish, A., Woodward, A., & Grossman, T. (2008). Not all emotions are created equal: The negativity bias in social-emotional development. *Psychological Bulletin, 134,* 383–403.

Vancouver, J. B., Thompson, C. M., Tischner, E. C., & Putka, D. J. (2002). Two studies examining the negative effect of self-efficacy on performance. *Journal of Applied Psychology, 87,* 506–516.

Walker, C. A. (2002). Saving your rookie managers from themselves. *Harvard Business Review, 80(*4), 97–102.

Wood, R., & Bandura, A. (1989). Social cognition theory of organizational management. *Academy of Management Review, 14*(3), 361–384.

4 Clarity: The Foundation of Crystal-Clear Expectations

Aronson, E. (1992). The return of the oppressed: Dissonance theory makes a comeback. *Psychological Inquiry, 3,* 353–356.

Bass, B. M. (1990). *Bass and Stogdill's handbook of leadership: Theory, research, and managerial applications* (3rd ed.). New York: Free Press.

Bauer, T. N., Bodner, T., Erdogen, B., Truxillo, D., & Tucker, J. S. (2007). Newcomer adjustment during organizational socialization: A meta-analytic review of antecedents, outcomes, and methods. *Journal of Applied Psychology, 92*(3), 707–721.

Berkowitz, L., & Devine, P. (1989). Research traditions, analysis, and synthesis in social psychological theories: The case of dissonance theory. *Personality and Social Psychology Bulletin, 15,* 493–507.

Bliese, P. D., & Castro, C. A. (2000). Role clarity, work overload and organizational support: Multilevel evidence of the importance of support. *Work & Stress, 14*(1), 65–73.

Chambers, H. E. (2004). *My way or the highway: The micromanagement survival guide.* San Francisco: Berrett-Koehler.

Chatman, J. A., & Kennedy, J. A. (2010). Psychological perspectives on leadership. In N. Nohria & R. Khurana (Eds.). *Handbook of leadership theory and practice.* Boston: Harvard Business Press.

Chen, G., & Bliese, P. D. (2002). The role of different levels of leadership in predicting self- and collective efficacy: Evidence for discontinuity. *Journal of Applied Psychology, 87,* 549–556.

Deal, J. J., Peterson, K., & Gailor-Loflin, H. (2001). *Emerging leaders: An annotated bibliography.* Greensboro, NC: Center for Creative Leadership.

Dotlich, D. L., Noel, J. J., & Walker, N. (2004). *Leadership passages: The personal and professional transitions that make or break a leader.* San Francisco: Jossey-Bass.

Eatough, E. M., Chang, C. H., & Miloslavic, S. A. (2011). The relationship of role stressors with organizational citizenship behavior: A meta-analysis. *Journal of Applied Psychology, 96*(3), 619–632.

Erez, M., Earley, P. C., & Hulin, C. L. (1985). The impact of participation on goal acceptance and performance: A two-step model. *Academy of Management Journal, 28*, 50–66.

Festinger, L. (1957). *A theory of cognitive dissonance.* Evanston, IL: Row, Peterson.

Graen, G. B., & Uhl-Bien, M. (1995). Relationship-based approach to leadership: Development of leader-member exchange (LMX) theory of leadership over 25 years: Applying a multi-level multi-domain perspective. *Leadership Quarterly, 6*, 219–247.

Hays, S. (1999). Generation X and the art of reward. *Workforce, 78*(11), 44–48.

Hill, L. A. (2003). *Becoming a manager.* Boston: Harvard Business School Press.

Hill, L. A., & Lineback, K. (2011). *Being the boss: The 3 imperatives for becoming a great leader.* Boston: Harvard Business Review Press.

Holtz, G. T. (1995). *Welcome to the jungle: The why behind generation X.* New York: St. Martin's Press.

Jafri, M. H. (2011). Influence of psychological contract breach on organizational commitment. *Synergy, 9*(11), 19–30.

Kahn, R., Wolfe, D., Quinn, R., Snoek, J. D., & Rosenthal, R. (1964). *Organizational stress: Studies in role conflict and ambiguity.* New York: John Wiley & Sons.

Katz, D., & Kahn, R. L. (1978). *The social psychology of organizations* (2nd edn). New York: John Wiley & Sons.

Lang, J., Thomas, J. L., Bliese, P. D., & Adler, A. B. (2007). Job demands and job performance: The moderating effect of psychological and physical strain and the moderating effect of role clarity. *Journal of Occupational Health Psychology, 12*, 116–124.

Latham, G. P., & Locke, E. A. (2007). New developments in and directions for goal-setting research. *European Psychologist, 12*(4), 290–300.

Lester, S., Turnley, W., Bloodgood, J., & Bolino, M. (2002). Not seeing eye-to-eye: Differences in supervisor and subordinate perceptions of and attribution for psychological contract breach. *Journal of Organizational Behavior, 23*, 39–56.

Lipkin, N. A., & Perrymore, A. J. (2009). *Y in the workplace: Managing the "me first" generation.* Pompton Plains, NJ: Career Press.

Locke, E. A. (1968). Toward a theory of task motivation and incentives. *Organizational Behavior and Human Performance, 3*, 157–189.

Locke, E. A., & Latham, G. P. (1990). *A theory of goal setting and task performance.* Upper Saddle River, NJ: Prentice Hall.

Locke, E. A., & Latham, G. P. (2002). Building a practically useful theory of goal-setting and task motivation: A 35-year odyssey. *American Psychologist, 57*(9), 705–717.

McClelland, D. C. (1971). *Motivational trends in society.* Morristown, NJ: General Learning Press.

Meyer, C., & Kirby, J. (2010). Leadership in the age of transparency. *Harvard Business Review, 88*(4), 38–46.

Restubog, S. L., Hornsey, M. J., Bordia, P., & Esposo, S. R. (2008). Effects of psychological contract breach on organizational citizenship behavior: Insights from the group value model. *Journal of Management Studies, 45,* 1377–1400.

Robinson, S. L. (1996). Trust and breach of the psychological contract. *Administrative Science Quarterly, 41,* 574–599.

Rousseau, D. M. (1989). Psychological and implied contracts in organizations. *Employee Responsibilities and Rights Journal, 12,* 121–139.

Rousseau, D. M. (2001). Schema, promise, and mutuality: The building blocks of the psychological contract. *Journal of Occupational and Organizational Psychology, 74,* 511–541.

Rousseau, D. M., & Tijoriwala, S. A. (1998). Assessing psychological contracts: Issues, alternatives and measures. *Journal of Organizational Behavior, 19,* 679–695.

Shore, L.M., & Barksdale, K. (1998). Examining degree of balance and level of obligation in the employment relationship: A social exchange approach. *Journal of Organizational Behavior, 19,* 731–744.

Taylor, M. S., Fisher, C. D., & Ilgen, D. R. (1984). Individuals' reactions to performance feedback in organizations: A control theory perspective. In K. M. Rowland & G. R. Ferris (Eds.). *Research in personnel and human resources management* (Vol. 2, pp. 81–124). Greenwich, CT: JAI Press.

Tulgan, B. (2007). *It's okay to be the boss: The step-by-step guide to becoming the manager your employees need.* New York: HarperCollins.

Twenge, J. M. (2006). *Generation me: Why today's young Americans are more confident, assertive, entitled—and more miserable than ever.* New York: Free Press.

Twenge, J. M., & Campbell, W. K. (2009). *The narcissism experiment: Living in an age of entitlement.* New York: Free Press.

Walumba, F. O., Avolio, B., Gardner, W., Wernsing, T., & Peterson, S. (2008). Authentic leadership: Development of a theory-based measure. *Journal of Management, 34*(1), 89–126.

Wang, C. (1999). You must have a moral compass. In T. J. Neff & J. M. Citrin (Eds.). *Lessons from the top: The search for America's best business leaders* (pp. 327–332). New York: Currency.

Whitaker, B., Dahling, J., & Levy, P. (2007). The development of a feedback environment and role clarity model of job performance. *Journal of Management, 33,* 570–591.

Zhao, H., Wayne, S. J., Glibkowski, B. C., & Bravo, J. (2007). The impact of psychological contract breach on work-related outcomes: A meta-analysis. *Personnel Psychology, 60,* 647–680.

5 Conflict: The Power of Successful Conflict Encounters

Bar-On, R. (2002). *The emotional quotient inventory.* North Towanda, NY: Multi-Help Systems.

Bartlett II, J. E., & Bartlett, M. (2011). Workplace bullying: An integrative literature review. *Advances in Developing Human Resources, 13*(1), 69–84.

Blake, R., & Mouton, J. (1964). *The Managerial Grid.* Houston, TX: Gulf.

Chen, G., Liu, C., & Tjosvold, D. (2005). Conflict management for effective top management teams and innovation in China. *Journal of Management Studies, 42,* 277–300.

Chen, M. J., & Ayoka, O. B. (2011). Conflict and trust: The mediating effects of emotional arousal and self-conscious emotions. *International Journal of Conflict Management, 23*(1), 19–56.

Davis, M. H., Capobianco, S., & Kraus, L. A. (2004). Measuring conflict-related behaviors: Reliability and validity evidence regarding the conflict dynamics profile. *Educational and Psychological Measurements, 64*(4), 707–731.

Ellis, J. J. (2002). *Founding brothers: The revolutionary generation.* New York: Vintage.

Fisher, R., Ury, W. L., & Patton, B. (1991). *Getting to yes: Negotiating agreement without giving in.* New York: Penguin.

Goleman, D. (1998). *Working with emotional intelligence.* New York: Bantam Books.

Goleman, D., Boyatzis, R., & McKee, A. (2002). *Primal leadership: Realizing the power of emotional intelligence.* Boston: Harvard Business School Press.

Heames, J., & Harvey, M. (2006). Workplace bullying: A cross-level assessment. *Management Decision, 44*(9), 1214–1230.

Jehn, K. A., & Mannix, E. A. (2001). The dynamic nature of conflict: A longitudinal study of intragroup conflict and group performance. *Academy of Management Journal, 44*(2), 238–251.

Leslie, J. B. (2003). *Leadership skills and emotional intelligence.* Greensboro, NC: The Center for Creative Leadership.

Mayer, J., & Salovey, P. (1997). What is emotional intelligence? In P. Salovey & D. Sluyter (Eds.). *Emotional development and emotional intelligence: Implications for educators* (pp. 3–31). New York: Cambridge University Press.

Nardone, G., & Watzlawick, P. (2005). *Brief strategic therapy: Philosophy, techniques, and research.* Latham, MD: Jason Aronson.

Perry, S. J., Marcum, T. M., & Stoner, C. R. (2011). Stumbling down the courthouse steps: Mediator perceptions of the stumbling blocks to successful mandated mediation in child custody and visitation. *Pepperdine Dispute Resolution Law Journal, 11*(3), 441–463.

Rizkalla, L., Wertheim, E. H., & Hodgson, L. K. (2008). The roles of emotion management and perspective taking in individuals' conflict management styles and disposition to forgive. *Journal of Research in Personality, 42,* 1594–1601.

Saam, N. J. (2010). Interventions in workplace bullying: A multi-level approach. *European Journal of Work and Organizational Psychology, 19*(1), 51–75.

Singh, K. (2007). *Counseling skills for managers.* New Delhi: Prentice-Hall of India Private Limited.

Song, M., Dyer, B., & Thieme, R. J. (2006). Conflict management and innovation performance: An integrated contingency perspective. *Journal of the Academy of Marketing Science, 34*, 341–356.

Sternberg, R., & Soriano, L. (1984). Styles of conflict resolution. *Journal of Personality and Social Psychology, 47*, 115–126.

Stone, D., Patton, B., & Heen, S. (2010). *Difficult conversations: How to discuss what matters most.* New York: Penguin.

Stoner, C. R., Perry, S. J., & Marcum, T. M. (2011). The court, the parent, and the child: Mediator perceptions of the purpose and impact of mandated mediation in child custody cases. *Journal of Law and Family Studies, 13*(1), 151–170.

Sutton, R. I. (2010). *The no asshole rule: Building a civilized workplace and saving one that isn't.* Boston: Grand Central Publishing.

Thomas, K. W. (1992). Conflict and negotiation processes in organizations. In M. D. Dunnette & L. M. Hough (Eds.). *Handbook of Industrial and Organizational Psychology* (2nd ed., Vol. 3, pp. 651–717). Palo Alto, CA: Consulting Psychologists Press.

6 Connection: The Language of Understanding

Adler, R. B., & Elmhorst, J. M. (2010). *Communicating at work: Principles and practices for business and professionals* (10th ed.). New York: McGraw-Hill.

Adler, R. B., Rosenfeld, L. B., & Proctor II, R. F. (2013). *Interplay: The process of interpersonal communication* (12th edn). New York: Oxford University Press.

Bambacas, M., & Patrickson, M. (2008). Interpersonal communication skills that enhance organisational commitment. *Journal of Communication Management, 12*(1), 51–72.

Baron-Cohen, S. (2011). The empathy bell curve. *Phi Kappa Phi Forum, 91*(1), 10–12.

Berlo, D. K. (1960). *The process of communication.* New York: Holt, Rinehart, & Winston.

Bohm, D. (1996). *On dialogue.* London: Routledge.

Calloway-Thomas, C., Cooper, P., & Blake, C. (1999). *Interpersonal communication: Roots and routes.* Upper Saddle River, NJ: Pearson.

Covey, S. R. (1989). *The 7 habits of highly successful people: Powerful lessons in personal change.* New York: Fireside.

Dainton, M., & Zelley, E. D. (2005). *Applying communication theory for professional life.* London: Sage.

Duck, J. D. (1998). Managing change: The art of balancing. *Harvard Business Review, 71*(6), 109–118.

Feiner, M. (2004). *The Feiner points of leadership: The 50 basic laws that will make people want to perform better for you.* New York: Warner Books.

Fromkin, V., & Rodman, J. (1983). *An invitation to language.* New York: CBS College Publishing.

Gabarro, J. J., & Kotter, J. P. (2005). Managing your boss. *Harvard Business Review, 83*(1), 92–99.

Goleman, D. (2006). *Social intelligence: The revolutionary new science of human relationship.,* New York: Bantam Books.

Goman, C. K. (2011). What's so great about face-to-face. *Harvard Business Review, 89*(3), 38–39.

Hamilton, C. (2010). *Communicating for results: A guide for business and the professions.* Boston: Wadsworth-Cengage Learning.

Hardy, C., Lawrence, T. B., & Grant, D. (2005). Discourse and collaboration: The role of conversations and collective identity. *Academy of Management Review, 30,* 58–77.

Harrell, T. W., & Harrell, M. S. (1984). *Stanford MBA careers: A 20-year longitudinal study.* Graduate School Business Research Paper, No. 723. Stanford, CA.

Hofstede, G. (1980). *Culture's consequences: International differences in work-related values.* Beverly Hills, CA: Sage.

Hofstede, G. (2001). *Culture's consequences: Comparing values, behaviors, institutions, and organizations across nations.* Thousand Oaks, CA: Sage.

Human, L. J., & Biesanz, J. C. (2011). Through the looking glass clearly: Accuracy and assumed similarity in well-adjusted individuals' first impressions. *Journal of Personality and Social Psychology, 100,* 349–364.

Johnson, S. D., & Beechler, C. (1998). Examining the relationship between listening effectiveness and leadership emergence: Perceptions, behaviors, and recall. *Small Group Research, 29,* 452–471.

Kirkman, B. L., Lowe, K. B., & Gibson, C. B. (2006). A quarter century of *Culture's Consequences*: A review of empirical research investigating Hofstede's cultural values framework. *Journal of International Business Studies, 31,* 285–320.

Lenhart, A. (2010). Teens, cell phones and texting. Retrieved from http://www.pewinternet.org.

Maruca, R. F., & Milhaven, J. (2000). When the boss won't budge. *Harvard Business Review, 78*(1), 25–35.

Nellermoe, D. A., Weirich, T. R., & Reinstein, A. (1999). Using practitioners' viewpoints to improve accounting students' communication skills. *Business Communication Quarterly, 62*(2), 41–60.

Patterson, K., Grenny, J., McMillan, R., & Switzler, A. (2002). *Crucial conversations: Tools for talking when stakes are high.* New York: McGraw-Hill.

Roethlisberger, F. J. (1989). The Hawthorne experiments. In J. S. Ott (Ed.). *Classic readings in organizational behavior* (pp. 36–47). Pacific Grove, CA: Brooks/ Cole.

Simon, P. (1964). Sounds of silence. On *Sounds of Silence* [CD]. New York: Columbia Recording Co.

Smith, A., & Brenner, J. (2012). Twitter use 2012. Retrieved from http://pew internet.org/Reports/2012/Twitter-use-2012.aspx.

Staw, B. M. (1976). Knee-deep in the big muddy: A study of escalating commitment to a chosen course of action. *Organizational Behavior and Human Performance, 16*(1), 27–44.

7 Commitment: The Strength of Performance through People

Adams, J. S. (1963). Toward an understanding of inequity. *Journal of Abnormal and Social Psychology, 67*, 422–436.

Adams, J. S. (1965). Inequity in social exchange. In L. Berkowitz (Ed.). *Advances in experimental social psychology* (Vol. 2, pp. 267–299). New York: Academic Press.

Amabile, T. M. (1998). *Creativity in context.* Boulder, CO: Westview.

Anderson, N. J., & Butzin, C. A. (1974). Performance = Motivation X Ability: An integration-theoretical analysis. *Journal of Personality and Social Psychology, 30*, 598–604.

Babb, H. W. & Kopp, D. G. (1978). Applications of behavior modification in organizations: A review and critique. *Academy of Management Review, 3*(2), 281–292.

Bandura, A. (1977). Self-efficacy: Toward a unifying theory of behavioral change. *Psychological Review, 84*, 191–215.

Bies, R. J., & Moag, J. S. (1986). Interactional justice: Communication criteria of fairness. *Research on Negotiation in Organizations, 1*, 43–55.

Bies, R. J., & Shapiro, D. L. (1987). Interactional fairness judgments: The influence of causal accounts. *Social Justice Research, 1*, 160–169.

Buckingham, M. (2005). What great managers do. *Harvard Business Review, 83*(3), 70–79.

Buckingham, M., & Coffman, C. (1999). *First break all the rules: What the world's greatest managers do differently.* New York: Simon & Schuster.

Burchell, M., & Robin, J. (2011). *The great workplace: How to build it, how to keep it, and why it matters.* San Francisco: Jossey-Bass.

Carson, S. J., Madhok, A., Varman, R., & John, G. (2003). Information processing moderators of the effectiveness of trust-based governance in interfirm R & D collaboration. *Organization Science, 14*(1), 45–56.

Coelho, F., & Augusto, M. (2010). Job characteristics and the creativity of frontline service employees, *Journal of Service Research, 13*, 426–438.

Collins, J. (2001). *Good to great: Why some companies make the leap . . . and others don't*. New York: HarperCollins.

Colquitt, J. A., Conlon, D. E., Wesson, M. J., Porter, C. O. L. H., & Ng, K. Y. (2001). Justice at the millennium: A meta-analytic review of 25 years of organizational justice research. *Journal of Applied Psychology, 86*(3), 425–445.

Csikszentmihalyi, M. (1990). *Flow: The psychology of optimal experience*. New York: Harper and Row.

Cummings, L. L., & Brimley, P. (1996). The organizational trust inventory (OTI): Development and validation. In R. Kramer & T. Tyler (Eds.). *Trust in organizations* (pp. 302–330). Thousand Oaks, CA: Sage.

Deal, J. J., Peterson, K., & Gailor-Loflin, H. (2001). *Emerging leaders: An annotated bibliography*. Greensboro, NC: The Center for Creative Leadership.

Donohue, R. (2007). Examining career persistence and career change intent using career attitudes and strategy inventory. *Journal of Vocational Behavior, 70*, 259–276.

Druskat, V. U., & Pescosolido, A. T., (2002). The content of effective teamwork mental models in self-managing teams: Ownership, learning, and heedful interrelating. *Human Relations, 55*, 283–314.

Freud, S., Dufresne, T., & Richter, G. C. (2011). *Beyond the pleasure principle*. Buffalo, NY: Broadview Press.

Hackman, J. R., & Oldham, G. R. (1976). Motivation through the design of work: Test of a theory. *Organizational Behavior and Human Performance, 16*, 250–279.

Hackman, J. R. & Oldham, G. R. (1980). *Work redesign*. Reading, MA: Addison-Wesley.

Heider, F. (1958). *The psychology of interpersonal relations*. New York: John Wiley & Sons.

Herman, J. L., Deal, J. J., Lopez, J., Gentry, W. A., Shively, S., Ruderman, M., & Zukin, L. (2011). *Motivated by the organization's mission or their career: Implications for leaders in turbulent times*. Greensboro, NC: The Center for Creative Leadership.

Hill, L. A. (2003). *Becoming a manager: How new managers master the challenges of leadership*. Boston: Harvard Business School Press.

Hill, L. A., & Lineback, K. (2011). *Being the boss: The 3 imperatives for becoming a great leader*. Boston: Harvard Business Review Press.

Homans, G. C. (1961). *Social behavior: Its elementary forms*. New York: Harcourt, Brace, & World.

Human, L. J., & Biesanz, J. C. (2011). Through the looking glass clearly: Accuracy and assumed similarity in well-adjusted individuals' first impressions. *Journal of Personality and Social Psychology, 100*, 349–364.

Isaac, R. G., Zerbe, W. J., & Pitt, D. C. (2001). Leadership and motivation: The effective application of expectancy theory. *Journal of Managerial Issues, 13*(2), 212–226.

Izzo, J. B., & Withers, P. (2001). *Values shift: The new work ethic and what it means for business.* Lions Bay, BC: Fairwinds Press.

Karau, S. J., & Kipling, W. D. (2001). Understanding individual motivation in groups: The collective effort model. In M. E. Turner (Ed.). *Groups at work: Theory and research* (pp. 113–141). Mahwah, NJ: Erlbaum.

Kazdin, A. (2008). *Behavior modification in applied settings.* Long Grove, IL: Waveland Press.

Kerr, S. (1975). On the folly of rewarding A, while hoping for B. *Academy of Management Journal, 18,* 769–782.

Komaki, J. L., Coombs, T., & Shepman, S. (1990). *A review of two decades of operant conditioning literature in business and industry.* West Lafayette, IN: Purdue University.

Kristof-Brown, A. L., Zimmerman, R. D., & Johnson, E. C. (2005). Consequences of individuals' fit at work: A meta-analysis of person-job fit, person-organization, person-group and person-supervisor fit. *Personnel Psychology, 58,* 281–342.

Latham, G. P. (2012). *Work motivation: History, theory, research, and practice* (2nd edn). Thousand Oaks, CA: Sage.

LePine, J. A., LePine, M. A., & Jackson, C. L. (2004). Challenge and hindrance stress: Relationships with exhaustion, motivation to learn and learning performance. *Journal of Applied Psychology, 98,* 883–891.

Leventhal, G. S. (1980). What should be done with equity theory? In R. J. Gergen, M. S. Greenberg, & R. H. Willis (Eds.). *Social exchange: Advances in theory and research* (pp. 27–55). New York: Plenum Press.

Lind, A. E., & Tyler, T. R. (1988). *The social psychology of procedural justice.* New York: Plenum Press.

Locke, E. A., & Latham, G. P. (1990). *A theory of goal setting and task performance.* Englewood Cliffs, NJ: Prentice Hall.

Locke, E. A., & Latham, G. P. (2004). What should we do about motivation theory? Six recommendations for the twenty-first century. *Academy of Management Review, 29*(3), 388–403.

Locke, E. A., Shaw, K. M., Saari, L. M., & Latham, G. P. (1981). Goal setting and task performance: 1969–1980. *Psychological Bulletin, 90,* 125–152.

Luthans F., & Kreitner, R. (1985). *Organizational behavior modification and beyond.* Glenview, IL: Scott, Foresman.

Luthans, F., Maciag, W. S., & Rosenkrantz, S. A. (1983). OB Mod: Meeting the productivity challenge with human resources management. *Personnel, 60*(2), 28–36.

Marks, M. A., & Mathieu, J. E. (2000). Performance implications of leader briefings and team-interaction training for team adaptation to novel environments. *Journal of Applied Psychology, 85,* 971–986.

Miller, D. T., & Ross, M. (1975). Self-serving biases in attribution of causality: Fact or fiction? *Psychological Bulletin, 82,* 213–225.

Mowday, R. T. (1996). Equity theory predictions of behavior in organizations. In R. M. Steers, L. W. Porter, & G. A. Bigley (Eds.). *Motivation and leadership at work* (6th ed.). New York: McGraw-Hill.

Nowakowski, J. M., & Conlon, D. E. (2005). Organizational justice: Looking back, looking forward. *International Journal of Conflict Management, 16*(1), 4–29.

Phillips, J. M., Douthitt, E. A., & Hyland, M. M. (2001). The role of justice in team member satisfaction with the leader and attachment to the team. *Journal of Applied Psychology, 86,* 316–325.

Pinder, C. C. (1998). *Motivation in work organizations.* Upper Saddle River, NJ: Prentice Hall.

Pink, D. H. (2011). *Drive: The surprising truth about what motivates us.* New York: Riverhead Books.

Porter, L. W., & Lawler III, E. E. (1968). *Managerial attitudes and performance.* Homewood, IL: Richard D. Irwin.

Porter, L., Steers, R. M., & Bigley, G. A. (2002). *Motivation and work behavior* (7th ed.). New York: McGraw-Hill.

Roberts, K., & Glick, W. (1981). The job characteristics approach to task design: A critical review. *Journal of Applied Psychology, 66,* 193–217.

Ross, L. (1977). The intuitive psychologist and his shortcomings: Distortions in the attribution process. In L. Berkowitz (Ed.). *Advances in experimental social psychology* (pp. 173–220). New York: Academic Press.

Ruch, W. (2012). Full engagement, *Leadership Excellence, 22,* 11.

Sarker, S., Ajuja, M., Sarker, S., & Kirkeby, S. (2011). The role of communication and trust in global virtual teams: A social network perspective. *Journal of Management Information Systems, 28*(1), 273–309.

Stajkovic, A. D., & Luthans, F. (1997). A meta-analysis of the effects of organizational behavior modification of task performance: 1975–1995. *Academy of Management Journal, 40,* 1122–1149.

Stawiski, S., Deal, J. J., & Ruderman, M. (2010). *Building trust in the workplace: A key to retaining women.* Greensboro, NC: The Center for Creative Leadership.

Steers, R. M., Mowday, R. T., & Shapiro, D. L. (2004). The future of work motivation theory. *Academy of Management Review, 29*(3), 379–387.

Steers, R. M., Porter, L. W., & Bigley, G. A. (1996). *Motivation and leadership at work* (6th ed.). New York: McGraw-Hill.

Stewart-Williams, S., & Podd, J. (2004). The placebo effect: Dissolving the expectancy versus conditioning debate. *Psychological Bulletin, 130,* 324–340.

Twenge, J. (2006). *Generation me: Why today's young Americans are more confident, assertive, entitled—and more miserable than ever.* New York: Free Press.

Tyler, T. R. (1987). Conditions leading to value expressive effects in judgments of procedural justice: A test of 4 models. *Journal of Applied Social Psychology, 52,* 333–344.

Tyler, T. R. (1989). The psychology of procedural justice: A test of the group-value model. *Journal of Personality and Social Psychology, 57*, 830–838.

Vroom, V. H. (1964). *Work and motivation.* New York: John Wiley & Sons.

Weick, K. E. (1993). The collapse of sensemaking in organizations: The Mann Gulch disaster. *Administrative Science Quarterly, 38*, 628–652.

Weiner, B. (1985). An attributional theory of achievement motivation and emotion. *Psychological Review, 92*, 548–573.

Woodward, N. H. (1999). The coming of the manager. *HR Magazine, 44*, 74–80.

Zenger, J. H., & Folkman, J. R. (2009). *The extraordinary leader: Turning good managers into great leaders.* New York: McGraw-Hill.

Zenger, J., Folkman, J., & Edinger, S. (2009). *The inspiring leader.* New York: McGraw-Hill.

8 Change: The Call to Opportunity and Possibility

Allen, J., Jimmieson, N. L., Bordia, P., & Irmer, B. E. (2007). Uncertainty during organization change: Managing perceptions through communication. *Journal of Change Management, 7*, 187–210.

Barling, J., Kelloway, E. K., & Frone, M. R. (2005). *Handbook of work stress.* Thousand Oaks, CA: Sage.

Beer, M., & Nohria, N. (2000). Cracking the code of change. *Harvard Business Review, 78*(3), 133–141.

Bies, R. J., & Moag, J. S. (1986). Interactional justice: Communication criteria of fairness. In R. J. Lewicki, B. H. Sheppard, & M. H. Bazerman (Eds.). *Research on negotiation in organizations* (pp. 43–55). Greenwich, CT: JAI Press.

Brockner, J., Konovsky, M., Cooper-Schneider, R., Folger, R., Martin, C., & Bies, R. J. (1994). Interactive effects of procedural justice and outcome negativity on victims and survivors of job loss. *Academy of Management Journal, 37*, 397–409.

Buchanan, D., Fitzgerald, L., Ketley, D., Gollop, P., Jones, J. L., Lamont, S. S., Neath, A., & Whitby, E. (2005). No going back: A review of the literature on sustaining organizational change. *International Journal of Management Reviews, 7*(3), 189–205.

Burke, W. W., Lake, D. G., & Paine, J. W. (Eds.). (2009). *Organizational change: A comprehensive reader.* San Francisco: Jossey-Bass.

Doyle, M., Claydon, T., & Buchanan, D. (2000). Mixed results, lousy process: Contrasts and contradictions in the management experience of change. *British Journal of Management, 11*, 59–80.

Duck, J. (1998). Managing change: The art of balancing. *Harvard Business Review on Change* (pp. 55–81). Boston: Harvard Business School Press.

Fable, C. M., & Yukl, G. (1992). Consequences for managers using single influence tactics and combinations of tactics. *Academy of Management Journal, 35*, 638–652.

Fedor, D. B., Caldwell, S., & Herold, D. M. (2006). The effects of organizational changes on employee commitment: A multi-level investigation. *Personnel Psychology*, 59, 1–29.

Fiss, P. C., & Zaja, E. J. (2006). The symbolic management of strategic change: Sensegiving via framing and decoupling. *Academy of Management Journal*, 49, 1173–1193.

Ford, J. D., & Ford, L. W. (2009). Decoding resistance to change. *Harvard Business Review, 87*(2), 99–104.

Ford, J. D., Ford, L. W., & D'Amelio, A. (2008). Resistance to change: The rest of the story. *Academy of Management Journal*, 33, 362–377.

French, J. R. P., & Raven, B. (2001). The bases of social power. In I. Asherman & S. Anderman (Eds.). *Negotiation sourcebook* (2nd ed., pp. 61–73). Amherst, MA: HRD Press.

Gioia, D. A., & Chittipeddi, K. (1991). Sensemaking and sensegiving in strategic change initiation. *Strategic Management Journal, 12*, 433–448.

Gioia, D. A., Thomas, J. B., Clark, S. M., & Chittipeddi, K. (1994). Symbolism and strategic change in academia: The dynamics of sensemaking and influence. *Organization Science*, 5, 363–383.

Greenberg, J. (1994). Using socially fair treatment to promote acceptance of a work site smoking ban. *Journal of Applied Psychology, 79*, 288–97.

Greve, H. R. (1998). Performance, aspirations, and risky organizational change. *Administrative Science Quarterly, 43*, 58–86.

Heath, C., & Heath, D. (2010). *Switch: How to change when change is hard.* New York: Broadway Books.

Herold, D. M., Fedor, D. B., Caldwell, S., & Liu, Y. (2008). The effects of transformational and change leadership on employees' commitment to change: A multilevel study. *Journal of Applied Psychology, 93*(2), 346–357.

Hersovitch, L., & Meyer, J. P. (2002). Commitment to organizational change: Extension of a three-component model. *Journal of Applied Psychology, 87*, 474–487.

Hiatt, J. M. (2006). *ADKAR: How to implement successful change in our personal lives and professional careers.* Loveland, CO: Prosci.

Hirschman, A. (1970). *Exit, voice and loyalty.* Cambridge, MA: Harvard University Press.

Holmes, T. H., & Rahe, R. H. (1967). The social readjustment rating scale. *Journal of Psychosomatic Research, 11*, 213–218.

Hulin, C. L., & Judge, T. A. (2003). Job attitudes. In W. C. Borman & D. R. Ilgen (Eds.). *Handbook of psychology: Industrial and organizational psychology* (pp. 255–276). New York: John Wiley & Sons.

IBM Business Consulting Services. (2004). *Your turn: The global CEO study 2004.* Retrieved from http://www-05.ibm.com/no/news/publications/IBI.

Jex, S. M. (1998). *Stress and job performance.* Thousand Oaks, CA: Sage.

Kanter, R. M. (1983). *The change masters: Innovation and entrepreneurship in the American corporation.* New York: Simon & Schuster.

Karp, T., & Helgo, T. I. T. (2009). Reality revisisted: Leading people in chaotic change. *Journal of Management Development, 28*(2), 81–93.

Kerr, S. (1975). On the folly of rewarding A, while hoping for B. *Academy of Management Journal, 18*(4), 769–783.

Klein, S. M. (1996). A management communication strategy for change. *Journal of Organizational Change Management, 9,* 32–46.

Kotter, J. (1995). Leading change: Why transformational efforts fail. *Harvard Business Review, 73*(1), 59–67.

Kotter, J. (1996). *Leading change.* Boston: Harvard Business School Press.

Kotter, J. P. (2008). *A sense of urgency.* Boston: Harvard Business Press.

Kotter, J. P., & Cohen, D. S. (2002). *The heart of change: Real-life stories of how people change their organizations.* Boston: Harvard Business School Publishing.

Kotter, J., & Schlesinger, L. (1979). Choosing strategies for change. *Harvard Business Review, 57,* 106–114.

Labianca, G., Gray, B., & Brass, D. J. (2000). A grounded model of organizational schema change during empowerment. *Organization Science, 11,* 235–257.

Lazarus, R. S., & Folkman, S. (1987). Transactional theory and research on emotions and coping. *European Journal of Personality, 1,* 141–169.

Leung, K., Huang, K., Su, C., & Lu, L. (2011). Curvilinear relationship between role stress and innovative performance: Moderating effects of perceived support for innovation. *Journal of Occupational and Organizational Psychology, 84*(4), 741–758.

Leung, K., Su, S., & Morris, M. W. (2001). When is criticism not constructive? The roles of fairness perceptions and dispositional attributions in employee acceptance of critical supervisory feedback. *Human Relations, 54,* 1155–1187.

Lewin, K. (1947). Frontiers in group dynamics. *Human Relations, 1,* 5–41.

Lind, E. A., & Tyler, T. (1988). The social psychology of procedural justice. New York: Plenum Press.

Lind, E. A., Kulik, C. T., Ambrose, M., & de Vera Park, M. V. (1993). Individual and corporate dispute resolution: Using procedural fairness as a decision heuristic. *Administrative Science Quarterly, 38,* 224–51.

Maitlis, S., & Lawrence, T. B. (2007). Triggers and enablers of sensegiving in organizations. *Academy of Management Journal, 50*(1), 57–84.

Mantere, S., Schildt, H. A., & Sillince, J. A. A. (2012). Reversal of strategic change. *Academy of Management Journal, 55*(1), 172–196.

NHS Modernisation Agency (2002). *Improvement leaders' guide to sustainability and spread.* Ipswich: Ancient House Printing Group.

Noer, D. M. (2009). *Healing the wounds: Overcoming the trauma of layoffs and revitalizing downsized organizations.* San Francisco: Jossey-Bass.

Ravasi, D., & Schultz, M. (2006). Responding to organizational identity threats: Exploring the role of organizational culture. *Academy of Management Journal, 49*, 433–458.

Reeves, M., & Deimler, M. (2011). Adaptability: The new competitive advantage. *Harvard Business Review, 89*(7/8), 135–141.

Salem, P. (2008). The seven communications reasons organizations do not change. *Corporate Communications: An International Journal, 13*, 333–348.

Schein, E. H. (1996). Culture: The missing concept on organizational studies. *Administrative Science Quarterly, 41*, 229–240.

Schein, E. H. (2010). *Organizational culture and leadership* (4th ed.). San Francisco: Jossey-Bass.

Selye, H. (1978). *The stress of life* (2nd ed.), New York: McGraw-Hill.

Smith, A. D., Plowman, D. A., & Duchon, D. (2010). Everyday sensegiving: A closer look at successful plant managers. *Journal of Applied Behavioral Science, 46*(2), 220–244.

Tyler, T. R., & Bies, R. J. (1990). Interpersonal aspects of procedural justice. In J. S. Carroll (Ed.). *Applied social psychology and organizational settings* (pp. 77–98). Hillsdale, NJ: Erlbaum.

Van de Ven, A. H., & Sun, K. (2011). Breakdowns in implementing models of organizational change. *Academy of Management Perspectives, 25*(3), 58–74.

Vuori, T., & Virtaharju, J. (2012). On the role of emotional arousal in sensegiving. *Journal of Organizational Change Management, 25*(1), 48–66.

Weick, K. E. (1995). *Sensemaking in organizations.* Thousand Oaks, CA: Sage.

Yerkes, R. M., & Dodson, J. D. (1908). The relation of strength of stimulus to rapidity of habit-formation. *Journal of Comparative Neurology and Psychology, 18*, 459–482.

9 Crisis: Developing through the Cauldron of Adversity

Abramson, L. Y., Seligman, M. E. P., & Teasdale, J. (1978). Learned helplessness in humans: Critique and reformulation. *Journal of Abnormal Psychology, 87*, 32–48.

Adams, J. S. (1963). Toward an understanding of inequity. *Journal of Abnormal Psychology, 67*, 422–436.

Adams, J. S. (1965). Inequity in social exchange. *Advances in Experimental Social Psychology, 62*, 335–343.

Bailyn, L., Drago, R., and Kochan, T. A. (2001). Integrating work and family: A holistic perspective. *A Report of the Sloan Work-Family Policy Network.* Boston: Boston College.

Bennis, W. G., & Thomas, R. J. (2002a). *Geeks and geezers.* Boston: Harvard Business School Press.

Bennis, W. G. & Thomas, R. J. (2002b). Crucibles of leadership. *Harvard Business Review, 80*(9), 39–45.

Ben-Shahar, T. (2007). *Happier.* New York: McGraw-Hill.

Ciulla, J. B. (2002). *The working life: The promise and betrayal of modern work.* New York: Three Rivers Press.

Collins, J. (2001). *Good to great: Why some companies make the leap . . . and others don't.* New York: HarperCollins.

Duckworth, A. L., Peterson, C., Matthews, M. D., & Kelly, D. R. (2007). Grit: Perseverance and passion for long-term goals. *Personality Processes and Individual Differences, 92*(6), 1087–1101.

Ezzedeen, S. R., & Swiercz, P. M. (2002). Rethinking work-life balance: Development and validation of the cognitive intrusion work scale—a dissertation proposal. *Proceedings of the 2002 Eastern Academy of Management Meeting.* New Haven, CT: Eastern Academy of Management.

Friedman, S. D., & Greenhaus, J. H. (2000). *Work and family—allies or enemies? What happens when business professionals confront life choices.* Oxford: Oxford University Press.

Greenhaus, J. H., & Powell, G. N. (2005). When work and family are allies: A theory of work-family enrichment. *Academy of Management Review, 31*(1), 79–92.

Hamel, G. (2012). *What matters now: How to win in a world of relentless change, ferocious competition, and unstoppable innovation.* New York: John Wiley & Sons.

Hill, L. A. (2003). *Becoming a manager: How new managers master the challenges of leadership.* Boston: Harvard Business School Press.

Hochchild, A. (1997). *The time bind: When work becomes home and home becomes work.* New York: Metropolitan Books.

Jackson, D., & Daly, J. (2011). All things to all people: Adversity and resilience in leadership. *Nurse Leader, 21,* 22–30.

Jamison, K. R. (1995). *An unquiet mind: A memoir of moods and madness.* New York: Vintage.

Kirkpatrick, S. A., & Locke, E. A. (1991). Leadership: Do traits matter? *Academy of Management Executive, 5*(2), 48–60.

Lewis, S., & Dyer, J. (2002). Towards a culture of work-life integration? In C. L. Cooper & R. J. Burke (Eds.). *The new world of work: Challenges and opportunities* (pp. 302–316). Oxford: Blackwell.

Lockwood, N. R. (2003). Work/life balance: Challenges and solutions. *HR Magazine, 48*(6), 2–10.

Maddi, S. R., & Kobasa, S. C. (1984). *The hardy executive: Health under stress.* Homewood, IL: Dow Jones-Irwin.

Manzoni, J. F., & Barsoux, J. L. (2009). The interpersonal side of taking charge. *Organizational Dynamics, 38*(2), 106–116.

McCall, M., & Hollenbeck, G. (2002). *Developing global executives: The lessons of international experience.* Boston: Harvard Business School Press.

McCall, M., Lombardo, M., & Morrison, A. (1988). *The lessons of experience: How successful executives develop on the job.* Lexington, MA: Lexington Books.

McCall Jr., M. W. (2010). The experience conundrum. In N. Nohria & R. Khurana (Eds.). *Handbook of leadership theory and practice* (pp. 679–707). Boston: Harvard Business Press.

McCauley, C., Ruderman, M., Ohlett, P., & Morrow, J. (1994). Assessing the developmental components of managerial jobs. *Journal of Applied Psychology, 79*(4), 544–560.

Moxley, R. S. (1998). Hardships. In C. D. McCauley, R. S. Moxley, & E. Van Velsor (Eds.). *The Center for Creative Leadership handbook of leadership development* (pp. 194–215). San Francisco: Jossey-Bass.

Rosenthal, R., & Jacobson, L. (1992). *Pygmalion in the classroom.* New York: Irvington.

Schulman, P. (1999). Applying learned optimism to increase sales productivity. *Journal of Personal Selling and Sales Management, 19*(1), 31–37.

Seligman, M. E. P. (2006). *Learned optimism: How to change your mind and your life.* New York: Vintage Books.

Seligman, M. E. P. (2011). Building resilience. *Harvard Business Review, 89*, 100–106.

Seligman, M. E. P., Abramson, L. Y., Semmel, A., & von Bacyer, C. (1979). Depressive attributional style. *Journal of Abnormal Psychology, 88*, 242–247.

Stoner, C. R., & Gilligan, J. F. (2002). *The adversity challenge: How successful leaders bounce back from setbacks.* Provo, UT: Executive Excellence Publishing.

Stoner, C. R., & Robin, J. (2006). *A life in balance: Finding meaning in a chaotic world.* Lanham, MD: University Press of America.

Stoner, C. R., Robin, J., & Russell-Chapin, L. (2005). On the edge: Perceptions and responses to life imbalance. *Business Horizons, 48*, 337–346.

Stoner, C. R., Stephens, P., & McGowan, M. K. (2009). Connectivity and work dominance: Panacea or pariah? *Business Horizons, 52*, 67–78.

Sturges, J., & Guest, D. (2004). Working to live or living to work? Work/life balance early in the career. *Human Resource Management Journal, 14*(4), 5–20.

Weinzimmer, L. G. (2001). *Fast growth: How to attain it, how to sustain it.* Chicago: Dearborn Financial Publishing.

Whitehead, M. (1999). Work/life balance hits the top of graduate wish list. *People Management, 5*, 14–16.

10 Codas and Continuations

Boyatzis, R., & McKee, A. (2006). Intentional change. *Journal of Organizational Excellence, 25*(3), 49–60.

Collingwood, H. (2001). Personal histories: Leaders remember the moments and people that shaped them (pp. 1–23). *Harvard Business Review on breakthrough leadership.* Boston: Harvard Business School Press.

Goffee, R., & Jones, G. (2000). Why should anyone be led by you? *Harvard Business Review, 78*(5), 62–70.

Kegan, R., & Lahey, L. L. (2009). *Immunity to change: How to overcome it and unlock the potential in yourself and your organization.* Boston: Harvard Business Press.

Kets de Vries, M., & Engellau, E. (2010). A clinical approach to the dynamics of leadership and executive transformation. In N. Nohria & R. Khurana (Eds.). *Handbook of leadership theory and practice* (pp. 183–222). Boston: Harvard Business Press.

Morin, J. J. (2010). *Better make it real: Creating authenticity in an increasingly fake world.* Santa Barbara, CA: Praeger.

Palmer, P. J. (2011). *Healing the heart of democracy: The courage to create a politics worthy of the human spirit.* San Francisco: Jossey-Bass.

Index